FIFTY

D[...]

D0801078

Fifty Key Theatre Directors covers the work of practitioners who have shaped and pushed back the boundaries of theatre and performance. The authors provide clear and insightful overviews of the approaches and impact of fifty of the most influential directors of the twentieth and twenty-first centuries from around the world. They include:

- Anne Bogart
- Peter Brook
- Lev Dodin
- Declan Donnellan
- Jerzy Grotowski
- Elizabeth LeCompte
- Joan Littlewood
- Ariane Mnouchkine

Each entry discusses a director's key productions, ideas and rehearsal methods, effectively combining theory and practice. The result is an ideal guide to the world of theatre for practitioners, theatregoers and students.

Shomit Mitter is a freelance writer and author of *Systems of Rehearsal* (Routledge, 1992).

Maria Shevtsova is Professor of Drama and Theatre Arts at Goldsmiths College, University of London, and author of *Dodin and the Maly Drama Theatre: Process to Performance* (Routledge, 2004).

You may also be interested in the following Routledge Student Reference titles:

Fifty Contemporary Choreographers
Edited by Martha Bremser

Who's Who in Contemporary World Theatre
Edited by Daniel Meyer-Dinkgräfe

FIFTY KEY THEATRE DIRECTORS

Edited by Shomit Mitter and Maria Shevtsova

Routledge
Taylor & Francis Group

LONDON AND NEW YORK

First published 2005
by Routledge
2 Park Square, Milton Park, Abingdon, Oxon. OX14 4RN

Simultaneously published in the USA and Canada
by Routledge
270 Madison Avenue, New York, NY 10016

Reprinted 2007

Transferred to Digital Printing 2007

Routledge is an imprint of the Taylor & Francis Group, an informa business

Selection and editorial matter © 2005 Shomit Mitter and Maria
Shevtsova
Individual entries © 2005 the contributors

Typeset in Bembo by Taylor & Francis Books Ltd
Printed and bound in Great Britain by TJI Digital, Padstow,
Cornwall

British Library Cataloguing in Publication Data
A catalogue record for this book is available from the British Library

Library of Congress Cataloging in Publication Data
A catalog record for this book has been requested

ISBN10: 0–415–18731–1 (hbk)
ISBN10: 0–415–18732–X (pbk)

ISBN13: 978–0–415–18731–2 (hbk)
ISBN13: 978–0–415–18732–9 (pbk)

CHRONOLOGICAL LIST OF CONTENTS

ALPHABETICAL LIST OF CONTENTS

CONTRIBUTORS

Birgit Beumers is Senior Lecturer in the Russian Department at Bristol University. She specialises in contemporary Russian culture, especially cinema and theatre. Her publications include *Yury Lyubimov at the Taganka Theatre 1964–1994* (Amsterdam: Harwood, 1997), *Burnt by the Sun* (London: I.B. Tauris, 2000) and her edited *Russia on Reels: The Russian Idea in Post-Soviet Cinema* (I.B. Tauris, 1999).

Ian Carruthers has taught in the Theatre and Drama Department of La Trobe University since 1985. He is a co-editor (with Minami Ryuta and John Gillies) of *Performing Shakespeare in Japan* (Cambridge University Press, 2001) and co-author (with Takahashi Yasunari) of *The Theatre of Suzuki Tadashi* (CUP, 2004).

Jean Chothia is Reader in Drama and Theatre in the Cambridge University Faculty of English and a Fellow of Selwyn College. Her publications include *Forging a Language: A Study of the Plays of Eugene O'Neill* (Cambridge University Press, 1979), *Directors in Perspective: André Antoine* (CUP, 1991), *English Drama, 1890–1940* (Harlow: Longman, 1996) and *'The New Woman' and Other Emancipated Woman Plays* (Oxford University Press, 1998). Research interests include dramatic language and Shakespeare in the theatre and on film. She is currently working on the staging of crowds and insurgency.

Scott T. Cummings teaches and directs plays in the Theatre Department of Boston College. Author of *Anne Bogart and Charles Mee: Remaking American Theatre* (Cambridge University Press, 2005), he has published in various journals and newspapers, including *Modern Drama, Theatre Journal, American Theatre* and the *Boston Phoenix*.

Maria M. Delgado is Professor of Drama and Theatre Arts at Queen Mary, University of London. She is author of *'Other' Spanish Theatres: Erasure and Inscription on the Twentieth-Century Spanish Stage* (Manchester University Press, 2003) and co-editor of *In Contact with the Gods?: Directors Talk Theatre* (with Paul Heritage, MUP, 1996), *Conducting a Life: Reflections on the Theatre of Maria Irene Fornes* (with Caridad Svich, Lyme, NH: Smith & Kraus, 1999), *The Paris Jigsaw: Internationalism and the City's Stages* (with David Bradby, MUP, 2002), *Theatre in Crisis?: Performance Manifestos for a New Century* (with Caridad Svich, MUP, 2002) and *Bernard-Marie Koltès Plays: 2* (London: Methuen, 2004). She is co-editor of *Contemporary Theatre Review* and of the MUP series 'Theatre: Theory/Practice/Performance', a member of the advisory board of *TheatreForum* and a contributing editor for *Western European Stages*.

Nadine Holdsworth is Senior Lecturer in Theatre and Performance Studies at the University of Warwick. She has written on 7:84, Theatre Workshop, Glasgow Unity and contemporary Scottish theatre. She edited John McGrath's *Plays for England* and his collected writings on theatre, *Naked Thoughts That Roam About* (London: Nick Hern, 2002). She is currently writing a book on Joan Littlewood for the Routledge Performance Practitioners series.

Michal Kobialka is Chair and Professor of Theatre at the Department of Theatre Arts and Dance, University of Minnesota. He is the author of *A Journey Through Other Spaces: Essays and Manifestos, 1944–1990* (Berkeley: University of California Press, 1993) and *This Is My Body: Representational Practices in the Early Middle Ages* (Ann Arbor: University of Michigan Press, 1999), which received the 2000 ATHE Annual Research Award for Outstanding Book in Theatre Practice and Pedagogy. He is the editor of *Of Borders and Thresholds: Theatre History, Practice, and Theory* (Minneapolis: University of Minnesota Press, 1999) and a co-editor (with Barbara Hanawalt) of *Medieval Practices of Space* (Minneapolis: University of Minnesota Press, 2000).

Dasha Krijanskaia is Assistant Professor of Theatre at Roosevelt Academy in the Netherlands. She is an editor of *Teatr: Russian Theatre Past and Present*. Her research interests include contemporary Russian and Eastern European theatre, modernist theatre in Russia and Europe as well as the directing methods of the twentieth century. Recent publications include articles in *Slavic and Eastern European Performance*, *Theatre History Studies* and the Moscow newspaper *Kultura*.

Kazuko Matsuoka is a theatre critic and translator of numerous Shakespeare plays, including *Richard III*, *King Lear* and *Pericles*. In 1995 she was awarded the Yuasa Yoshiko Prize for her translation of *The Comedy of Errors*, *A Midsummer Night's Dream* and *Romeo and Juliet*. She has also translated Caryl Churchill's *Cloud 9* and *Rosencrantz and Guildenstern Are Dead* by Tom Stoppard. She is the author of works of criticism, including *Kaidoku Shakespeare (Invigorating Reading of Shakespeare)[a conversation on Shakespeare's plays with psychotherapist Dr Hayao Kawai]* (Tokyo: Shinchosha, 1999) and *Shakespeare Mono-Gatari* (Tokyo: Shinchosha, 2004).

Ian Maxwell is Chair of the Department of Performance Studies at the University of Sydney. He is the author of *'Phat Beats, Dope Rhymes': Hip Hop Down Under Comin' Upper* (Middletown, CT: Wesleyan University Press, 2003), an ethnography of rap culture in Sydney's western suburbs. He trained as a theatre director at the Victorian College of Arts School of Drama and has written extensively on a wide range of performance practices, from Australian Rules Football and community theatre to legal advocacy.

Shomit Mitter has an MPhil from Oxford University and a PhD from Cambridge University. In 1992 he published *Systems of Rehearsal*, a book on performance theory based in part on his work with Peter Brook, Augusto Boal and Richard Schechner. Having taught English Literature and Drama for some years at Cambridge and Nottingham universities, he is now involved both with running an aviation business and with writing and producing films.

Aoife Monks completed her PhD studies at Trinity College, Dublin, and lectures in theatre at the Department of Film, Theatre and Television at the University of Reading. She worked as an intern with the Wooster Group in 2003 and has published articles in *Modern Drama* and *Australasian Drama Studies*.

Arkady Ostrovsky was born in Moscow and graduated from the Russian Academy of Theatre Arts in 1993. He received a PhD from Cambridge University in 1999. The title of his thesis was *Stanislavsky Meets England: Shakespeare, Byron, Dickens and the Moscow Art Theatre and its First Studio*. He is currently working for the *Financial Times*.

Gerald Rabkin is Professor Emeritus of Theatre Arts in the Mason Gross School of the Arts at Rutgers University. He is the author of *Drama and Commitment: Politics in the American Theatre of the 1930s* (Indianapolis: Indiana University Press, 1964). He has written extensively on theatre for popular and scholarly journals including the *Soho Weekly News*, the *Kansas City Star*, the *New Statesman* and *The Drama Review*. He is a member of the American Theatre Critics Association, Drama Desk and the Lucille Lortel Off-Broadway Nominating Committee.

John Rudlin is Director of Centre Selavy in rural France, which is devoted to research and training in outdoor performance. He is the author of *Jacques Copeau* (Cambridge University Press, 1986) and *Copeau: Texts on Theatre* (with Norman Paul, London: Routledge, 1989). He also contributed the chapter 'Copeau' in *Twentieth Century Actor Training* (ed. Alison Hodge, Routledge, 2000). He has written *Commedia dell'arte: an Actor's Handbook* (Routledge, 1993) and *Commedia dell'arte: a Resource Book for Troupes* (with Olly Crick, Routledge, 2001).

Deborah Saivetz is a New York-based director whose work has been performed at such theatres as Clubbed Thumb, New Georges, The Drama League, Women's Project & Productions, New Dramatists, Powerhouse/New York Stage and Film, and the New Jersey Shakespeare Festival. Her translation of Mexican playwright María Morett's *Mujeres en el Encierro/Women in Confinement* was published in *TheatreForum* (June 2003). She teaches at Baruch College of the City University of New York.

Maria Shevtsova is Professor of Drama and Theatre Arts at Goldsmiths College, University of London, having previously held Chairs at the University of Connecticut and Lancaster University. She is the author of *Theatre and Cultural Interaction* (University of Sydney Press, 1993) and *Dodin and the Maly Drama Theatre: Process to Performance* (Routledge, 2004). She has edited the focus issues *Theatre and Interdisciplinarity* (2001) for *Theatre Research International* and *The Sociology of the Theatre* (2002, with Dan Urian) for *Contemporary Theatre Review*, which features her article 'Appropriating Pierre Bourdieu's *Champ* and *Habitus* for a Sociology of Stage Productions'. She is the co-editor of *New Theatre Quarterly*, contributing editor of *Theatre Research International* and advisory editor of *Literature and Aesthetics*.

David Williams is Professor of Theatre at Dartington College of Arts, England and has worked as a teacher, writer, translator, director, dramaturg and performer in Australia and England. He has compiled and edited *Peter Brook: A Theatrical Casebook* (London: Methuen, 1988), *Peter Brook and the Mahabharata: Critical Perspectives* (London: Routledge, 1991) and *Collaborative Theatre: The Théâtre du Soleil Sourcebook* (Routledge, 1999). He is consultant editor of *Performance Research* and a contributing editor to *Writings on Dance*.

INTRODUCTION

It is in the spirit of generating a lively debate that we have selected the directors whose work is discussed in this book. Our purpose is to stimulate an interest in the theatre-making processes of some of the directors of the twentieth and twenty-first centuries who have marked theatre practice, not to generate a definitive list that claims somehow to enshrine for all time the achievements of those who are in at the cost of those who are out. We wanted an intriguing mixture of gender, and of older and newer figures in the field. We have deliberately mixed in, with entries on very visible directors, articles on the work of those who are less well known, but just as exciting.

The decision not to put together a United Nations of the theatre, with proportional representation from five continents, is also a consequence of our decision to make the book more analytical than descriptive. While the book provides a basic minimum amount of information, the emphasis of the entry could, we felt, be less concerned with presenting the bare bones of biographical fact than with reaching into the heart of a body of work and distilling its essence into a few critical paragraphs. We see each article as a guide to the core of the work of certain directors, to the principles that animate their work. It seemed important that the book limit itself geographically so as to allow readers meaningfully to apply their understanding of the work of some directors to that of others.

A *Fifty Key* book serves several purposes. It can be used by a reader intermittently as a reference book, to look up entries discretely. It should also be structured in such a way as to reward the interested layperson who wants to 'look something up' and the student, actor, director or any other practitioner who may wish to read it through from beginning to end. In order to satisfy the theatre-goer, student and practitioner, entries seek to relate the vision of each of the directors discussed to the measures taken to realise his or her ideas in practice. The analysis is therefore rooted, when possible, in a study of rehearsal and other working methods. These, more than performance, are the areas in which the work of the director is most clearly seen. It seems significant that contributors, working independently, have chosen to focus on the relationship between the director and the actor as constituting the core of the work of the director. In a century that has produced theatre in virtually every style and genre imaginable, the bond between actor and director and the research carried out by both of them together into the potentiality of acting have emerged as two of the few themes that unite a multifaceted body of work. There are directors who have worked obsessively within a naturalistic or realistic framework and those who have been just as fixated, often for political reasons, on giving their productions the poetry and flexibility that come from working with a more relaxed attitude to theatricality. However diverse these sets of assumptions, they have, almost without exception, generated actor-training methods that comprise the most telling contributions made by each of the selected directors to twentieth-century theatre and its development into the opening decade of the present century.

Given the very different goals these directors have had for their theatres, the exercises and routines developed by them have been numerous and distinctive. If there is a common thread that runs through this material, it is the inclination to work with the body rather than exclusively through the mind and, most frequently, not to effect a separation between them at all. From the early days of Stanislavsky's 'method of physical actions' and Meyerhold's 'biomechanics' to Ariane Mnouchkine and Anne Bogart's more recent determination to create performances through workshops rather than from pre-written texts, there has been a strong move to make and view theatre as a plastic rather than an intellectual art form. The ability of the theatre to generate a plethora of visual, aural and physical images all at once is a function of its new-found willingness to make action rather than language the medium in which performances are constructed. This move away from the dominance of the word to the primacy of the moving body constitutes the seminal contribution of the art of the director to the theatre in all its multiplicity today.

Shomit Mitter
Maria Shevtsova

FIFTY KEY THEATRE DIRECTORS

ANDRÉ ANTOINE (1858–1943)

Antoine's vision in creating his first company, the Théâtre Libre (1887–94), was of a *théâtre d'essai*, a workshop theatre, where plays could be tried out regardless of their commercial prospects. He would provide a stage for new writing whose challenging subject matter or form had led to its rejection elsewhere. The playwrights would be part of the company and the company would develop its methods in the service of the text. The staging in the course of seven years of some 111 plays – verse drama, symbolism, black farce, notorious naturalist pieces and one-act slices of low life – suggests that the vision was triumphantly fulfilled.

It was evident from the outset, however, that audiences were compelled at least as much by the *mise-en-scène*, the acting and the sense of ensemble, as by the plays themselves. This was even more apparent in Antoine's better-resourced, professional repertory companies, the Théâtre Antoine (1897–1906) and the Théâtre National de L'Odéon (1906–14). Whilst staunchly upholding the integrity of the dramatist's text, in an age of casual adaptation, Antoine saw his task as the accurate interpretation for the stage of the writer's imagined world. It was precisely because he attended so assiduously to the needs of the play that this champion of the playwrights' theatre became one of the initiators of the directors' theatre.

Antoine's practice in mounting a play was established early and remained consistent. First, the playwright read his work to the full company. Then Antoine cast the play and, alone with the text, worked out a preliminary *mise-en-scène*. This involved locating the play in numerous sketches and stage plans, marking exits and entrances, and, by means of crosses and small arrows, plotting the actors' positions and movements. In developing the *mise-en-scène* Antoine rarely altered dialogue, but his working texts often show the dramatist's stage directions boldly crossed out and his own substituted. Interestingly, not only is there no record of a writer objecting to his alterations, but many playwrights incorporated his stage directions into subsequent printings of their plays.

The acting style developed in Antoine's theatres was evidently an extension of his own intuitive sensibility. It was deliberately low-key, rejecting the 'exaggerated a-r-t-i-c-u-l-a-t-i-o-n' (*Le Théâtre Libre*, May 1890: 82) taught at the Conservatoire. The difference from the norm frequently drew comment: 'nothing forced, nothing melodramatic, no effects, no cries, no big gestures' (*Le Gaulois*, 12 October 1887); 'no taking the stage, no playing to the gallery' (George Moore, *Pall Mall Gazette*, 5 February 1889). Critics praised the 'truth', 'simplicity' and 'naturalness' of the acting but also its 'intelligence' and 'understanding'. It is in the conjunction of these elements that both the power and the contradictions of Antoine's practice lie. For Antoine, the persuasive actor must not only lose self-consciousness and be seen to become the character, but must also be thoroughly in control of the role, with every movement and intonation prepared through intensive rehearsal.[1]

Antoine's rehearsals took place, whenever possible, on the stage, with set, costumes and props as available so that his actors learned to live in and with them. The world of the drama was presumed to continue beyond the confines of the stage: actors always knew whether they were entering from the street or from another room. Even worlds as remote and fanciful as that of Émile Bergerat's magical verse comedy, La Nuit Bergamasque (1887) were solidly present, with the gardens furnished with real plants rather than paintings on a back-cloth. The action was conceived not as a series of individual turns but as an interactive process. Mutual physical awareness, eye-contact and the art of listening when not speaking were paramount. Doubling, even of the smallest roles, was not allowed within a play because of the need for the actor to 'live' the role. Scenes were worked over and over. Lines, gestures and interactions were explored until they became second nature. Actors were sent out to observe real people – a woman in the market, a police informer, a patron of a local bar – so that the bearing, movement and manner of speech they adopted genuinely evinced the physical, social and psychological being of the character. Once Antoine was satisfied with the preliminaries, the mise-en-scène was written up by the régisseurs and had to be followed scrupulously. The paradox of the actors was that they had to 'live' their parts without missing a single previously recorded move.

The habitual playing place in the French theatre had been the front of the stage, with dialogue directed forwards to the audience. In Antoine's theatre, the relationship between the stage and the audience changed. The middle of the stage became the centre of the action, with actors required to play to each other rather than out to the auditorium. The auditorium was darkened (from 1888) and the actors did not acknowledge the presence of the audience. This was, of course, nothing less than a shift from presentational to illusionist acting. As the audience was no longer located at the core of the action, they began to experience the illusion of being eavesdroppers, unacknowledged witnesses of a self-contained world in which the most intimate concerns of the characters were revealed. As John

Jullien put it, the barrier between the stage and the audience was now 'a fourth wall, transparent for the public, opaque for the actor'.[2]

The audience, of course, only appeared to be ignored. Precisely because he aimed at an effect of complete realism, Antoine had to use artifice to sustain it. An inappropriate fixture, a hammy simulation of drunkenness, a rain effect stopping too abruptly, could disrupt the illusion. So stage furnishings had to be practical and lighting had to be directed as if not in from windows. The peasants in Verga's *Chevalerie rustique* (1888) had to seem Sicilian, not French, and those in Hauptmann's *The Weavers* (1893) had to be Silesian. The 1888 *Powers of Darkness*, with its antique costumes, icons and samovars borrowed from the Russian émigré community, became a byword for authentic staging. But, in each case, it was the *impression* of authenticity that was achieved, often by sleight of hand. The 'authentic' Russian items, for example, emanated from a social class quite different from that of Tolstoy's play. The 'realistic' lighting was in fact subtly boosted to give the action greater clarity. Lanterns were placed so as to catch tormented expressions in a shaft of light. Most significantly, the set was arranged to look as natural as possible – without ever obscuring the action.

The more wild and random a scene seemed, the more carefully orchestrated it had to be. Antoine's much admired crowd sequences were created through a mixture of strategic blocking, explanation and operant conditioning: he used a foreman's whistle to train his actors to respond promptly. He followed the Meininger practice of dividing the 200 or more extras into small groups, each of which had a leader and was allotted a specific activity. Sounds of marching footsteps, drums and shots were generated backstage to create the impression of distant turmoil. The voices of small groups of extras advancing from deep in the theatre were positioned closer and closer to the stage to simulate an approaching riot. Antoine's first attempt at creating a revolutionary crowd in *La Patrie en danger* (1889), whilst wonderfully convincing to the audience, had the leading actor Mévisto straining so realistically against the crowd that he lost his voice. In the forum scene in *Julius Caesar* (1906), groups of actors coughed, murmured and hushed others through Antony's 'Friends, Romans, countrymen' speech, giving a fleeting sense of variant opinions and attitudes among the masses.

Antoine was the creative centre of his theatre and everything derived from, and returned to, the man universally called '*le patron*'. Although he worked closely with actors, designers and writers, his practice was fundamentally despotic. No actor contradicted his

interventions. He held his position by the force of his own commitment. In his theatres, the co-ordinating function of the old stage
manager gave way to the interpreting functions of the modern
director. Acting in virtually every production until his move to the
Odéon, taking responsibility for selecting and staging plays, audi-
tioning actors, employing stage hands, overseeing the design and
mounting of the set, as well as bearing ultimate financial responsibility for the whole enterprise, Antoine was much more a practical
man of the theatre than a theoriser. His actors were obliged to learn
on the job, not in the acting school of which he dreamed. He
demanded, and got, remarkable loyalty from the company, many of
whom stayed with him for years. His theatres became magnets for
writers, actors and *régisseurs*, all anxious to learn.

Finally, it was Antoine's idea of a playwrights' theatre that would
work independently of commercial considerations that had greatest
impact on subsequent theatre. This was the thinking that had
animated Antoine's first project, the Théâtre Libre, which generated
some 12,000 newspaper articles during its first three years. Many of
the tactics Antoine developed to sustain such a theatre – a seasonal
subscription list to enable financial security, closed house performances to elude the censor, single performance showings or very
short runs, a team of amateur actors intermixed with moonlighting
professionals – informed the practice of a number of alternative
theatre companies such as the Freie Bühne of Berlin, Lugné Poe's
Théâtre d'Œuvre, Strindberg's Intimate Theatre and the Moscow Art
Theatre.

Notes

1   Antoine, André (1919) 'Mounet-Sully et le paradoxe sur le comédien',
    L'Information, July.
2   (1892) *Le Théâtre Vivant*, Paris: 11.

Further reading

Chothia, J. (1991) *Directors in Perspective: André Antoine*, Cambridge:
    Cambridge University Press.
Henderson, J.A. (1971) *The First Avant-Garde*, London: Lawrence Verry.
Stokes, J. (1972) *Resistible Theatres*, London: Elek.

JEAN CHOTHIA

VLADIMIR NEMIROVICH-DANCHENKO
(1858–1943)

The Moscow Art Theatre is largely known in the West as the theatre of Konstantin **Stanislavsky**. Vladimir Nemirovich-Danchenko, its co-founder, is usually seen as performing a secondary role. Yet, without Nemirovich there would have been no theatre. It was Nemirovich who initiated the famous meeting with Stanislavsky at the Slavyansky Bazar restaurant in the summer of 1897 that led to the creation of the theatre. Of course, unlike Stanislavsky, Nemirovich did not create a system of acting. So while Stanislavsky's legacy transcends the Moscow Art Theatre, the legacy of Nemirovich is inseparable from that of the 'MKhT', one of the most unique cultural institutions of the twentieth century.

In 1897, Nemirovich was a prize-winning playwright whose plays had been performed at the Imperial Maly Theatre. He was also a recognised theatre critic and teacher who sought to reform Russian theatre art which, in the late 1890s, was divorced from both real life and the literary and artistic aspirations of the time. During the memorable meeting at the Slavyansky Bazar, Nemirovich and Stanislavsky formulated the main principles of the Moscow Art Theatre. The new theatre was to dispose of the system of star actors and stock-cast types such as 'leading man' and 'juvenile lead' in favour of ensemble acting. Its repertoire was to consist of artistically substantial dramas that would enable the theatre to play an important social and educational role. 'A meaningful and significant theatre must talk about meaningful and significant matters', wrote Nemirovich. 'When art stops serving this purpose it becomes an entertainment for the rich.'[1]

It was also agreed that, while Stanislavsky would have the last word in matters of staging, Nemirovich would have the last word in questions of repertoire and dramaturgy. They soon realised, however, that this division of responsibilities was more symbolic than practical. Nemirovich was very keen that the repertoire of the new theatre should consist mainly of contemporary plays. 'If the theatre were to dedicate itself exclusively to the classical repertoire, and not to reflect modern life, it would soon become dead',[2] he argued. For Nemirovich, one of the main purposes of the new theatre was to accommodate Chekhov's plays. For Stanislavsky, mostly interested in the classical repertoire, Chekhov hardly stood out amongst contemporary playwrights. Years later, Nemirovich and Stanislavsky would both confess that the creation of the Moscow Art Theatre was the

7

result of the merger of two different, and often alien, creative wills. The conflict in the relationship between Stanislavsky and Nemirovich was as essential for the Moscow Art Theatre as a conflict of characters is on stage.

Stanislavsky agreed to the 1898 staging of *The Seagull*, but remained cold towards the play. For Nemirovich the success of the production was a question of both personal and artistic self-esteem. It was decided that Stanislavsky would write a production plan according to which Nemirovich would then rehearse with the actors. Stanislavsky suggested a *mise-en-scène* that was 'true to life', while Nemirovich concentrated on conveying to the audience the 'music' of the play, which he claimed Stanislavsky did not feel. The outstanding feature of rehearsals was Nemirovich's ability to identify the half tones with which to create a 'natural' atmosphere. This was later to become the hallmark of Moscow Art Theatre productions. Nemirovich brought to his work an acute sensitivity to the author's style, the colour of a play and the tone that it required from the actors. Stanislavsky's unique talent, on the other hand, was to be able to see the life that lay behind the play. A play for Stanislavsky was not so much a literary text as a record of a real situation that could be re-lived on stage. When he talked about Othello he talked not about Shakespeare's play but about a story of the Moor in Venice that Shakespeare had simply recorded.

In contrast to Stanislavsky, who did not possess a tragic sense of the world, Nemirovich had a feel for tragedy and was capable of staging it successfully. In 1903, two years before the first Russian Revolution, he directed *Julius Caesar* 'as a tragedy of history itself, as the tragedy of the inevitable movement of history which brings the end to the republican freedoms and brings triumph to the empire'.[3] The production was notable for a vibrant, colourful and all-consuming mob that had plenty of energy but very little reason. Rome was not an imperial capital, as it was portrayed in nineteenth-century paintings, but a seething, southern city, a city ripe for slavery.

The production that best expressed Nemirovich's feel for tragedy as well as his sense of literary style was his adaptation of Dostoevsky's novel, *The Brothers Karamazov*. This most significant of Moscow Art Theatre productions, the legacy of which can be felt in many of today's stage adaptations of novels, appeared almost by accident. The theatre was in the middle of its work on *Hamlet*, directed jointly by Gordon **Craig** and Stanislavsky, when the latter fell gravely ill and the plan to open the season of 1910/11 with *Hamlet* had to be abandoned. After an emergency meeting of the board of directors of the

Moscow Art Theatre, Nemirovich decided to open the season with a performance of *The Brothers Karamazov* spread over two evenings. In a letter to Stanislavsky, Nemirovich described the eventual success of the production as 'not a triumph or a victory, but some colossal bloodless revolution'[4] which introduced the Moscow Art Theatre, and indeed theatre in general, to a new, non-dramatic form of literature. Novels had obviously been dramatised and adapted for the stage before, but nobody had ever attempted to stage a novel in its entirety without first converting it into a play. In the case of *The Brothers Karamazov*, no fixed dramatic text even existed: Nemirovich worked straight from the novel. The significance of the Moscow Art Theatre's achievement was in the fact that, by breaking all known theatre conventions, it managed to preserve the non-dramatic structure of the novel on stage. Nemirovich did not adapt the novel for the stage; he adapted the stage for the novel.

Nemirovich divided Dostoevsky's novel into twenty-one scenes that varied in length from 7 to 80 minutes and were linked by a narrator, who read the non-dialogue parts of the novel, some sections of which lasted up to 30 minutes. Scenes changed with cinematic speed. The production was performed on an empty stage of reduced size. There was no curtain, no illusory scenery. Walking into the auditorium, the audience saw a parted curtain of the Moscow Art Theatre with a seagull on it, a pulpit for the narrator with a book on it lit by a lamp with a green shade. To the right of the pulpit there was a drape that, every time the narrator stopped reading, would move to the right, revealing an almost empty platform on which a few key objects signalled a new scene. One of the most memorable scenes was Ivan Karamazov's encounter with the devil. Vasiliy Kachalov played both Ivan and the devil. For 32 minutes, Kachalov spoke for both Ivan and the devil, giving an impression of the devil with just a slight change of intonation on a dark and almost empty stage. Thus in *The Brothers Karamazov* Nemirovich managed to find that unique combination of Moscow Art Theatre principles – of psychological realism and elevated tragedy – which Stanislavsky and Craig had tried to create in *Hamlet*.

The Brothers Karamazov was the first tragedy to be staged by the Moscow Art Theatre. It was followed, in 1913, by a dark and burning production of Dostoevsky's *The Devils*. If Nemirovich's work on Dostoevsky offered the theatre's actors an opportunity to reveal their tragic temperament to the full (something that Chekhov's plays did not allow them to do), it also allowed Nemirovich to demonstrate his taste for epic, monumental and emotionally charged forms of theatre.

This taste for scale and big, broad lines partly ensured the success of his productions in the Soviet period, which included Gorky's *The Enemies* (1935) and *Anna Karenina* (1937). *The Enemies*, with its clear-cut division into enemies and friends, had a diagonal line dividing the stage into two worlds: for the first time in its history, the Moscow Art Theatre fully shared the position of the 'winners' and refused the 'losers' any sympathy. The principle of binary oppositions also defined the style of *Anna Karenina*, where Nemirovich drew a similarly straight line – this time between Anna, full of life forces and engulfed by untamed passion, and the hypocritical and emotionally dead world that surrounds her. The production was warmly embraced by the Soviet government and took its place at the forefront of artistic life within what was then the Soviet Empire. Nemirovich's productions had become examples of the grand 'classicist' style of the 1930s.

Yet in the same period, Nemirovich also created one of his most lyrical and sincere productions. The 1940 *Three Sisters*, with its themes of hope, endurance and humility, became a tribute to the Moscow Art Theatre that had been founded on the principles of sincerity and truthfulness to life, which had become all but extinct in Soviet Russia. By 1940, few in Russia 'breathed in the same way'[5] as Chekhov's characters. What had come naturally to the actors of the Moscow Art Theatre in 1901 had to be recreated artistically in 1940. Wary of the danger of turning half tones into clichés, Nemirovich now looked for clear diction. He sought the seed of the play in the anguished need for a better life that is buried in the sub-text. 'Each character carries something unspoken, some hidden drama', he wrote, 'a hidden dream, hidden feelings, the whole big life which is not expressed in words.'[6] Talking to the actors, Nemirovich emphasised the musical and poetic nature of Chekhov's language: 'The whole play, even though it shows prosaic life, is musical: its language is musical and its feelings are musical. Even the faces which express this reality … are musical.'[7]

The success of this, his most poetic production, encouraged Nemirovich once again to turn to Shakespeare. Thirty-seven years earlier, after the original production of *Three Sisters* in 1901, he had directed *Julius Caesar*. This time he turned to *Hamlet* and to *Antony and Cleopatra*, both Boris Pasternak's translations. He created a special 'head-quarters for staging Shakespeare', whose function was not limited to staging *Hamlet* but was extended to manage the staging of Shakespeare at the Moscow Art Theatre generally. Neither *Antony and Cleopatra* nor *Hamlet* was completed. The death of Nemirovich in 1943 was one reason. Stalin's dislike of the latter work was another: the country was immersed in blood and had no time for a play such as *Hamlet*.

Notes

1 Nemirovich-Danchenko, V.I. (1979) *Izbrannye pis'ma*, Vol. I, ed. V. Vilenkin, Moscow: Iskusstvo: 297–298.
2 Ibid.: 118.
3 Bartoshevich, A. (1998) 'Julius Caesar' in Smelyanky, A.M., Solovyova, I.N. and Egoshina, O.V. (eds) *Moscow Art Theatre: One Hundred Years*, Vol. 1, Moscow: Moskovskii Khudozhestvennyi Teatr: 36.
4 Nemirovich-Danchenko, V.I. (1979) *Izbrannye pis'ma*, Vol. II, ed. V. Vilenkin, Moscow: Iskusstvo: 40.
5 Vilenkin, V. (ed.) (1956) *V.I. Nemirovich-Danchenko vedet repeitsiyu*, Moscow: Iskusstvo: 147–148.
6 Ibid.: 152.
7 Ibid.: 151.

Further reading

Leach, R. and Borovsky, V. (eds) (1999) *A History of Russian Theatre*, Cambridge: Cambridge University Press.
Nemirovich-Danchenko, V.I. (1987) *My Life in the Russian Theatre*, trans. John Cournos, New York: Theatre Arts Books.
Worrall, N. (1996) *The Moscow Art Theatre*, London: Routledge.

ARKADY OSTROVSKY

KONSTANTIN STANISLAVSKY (1863–1938)

Director, actor and drama teacher, Konstantin Stanislavsky was a co-founder of the Moscow Art Theatre (1898) who believed that the highest condition to which an actor could aspire was that in which there was no distinction between the self and the role. In Nikolai Gorchakov's log of a rehearsal of Griboyedov's comedy *Much Woe from Wisdom* (1924), Stanislavsky exhorts his actors to 'fill the text with Griboyedov's feelings. You must create those feelings in your heart; you must live them on the stage' (Gorchakov 1954: 179). The actor must not pretend to be someone else; he must actually achieve a condition of total metamorphosis. The theatrical act is ineffectual unless there is a 'complete transformation of the actor himself into the character of the play' (ibid.: 396). This is not a matter of expediency, of manipulating the audience's perception so as to beget the illusion that the action taking place on the stage is 'real'. There is a more profound sense in which Stanislavsky's actor actually *creates* reality on stage. The audience believes in the action because the actor does so as well. Stage action is plausible because it is true.

For Stanislavsky, actors must 'become' their characters. They must think as their characters think and feel as their characters feel. The task of the director in such a situation is to generate in rehearsal the conditions under which this identification is most likely to occur. The interesting thing about the Stanislasky legacy is that the answers he put together in his famous books on the subject do not in fact derive from the techniques he actually used in rehearsal. The much lauded Stanislavsky system was, in reality, largely a failure. To understand Stanislavsky is to understand the nature of this contradiction.

On paper the solution to the challenge of 'becoming' the character is simple enough. If the essence of the actor's problem is that the character is initially an alien entity with whom it is hard to identify, it seems logical to suggest that the actor must begin by researching the character's world well enough to be able to enter it at will. As Stanislavsky puts it: '[I]n the language of the actor *to know* is synonymous with *to feel*' (Stanislavsky 1983: 5).

One of Stanislavsky's methods of getting his actors to enter the world of the drama is to visualise the dramatic space in every detail:

> [T]wo floors of the actor's dressing rooms backstage were used ... to represent Orgon's home.... We were told to establish the location of the principal rooms of the house....
>
> 'If the mistress of the house is sick would she be comfortable in the room you have chosen for her? It might be very noisy....'
>
> We acted out such events.
>
> (Toporkov 1979: 165–166)

Once the physical environment in which the drama takes place is properly understood, the actors are invited to project themselves into the action and to ask how they themselves would react if faced with similar situations. Stanislavsky's actor 'must be able to put himself into the given circumstances. An actor must ask himself, "How would I behave if it happened to me in real life?" ' (Gorchakov 1953: 84–85). 'If' is a word that recurs incessantly in Stanislavsky's writings. By using the word 'if' the actor is able to acknowledge that the stage is merely a stage and not reality; but having done so the actor can go on to access that deeper level of identification which occurs when actors refer the circumstances of the drama to their own lives. 'If' is a trick the actors play on themselves, for only by admitting that the drama is a fiction can the actors convert that fiction into reality.

A character is a product not merely of circumstances but of intentions. To feel as the character feels actors must not only research the character's background but also apply themselves to understanding what the character intends to achieve, especially as plays often deal with the extent to which these ambitions are realised or thwarted. The second major aspect of Stanislavsky's approach to the problem of characterisation involves dividing the play into units which are then labelled with a verb that describes what precisely the character hopes to achieve in that unit of action:

> 'How will you get into the house of the Governor? In order to get in what will you need?'
> 'An invitation....'
> 'That is it.... The whole scene is for the sake of this. Everything leads to this, try to achieve only this. This is your task....'
>
> (Toporkov 1979: 95–96)

The analysis of the role in terms of units and objectives has the advantage of drawing actor and character together in a single thrust of action. By assigning a motive to the character, the verb used also supplies the actor with a reason for behaving as the character behaves. The character's motivation and the actor's justification are bracketed together in a single word.

The objectives assigned to each scene are then amalgamated into a sequence that spans the entire length of the play to create what is called a 'through-line' of action. The through-line is the map of the role, a scheme that helps the actor locate each moment of the play in terms of the character's 'superobjective', or ultimate goal:

> 'And what could the essence of this role be, Konstantin Sergeyvich?'
> 'Could it be to look after Pickwick? If so, try to subordinate all your behaviour to this one aim: to look after him. Choose what is necessary to carry out this aim, and throw away the rest.... Then the character will acquire purposeful activity in accordance with the inner line'.
>
> (Ibid.: 204)

It is important that the superobjective too is viewed in terms of a verb rather than an adjective. An adjective tells an actor what a character is like, but a verb tells an actor what to do. Finally, it is from these impulses to action that the play gets its drive.

With the character's past minutely researched and the future mapped precisely, Stanislavsky felt his actors should be well on their way to achieving his vision of complete identification between actor and character. However, when he put what he had written into practice, his actors failed miserably. The first two productions after the publication of his so-called system, Hamsun's *Drama of Life* (1907) and Andreyev's *Life of Man* (1907), were characterised by a crippling self-consciousness. Famously, **Nemirovich-Danchenko** had to insist that Stanislavsky himself withdraw from playing the part of Rostanov, the role in which he had had his greatest success as a young actor.

When he looked back on this period Stanislavsky realised that the more consciously an actor works out what a character is about, the more self-conscious he becomes – and the less able he is to perform. In response to this problem Stanislavsky instituted the so-called 'Method of Physical Actions'. This was a system of work which was diametrically opposed to the 'system' in that it took as its starting point the assumption that a role is most effectively inhabited when approached not through the mind (through research and analysis), but through the body (through gait, for instance, or make-up). Under this regime, an actor uses the early stages of rehearsal to decide not what the character's childhood had been like, but what the character looks like, or how he walks, or what sort of hair he has.

This had been Stanislavsky's own way of working: if he had to play an old man he would simply begin by physically imitating an elderly person he knew. What Stanislavsky had discovered as a practising actor over the years was that a mastery over the physical attributes of the character almost always led by some mysterious process to a sense of the character's inner condition. Vasily Toporkov speaks of this as 'Konstantin Sergeyevich's secret: that through the correct execution of physical actions ... one penetrates into the deepest, most complicated feelings and emotional experiences' (ibid.: 87). The advantage of this method of working is that it avoids self-consciousness. Actions generate emotional conditions before actors have the opportunity to take account of this process. Actors 'become' their characters in spite of themselves.

Stanislavsky had used the technique often enough to know that it worked: when he assumed the external mannerisms of the characters he was playing off stage, the feelings and sensations of the character immediately arose in him. The question is, why did he not base his system on this method of working? Perhaps, as analysis is obviously inimical to the proper working of this method, he had never had reason to work out *why* 'it is possible to arrive at the inner characteristics of a part by way of the outer characteristics' (Stanislavsky, quoted in Magarshack 1950: 46). Perhaps, as the system was intended to be a work of explanation, that which was inexplicable had no place in it. Having decided to write his system, Stanislavsky probably succumbed to the demand language makes on the writer's capacity for reason. He produced a system that was coherent and logical. However, it was based not on what he had actually done in the theatre, but on his attempt to *rationalise* what he had achieved. The result was catastrophic: Stanislavsky did not appear in a single new part during the last twenty-three years of his life.

He continued to direct, however, and when he realised his error, he repudiated much of what he had written. This was the beginning of the third phase of his development as an actor and director. In the first phase he had instinctively, almost unwittingly, approached the problem of characterisation by working through the body. He had worked by imitating physical types, by using physical prompts such as make-up, gait and costume. In the second phase, following the publication of his system, his work had become more cerebral. He had encouraged his actors to study the character's background and motivation before going into rehearsal. When this failed he embarked upon the third phase. He explicitly rejected much of the system and reverted to working through the body. In a rehearsal of *Tartuffe* (1938), his last production, Stanislavsky repeatedly emphasised that '[w]hen the actor starts to reason the ... will is weakened. Don't discuss, just do it' (Toporkov 1979: 171).

> Why sit at a table for months and try and force out your dormant feelings? ... You would do better to go out on the stage and at once engage in action.
>
> (Stanislavksy 1983: 245)

Stanislavsky's work had come full circle. At the very end of his career he had returned to the techniques that had helped him achieve his greatest successes as a young actor.

Further reading

Gorchakov, N. (1954) *Stanislavsky Directs*, trans. Miriam Goldina, New York: Grosset & Dunlap.

Magarshack, D. (1950) *Stanislavsky: A Life*, London: Faber & Faber.

Stanislavsky, K. (1967) *An Actor Prepares*, trans. Elizabeth Reynolds Hapgood, London: Penguin Books.

—— (1968) *Building a Character*, trans. Elizabeth Reynolds Hapgood, London: Eyre Methuen.

—— (1983) *Creating a Role*, trans. Elizabeth Reynolds Hapgood, London: Methuen.

Toporkov, V.O. (1979) *Stanislavsky in Rehearsal: The Final Years*, trans. Christine Edwards, New York: Theatre Arts Books.

SHOMIT MITTER

EDWARD GORDON CRAIG (1872–1966)

As the son of the actress Ellen Terry and having toured as an actor under the tutelage of the legendary Henry Irving since the age of six, Edward Gordon Craig's credentials as a man of the theatre were impeccable. Yet, ironically, it was not until he gave up acting in 1897 and devoted himself to painting that he began to hone the skills that would make him one of the great British theatre directors. If indeed one can call him a director: Craig lived into his nineties having directed only a handful of productions, most of which he dismissed as having fallen far short of his ideals. Craig was better satisfied with his stage designs, in which he was able to realise his dreams of a revolutionary new form of theatre, unsullied by the tedious intervention of reality. Always more involved with space and light than with action, he generated a body of drawings and writing which were so proudly impervious to contemporary opinion that he found himself alienated from mainstream British theatre at a time when he had few friends abroad. However, his refusal to be drawn into compromise served to preserve the startling novelty of his ideas. Like **Artaud**, who was vastly influential without having actually produced much theatre, Craig was better able to reshape the course of twentieth-century theatre through theory than through practice.

At the core of Craig's work is the notion that the theatre is a place where the ineffable world of the spirit can find evanescent expression. For Craig the task of the director was not to represent reality as much as to transcend it. As Isadora Duncan once observed of Craig's need to find in the solidity of visual structures a means of gaining access to an incorporeal world:

> You are creating the only world that is worth living in – *the imagination* – ... releasing poor souls from the inferno of

16

reality and *matter* [you] lift them up out of 'life' into the *only life*, up where the spirit can fly – freed from this abominable bad dream of matter.

(Letter to Craig, June 1913, quoted in Innes 1983: 195)

For Craig the job of a director was to work with movement and light to distil that spiritual essence to which, he believed, all artists aspired. Craig's was a theatre in which subliminal forms embodied untarnished emotional states. It was an abstract world in which the interplay of stillness and action, shadows and light took precedence over trifling matters of plot and character. It was a vision as lofty as it was chimerical and Craig clung to it with a tenacity that was radiantly impervious to reason.

Comfortable as we are today with the notion of the director as an autonomous agent, the idea was radical in Craig's time and carried a number of uncomfortable implications. Chief amongst these was the concept of authority: a director could hardly be expected to produce a conceptually unified image if he did not have complete control over each of the constituent elements of production. In the context of the Victorian theatre, in which every element was geared merely to bolster the performance of the star actor, this was unacceptable. It is little wonder then that Craig worked best with amateurs, having repeatedly alienated professional actors with his overbearing attitude:

> [T]he company, in contrast to his devoted Hampstead amateurs, demanded to know why he should choose to *interpret* Ibsen rather than merely execute his detailed stage directions. In particular, two of them objected strongly to fighting with massive swords on a rock structure that sloped between thirty and forty degrees, especially as the lighting did not even reveal their faces to the audience. Craig's work with the actors soon degenerated into a running fight....[1]

Braun's observations on rehearsals of *The Vikings at Helgeland* (1903) show that the indignity of the actors was a function not merely of their theoretical disagreement with Craig but of the inconsiderate impracticality of Craig's staging.

Craig clashed with his actors not merely because they objected to their loss of status as 'stars' but also because their training made it virtually impossible for them to generate the abstract quality Craig required. Whereas actors revelled in the extent to which their performances were psychologically perceptive or emotionally riveting,

Craig wanted feelings and psychology to give way to his overriding preoccupation with form. Although he often toyed with the idea of training actors to achieve this condition of depersonalised materiality, the conclusion to which he was inevitably drawn was that the actor had to be dispensed with altogether and replaced with what Craig called the 'Uber-marionette'. The unfortunate consequence of Craig's use of the word 'marionette' was that his conflict with his actors was portrayed more as a matter of vanity than of art. In fact Craig sought not to *reduce* but to *elevate* his actors to puppets – puppets had for him a sublime quality that human beings lacked: 'Drama which is not trivial, takes us *beyond reality* and yet asks a human face, the realest of things, to express all that. It is unfair' (Walton 1983: 21). Craig wished to rid the theatre of actors not because of their insubordination but because they lacked the sacred and impersonal quality he required.

Like actors, words, too, fell foul of Craig for being too obviously tainted with mortality. 'Words are a bad means of communicating ideas', he wrote in his Daybook, '– especially transcendent ideas – ideas which fly' (quoted in Innes 1983: 113). For Craig, words were, by their nature, windows into the very world he was trying so hard to eclipse. Through language, feelings and psychology were able to infiltrate a drama and inhibit its capacity to express the ineffable. Only in his designs was Craig able to realise the formal purity of his imagination. Craig's designs, often created independently of the needs of specific productions, have the timeless quality of all great visual art. 'The Steps', for example, is a series of drawings that examine the effect of light on bodies moving through space. They are drawn with a painter's passion, not a designer's efficiency.

Unlike a purely visual artist, however, Craig did need movement to fulfil his vision. Even at his most poetic he was never an abstract expressionist painter: he was too enamoured of the dynamic thrust of drama.

> Look there to the right – something seems to unfold – something to fold – what has unfolded – ? slowly quick-ening, without haste, fold after fold loosens itself and clasps another, till that which was void has become palpable ... until there stand before us vast columns of shapes....
>
> (Craig 1985: 238)

As long as Craig needed a vision to 'unfold' he needed a stage peopled with actors. It was not until very late in his career that Craig retreated into a cocoon of pure theory. Until that time he worked not as the visionary draughtsman we have come so much to admire but as a man fiendishly preoccupied with overhauling the principles of staging. The magnificently impractical Craig is today so much admired that his vastly innovative contributions to the *functional* art of stage design are sometimes overlooked. Perhaps the most interesting of these is the idea of using moving screens which would, as Craig observed, enable the director to 'pass from one scene to another without a break of any kind' (Innes 1983: 141). As luck would have it, the first time Craig used moving screens – in his 1912 Moscow Art Theatre production of *Hamlet* – they collapsed in a heap and had to be fixed to the floor. It was as if the fates were conspiring to imprison Craig within his unjustly acquired reputation for vision at the cost of practicality.

Craig's reputation for unreasonable idealism is less a function of any apathy he may have had with regard to practical matters than of the sheer scale of his vision. The descriptions we have of lighting effects used by Craig, for instance, bear witness to the care he lavished on getting functional details right. In the 1902 *Acis and Galatea*, for instance:

> the tent of grey streamers slowly disappeared, and in the vast expanse of blue sky a 'Water God' gradually materialized in the form of a great fountain where the sparkling beads of water rose and fell. This beautiful effect ... was, in fact, achieved by piercing holes in the backcloth and backlighting them; then, by revolving large perforated discs in front of the lamps, the spots of light came and went, producing the cascade effect.
>
> (Craig 1985: 152)

For *The Vikings*, Craig was able to generate an atmosphere of sinister foreboding by removing the footlights and having the stage top-lit with shafts of angular light. Once again we have the juxtaposition of Craig's attraction to unrealisable infinities with sound and inventive pragmatism. Craig did not merely generate fanciful sketches; he applied himself assiduously to the task of realising the effects he wanted.

To overhaul an inanimate medium such as stage design is difficult but not impossible; far more difficult is the task of orchestrating appropriately disciplined movement from actors. Craig's solution to the problem of having his visuals unfold to unnatural and sometimes inordinately slow rhythms was to use music to provide the precise tempo he required from his actors:

> we hear outside a rustling and the sound of feet, which create mingled fear and expectation. Bacchanals enter, and the maskers flee like startled fawns. A hymn to Bacchus follows, with lively movement of hands and bodies, and an interweaving dance. While the eyes are fed, the measure of a bright country dance enchants the ear, the masque closing with the usual procession.
>
> (Ibid.: 136)

Craig's use of music is another example of his having contrived to ensure the realisation of an ideal through concrete and practical means. Craig was a man hunched over a woodcut, not a theorist staring vacantly at a sheet of paper.

In spite of all the attention his productions received, Craig virtually retired from active theatre work at the age of forty. Given that he died at the age of ninety-four, he spent an extraordinary proportion of his life outside the theatre. 'I want time to study the Theatre', he wrote in his Daybook. 'I do not want to waste time producing plays' (ibid.: 261). The question is, why did this man, who clearly enjoyed practical work, abandon the theatre and take up teaching and writing? Perhaps Craig's productions fell short of his own very high standard for them – not because they failed to give material expression to his vision but because that vision was not sufficiently taut in the *dramatic* sense of the term. Craig's spectacular visuals detracted from the action of the plays he presented. His actors were dwarfed by his sets and their concerns were rendered trivial by the scale of their environment. The abstract interplay of moods and pictures lacked the hustle and bustle of human warmth which a drama needs to be engaging.

Dissatisfied with his work but unable to find a reason for his private sense of failure, Craig took to blaming everyone around him. Accounts of Craig's behaviour in rehearsals are littered with stories of impatient outbursts and dramatic separations:

> Craig arrived in time for the first run-through, but half-way caused such a disturbance with his shouts of dissatisfaction that he was told to keep away until the final dress-rehearsals. When he was allowed to return a week later, he again brought the rehearsal to a halt with violent complaints....[2]

On another occasion, Craig reprimanded a stage manager for adjusting the height of a proscenium so severely that Duse, who had promised life-long co-operation with Craig, ended her association with him, commenting that it was impossible to work with someone whose reactions were so disproportionately vehement. It was five years before Craig worked on the stage again.

Craig's statements on the condition of contemporary theatre practice were often imperious and sweeping in their condemnation. Craig's contention that 'To save the theatre, the theatre must be destroyed, the actors and actresses must all die of the plague' (quoted in Innes 1983: 119) is typical both of his arrogance and his frustration. The sweeping reforms he envisaged were not always feasible but this did not worry him as much as is generally supposed. What Craig found far more infuriating was the need for compromise that is an inevitable aspect of working with others. Craig was a stubbornly independent artist. He felt that theatre should, like painting and sculpture, express the vision of a single artist. It was this freedom that writing afforded. Theatre was, in the final analysis, just too full of other people for a spirit as uncompromising as that of Craig.

Notes

1   Braun, E. (1982) *The Director and the Stage*, London: Methuen: 85.
2   Ibid.: 91–92.

Further reading

Craig, E.G. (1981) *Index to the Story of My Days*, Cambridge: Cambridge University Press.

—— (1985) *Gordon Craig: The Story of his Life*, New York: Limelight Editions.

Innes, C. (1983) *Edward Gordon Craig*, Cambridge: Cambridge University Press.

Walton, M.J. (ed.) (1983) *Craig on Theatre*, London: Methuen.

SHOMIT MITTER

MAX REINHARDT (1873–1940)

Max Reinhardt's appetite for the theatre was gargantuan. As a theatre director, actor and producer working initially in Austria and Germany and then in the United States, he managed thirty different companies and directed more than 600 productions. As each of these plays had to have its own kind of space and its own set of lighting rules, its own style of acting and its unique form of music, so Reinhardt adapted his methods of staging to accommodate his panoply of sources. Through the course of his career, Reinhardt became a master of the big scale and the small, of epics and of chamber pieces. He worked on Shakespeare and the Greeks, contemporary plays and foreign texts. He worked within proscenium arches and on thrust stages, he staged plays in the round and in public spaces.

Ironically, Reinhardt was repeatedly taken to task for his ability unfailingly to adhere to his view that 'there is no one form of theatre which is the only true artistic form' (Styan 1982: 10). In 1914 Sheldon Cheney remarked that Reinhardt 'worked too fast to be the deep thinker and original creator that Craig is' (ibid.: 7). The German critic Ihering derided him for leaving 'no style, only productions ... no theatre, only performances' (ibid.: 2). Reinhardt contributed to the view that he was shallow by refusing to write about his approach to theatre. Where directors gain immeasurably from publishing theories that complement their practical work, Reinhardt remained defiantly silent, content to let his productions speak for him. The productions of course spoke in many voices and the lack of an authoritative account of the principle underlying his understanding of these plays generated the impression that he was satisfied merely with churning out productions without pausing to consider the impact of each taken in isolation. The alternative was far too daunting: it required one to concede that Reinhardt possessed an almost superhuman capacity for theatrical invention and that his lack of a distinctive style was the product of an imagination too great to be contained within the orbit of an exclusive idea.

Of course, Reinhardt did not single-handedly invent each of the styles in which he worked. The styles had, for the most part, evolved independently. All Reinhardt did was to try each one out for himself. In doing this, Reinhardt's experience mirrored the experience of Europe as a whole at the turn of the century, where no single style ruled and rival paradigms vied with each other for the theatregoer's endorsement. Berlin had felt the influence both of Théâtre Libre naturalism and the symbolist drama of Maeterlinck and Hofmannsthal. If one considers in addition to this the excitement generated by the expressionist leanings of writers like Büchner and Wedekind, we have a melting pot of styles more various perhaps than at any other time in the history of the theatre. Reinhardt's achievement was to take on board the impact of each of these schools of theatre and to work without prejudice to realise their incompatible visions. Through all this, Reinhardt himself remained impenetrably transcendent, a still centre beyond the gaggle of warring fashions and factions.

One of the most interesting things about Reinhardt's handling of the various conventions with which he rapidly made himself conversant is that he often combined them to create performances of unprecedented intensity. The important thing about his 1906 *Ghosts*, for instance, is not that it helped consolidate his break from the Otto Brahm school of naturalism, but that he *retained* elements of naturalistic acting on a stage heavy with shadows and a threatening claustrophobia. Reinhardt's comments on the sets, which had been designed by Edvard Munch, are replete with references to the manner in which colour, line and rhythm determine the emotional impact of the drama: 'the dark colouring reflects the whole atmosphere of the drama. And then look at the walls: they're the colour of diseased gums. We must try to get that tone. It will put the actors in the right mood' (ibid.: 20).

The vocabulary here ('dark', 'atmosphere', 'diseased', 'tone', 'mood') is a far cry from the concern with authenticity that had been the hallmark of Brahm's naturalism. Munch's designs conceded a certain artificiality of means: colours were chosen not because they were plausible but because they reflected deep aspects of temperament and circumstance that a more externally lifelike portrayal would never have been able properly to capture. The designs externalised the interior world of the characters. They created in both the actors and the audience a sensitivity to the prevalent tensions by infiltrating the subconscious through a network of associations too complex to resist. However, instead of filling this space with a corresponding degree of non-naturalistic acting, Reinhardt deliberately cast a number of actors skilled in realism so as to secure what he felt would be the maximum impact. This was of course a risk – for the obvious reason that the amalgamation of styles could easily have contributed to the detriment of each element. But it worked. Reinhardt had broken free of the constraining clutches of naturalism – but had retained its appeal to the extent that suited him. Reinhardt had set about becoming a jack of many trades – and master of all.

The amalgamation of styles works only if the director can ensure the integration of each element into a unified whole geared to produce a single, premeditated impression. Reinhardt's early forays into symbolism had emphasised the importance of colour, sound and texture as bearers of dramatic meaning. Design was therefore no longer secondary, a matter of backdrops and locations, but a primary factor in the communication of an emotion.

Correspondingly, the contribution of language was downplayed so as to achieve a proper balance of elements. The 1910 *Sumurun*, for example, had little or no text, as the principal vehicle of the narrative was pantomime and dance. The appeal of the 1916 *The Ghost Sonata* was less a function of Strindberg's powerfully expressionistic text than Reinhardt's ability to meet it with a plethora of devices aimed at sustaining the macabre mood of the play: Reinhardt had church bells sound and shadows fall, colours fade and fingers drum on tables. The music even played through the interval so as to sustain the atmosphere of unrelenting tension. For the 1917 *The Beggar*, he had a spotlight pick out chalky white faces in a pitch black stage, disembodied expressions released from the constraints of time and place. For the 1920 *Danton's Death* he had spotlights come on and go off in accordance with the rhythm certain scenes required. When colour was used, it was in accordance with a painter's sense of the emotion associated with each shade on a carefully selected palette of moods: red, for example, suggested madness and prompted the use of red furnishings in *The Beggar*. Even the actor became yet another aspect of the overall mood of a scene, a body whose plasticity deserved no greater privilege than was afforded to the harps that played and the shouts that reverberated through a haze of indistinct silhouettes. The actor was an element in a picture, on par with every other element, one factor in a multitude of impressions that together conveyed the play.

With a plethora of elements all competing for a share of the overall appeal of each production, the need arose to harmonise their respective contributions. The secret of Reinhardt's success in this regard was the institution of the so-called *Regiebuch*, the detailed blueprint out of which each of his productions grew. These extraordinary documents betray a level of planning that is quite breathtaking in scale and detail, with notes not only on the inanimate elements such as design and lighting but on movement, gesture, expression, even tones of voice. The *Regiebuch* was the still point of control at the centre of Reinhardt's work. It gave him the confidence to move between styles and conventions without fear of being assailed by unforeseen hazards. It also permitted him to assemble productions on the scale of *Everyman* and *The Miracle* that required he play God to an extent that had never occurred before. With *Everyman* (1920) virtually the whole of central Salzburg became his stage. Actors entered not only from the audience but from nearby streets and houses.

Voices called out not only from within the church in front of which the play was staged but from the tops of castles and cathedrals in neighbouring squares and hillsides. Even the sunlight was used to best advantage, with the performance being timed so as to allow crucial moments in the story to be played in the light of the setting sun, and others to be glimpsed in the thickening darkness of night. The 1911 version of *The Miracle*, which Reinhardt staged at Olympia in London, involved 2000 actors, a choir of 500 and an orchestra of 200, all controlled by a network of messengers on bicycles who carried Reinhardt's instructions around a 100,000 square feet of playing space. This was Reinhardt at his best, the theatre director as field marshal, and it is this image of Reinhardt that has proved to be the most durable.

Reinhardt's reliance on the institution of the *Regiebuch* suggests that what his background in naturalism had in common with his subsequently more expressionistic and symbolist leanings was a heavy emphasis on directorial orchestration. But Reinhardt was chameleon enough to let go even of his determination to regulate every aspect of a production. Reinhardt revived *A Midsummer Night's Dream* many times between 1905 and 1939 – and the evolution of the production is the story of the gradual relinquishing of control. In the early days the impression of the wood was, for example, carefully cultivated through the interplay of a plethora of carefully lit screens:

> Through these silver screens the moon shines palely, and slowly the light increases. The screens are raised slowly one after another in individual trails of mist. Streams trickle.... On the right is seen a lake glinting between the trees.... Moonlight, which falls in patches on the grass through the leaf pattern. The lake is lit from behind.
>
> (Ibid.: 55–56)

By the time the production had reached Vienna in 1925, the stage was virtually bare, a playing-space in front of green curtains which merely suggested the wood. The scenic display had become less obtrusive, and the stage was given over principally to the actors. When, in 1933, Reinhardt adapted his production to an outdoor space in Oxford, this principle of ceasing obsessively to manage the production was carried one step further: control was, quite simply, handed over to nature. It was not that the *Regiebuch* had been abandoned but that the wood was now real, and Puck climbed real trees

25

from which to ply his loveable mischief. Reinhardt, who had spent a lifetime contriving to create a whole range of effects in a whole range of styles, had ceased to concoct, devise and fashion his playing environment.

It takes courage to release control, especially if one has spent a lifetime ensuring that one retains it. And it takes courage to assume that one will retain one's control in the face of the insuperable demands made by productions of the size of the *Everyman*. Courage is a moral term, not an aesthetic one – but it is the core of what is most fascinating about Reinhardt. It takes courage to undertake to work in every style and convention that the dramatic form has to offer. In this respect Reinhardt's work as a whole is itself a baroque spectacle, exercising a fascination that has more in common with the great tales of the triumph of the human spirit than with the work of this or that director. Reinhardt's greatness is a function of his infinitely capacious vision, his capacity to create as many worlds in as many ways as we believe could possibly exist.

Further reading

Styan, J.L. (1982) *Max Reinhardt*, Cambridge: Cambridge University Press.

SHOMIT MITTER

VSEVOLOD MEYERHOLD (1874–1940)

The Russian director Vsevolod Meyerhold is perhaps the most under-rated of the great modern theatre directors. Although theatre practitioners have long hailed Meyerhold as the 'father of modern theatre', the everyday theatregoer continues to be ignorant of the scale of the revolution Meyerhold instigated in European theatre at the turn of the century. There are two reasons for this. First, today's audiences are so accustomed to theatricality, to the absence of stage curtains and visible scene changes, to the minimalist use of sets and stage properties, that they are unable to appreciate just how radical the use of these devices was in Meyerhold's time. Second, a significant part of Meyerhold's achievement is still wrongly attributed to **Brecht**. The break with Stanislavskian realism, the use of episodic structures punctuated with music and song, the tendency to draw attention to the fictional basis of stage action, the use of projections and captions, the institution of a critical distance between the actor and the role are all devices which Meyerhold used well before

Brecht; yet in the mind of the casual theatre-lover these are all associated principally with the work of the Berliner Ensemble.

Meyerhold would be the first to acknowledge that he did not invent these devices as much as re-discover the theatricality that had always been a feature of the great dramatic traditions of the past, but which had been sacrificed to the nineteenth-century preoccupation with realism. Meyerhold's writings are replete with references to ancient Greek and Shakespearean theatre, to the tradition of the *commedia*, to the carnivals and festivals of sixteenth-century Europe – all of which flourished precisely because they were *not* tied to the needlessly restrictive fixation with sustaining stage illusion:

> Neither the antique stage nor the popular stage of Shakespeare's time had any need for the scenery which the striving for illusion demands nowadays.... It was the same in medieval Japan. In the Noh plays, with their refined ceremony in which movement, dialogue and singing were all rigidly stylized, ... special stage-assistants, known as 'kurogo' and clad in special black costumes resembling cassocks, used to prompt the actors in full view of the audience....
>
> (Braun 1969: 99–100)

In Meyerhold's production of *The Fairground Booth* (1906), the prompter and the stage hands were visible. Meyerhold's use of the fore-stage, of dance, of the absence of emotional motivation all derived in one way or another from his brief experience of Japanese theatre. Meyerhold was not 'original' in his use of these devices. His achievement was to have recognised the value of these techniques when realism was all-pervasive and to have had the courage to re-introduce theatricality to the theatre.

At the core of Meyerhold's revolution was an understanding of the manner in which theatre uses convention as a means of helping the audience to construe stage action as reality. 'Art and life are governed by different laws' (ibid.: 147), writes Meyerhold; 'the play of the actor differs from the behaviour of people in life by its special rhythm and by the special devices of playing' (Leach 1989: 127). The audience comes to the theatre equipped not merely with an understanding of these laws but with an appetite for the use of 'special devices' that comprise an essential part of the entertainment theatre affords: 'in the theatre the spectator's imagination is able to supply that which is left unsaid. It is this mystery and the desire to solve it which draw so many people to the theatre' (Braun 1969: 25).

By neutralising the distance between art and life, naturalism denies the spectator the pleasure of decoding stage action. 'More than anyone, the Moscow Art Theatre is to blame for the passivity of the spectator whom it held in thrall for so long' (ibid.: 174), wrote Meyerhold, proposing as an alternative a theatre in which there would be 'no pauses, no psychology, no "authentic emotions" ', all of which would be replaced by 'plenty of light, plenty of high spirits [and] … the participation of the audience in the corporate creative act of the performance' (Braun 1986: 154). For one tutored by **Nemirovich-Danchenko** and then raised on the hallowed traditions of the Moscow Art Theatre, such a project was revolutionary.

Not surprisingly, Meyerhold's relationship with the senior figures of the Moscow Art Theatre was almost always fraught with conflict. **Stanislavsky** did eventually encourage Meyerhold to open a Studio Theatre at the Moscow Art Theatre. Part of the reason for this was Stanislavsky's growing sense of the failure of realism to address the so-called 'New-Drama' of symbolist dramatists such as Maeterlinck, Verhaeren and Przybyszewski. At the core of the symbolist sensibility was a desire to penetrate beneath the surface of things, to evoke a reality that cuts across the appearances with which Stanislavsky had been so fastidiously involved. It was in his attempt to find appropriate ways of staging the new symbolist drama that Meyerhold forged his identity as a radical new director of the Russian avant-garde.

The concept of the symbol is not merely semantic, whereby something 'stands for' something else; it also implies a measure of economy whereby a large and complex phenomenon is distilled into a single image. The pleasure a symbol yields is a function both of the skill of the poet, who is able to find in a simple figure the synthesis of a more intricate and unstable reality, and the imagination of the reader, who travels this distance in reverse and deciphers the emblem. In the theatre this involves the deployment of a few telling features which, when interpreted, deliver a more elaborate reality. Thus, for example, when Meyerhold writes of the set for his production of *Schluck and Jau* (1905) that the 'mood of idleness and whimsy is *conveyed by* a row of arbours',[1] the arbours single-handedly signify what Stanislavsky would have communicated by cramming his stage full of decadent delights. Again, 'in giving Tesman a loose jacket with sloping shoulders, an exaggeratedly wide tie, and broad trousers tapering sharply towards the bottoms, the designer, Vassily Miliotti, has sought to express the essence of "Tesmanism" ' (Braun 1969: 65) – which is of course a far cry from the naturalistic obsession with establishing 'the exact style of sleeve worn in the time of Louis XV' (ibid.: 24). Instead of lifelike externals, we get an interior portrait of character that must actively be deciphered. The symbolic use of setting and costume not only achieves a greater density of expression – communicating more with a greater economy of means – but also involves the audience to a greater extent. Stylisation requires that the spectator engage creatively with the action and complete in his or her mind's eye what has merely been cryptically suggested on stage.

In the years immediately preceding the Russian Revolution, the participation of the audience in Meyerhold's dramas was less a matter of decoding symbols than of mutual involvement with the momentous political situation that was beginning to grip Russia. Just as Meyerhold had responded to the New Drama of the early 1900s with greater alacrity than his Moscow Art Theatre seniors, so also he was now better able than them to respond to the turmoil of revolution. By 1920 Meyerhold was putting on performances free of charge in unheated premises for leather jacket-clad Red Army men who would clamber up onto the stage periodically and stamp their feet in uproarious and vehement participation. This was theatre as a meeting place, complete with interruptions for hourly news updates and political speeches. Edward Braun describes the first performance of Emile Verhaeren's *The Dawn* (1920), a symbolist work which Meyerhold rapidly adapted into a play 'with one aim only: to serve the cause of the Revolution' (Braun 1986: 187).

> Admission was free, the walls were hung with hortatory placards, and the audience was showered at intervals during the play with leaflets. Also derived from the meeting was the declamatory style of the actors, who mostly remained motionless and addressed their speeches straight at the audience.... A fortnight after the production had opened, the actor playing the Herald interrupted his performance to deliver the news received the day before that the Red Army had made a decisive breakthrough into the Crimea.... As the applause died down, a solo voice began to sing the Revolutionary funeral march.... The action on stage then resumed its course.... *The Dawn* depended very much on the mood of the audience on the night for its success.[2]

The audience was now a segment of 'the people' who had to be 'served' by the theatre. Meyerhold, sensitive as ever to the spirit of the times, realised that it was no longer possible to keep art and politics apart.

What Meyerhold's political theatre had in common with his earlier symbolist work was the ease with which it measured its distance from reality and declared itself to be merely an artefact, a product of human contrivance. Thus Meyerhold's house lights often remained on and his stage lights remained unconcealed. He would seat his audience around the action and use the aisles and steps within the auditorium as playing areas so that spectators could see each other watching the drama. When Meyerhold's Harlequin leapt through a window, it turned out to be only a frame with blue paper stuck to it.

Meyerhold's problem was that his actors, trained in the naturalist mould, found such artificiality extremely difficult to sustain. Meyerhold's solution was to evolve an alternative system of actor training that would bring about what he called 'the advent of *the new actor*' (Braun 1969: 82):

> The Theatre Studio demonstrated to everybody who made its acquaintance that it is impossible to build a new theatre on old foundations. Either one must continue the construction of the Antoine-Stanislavsky theatre, or one must begin all over again....
>
> It was then that it struck me that an acting school ... must be organized so that a new theatre arises out of it.
>
> (Ibid.: 46)

In 1913 Meyerhold opened a studio to train actors in voice and movement techniques along with some grounding in the history of the popular theatre traditions such as the *commedia*. As Erast Garin recalls: 'beginning with elementary exercises in metrical patterns, we progressed to more complicated tasks: mastery of free rhythmical movement against a metrical pattern and, finally, to mastery of free movement in an unrestricted counterpoint' (Schmidt 1996: 40).

Along with training in gymnastics, Meyerhold's actors had to study anatomy and physiology. This combination of academic rigour and physical discipline led to the evolution of 'biomechanics', a system of movement which employed conflicts between opposing forces as a means of generating dramatic tension in the body.

In time the discipline of biomechanics came to influence the manner in which stage action was presented. Sequences of action were introduced into scenes that contradicted their overall momentum so as to heighten the significance of the action. Meyerhold would deliberately interrupt scenes requiring a quick tempo with moments of slow movement so as to create a rhythmic tension that would grip the spectator with its unexpectedness. Scenes would also be played in such a manner that opposing emotions were presented simultaneously:

> Bruno ... stood before the audience, his face pale and motionless, and with unvarying intonation ... uttered his grandiloquent monologues. But at the same time this Bruno was being ridiculed by the actor performing acrobatic stunts at the most impassioned moments of his speeches, belching and comically rolling his eyes whilst enduring the most dramatic anguish.
>
> (Boris Alpers in Braun 1969: 174)

One can see how biomechanics did not merely give the actor the physical means of executing such contortions but also the mental dexterity to be able to inhabit two positions – that of actor and character – at once. This was Meyerhold's 'new actor', one who was capable of retaining a critical distance from the character and was able, as a result, to persuade the audience to do so as well.

When Meyerhold's audience was buffeted around by abrupt changes of perspective it was as much to draw attention to certain elements in the drama as to generate in the audience an experience of the uncertainty which, in spite of Meyerhold's professed Bolshevism, was deeply symptomatic of the unpredictable world Meyerhold believed he inhabited. Meyerhold brought theatre into the twentieth century not merely by re-introducing theatricality but by fashioning a working image of a heterogeneous and uncertain world. At base, what is interesting about Meyerhold is not so much the issue of artificiality versus realism as much as the dawn of a deep-seated indeterminacy, of a multiplicity of viable world-views. It was in this sense that Meyerhold was truly modern before his time.

Notes

1　Braun, E. (1982) *The Director and the Stage*, London: Methuen: 111. My italics.
2　Ibid.: 131–133.

Further reading

Braun, E. (ed.) (1969) *Meyerhold on Theatre*, London: Eyre Methuen.
—— (1986) *The Theatre of Meyerhold*, London: Methuen.

Leach, R. (1989) *Vsevolod Meyerhold*, Cambridge: Cambridge University Press.

Schmidt, P. (ed.) (1996) *Meyerhold at Work*, London: Applause.

SHOMIT MITTER

JACQUES COPEAU (1879–1949)

Judged by his own standards, Copeau was a relative failure as a director and, one might add, as an actor, a playwright and a dramatic pedagogue. That judgement should not surprise us, since his role-models were Aeschylus, Molière, Shakespeare and Zeami. Copeau's writings are permeated with regret that he did not live in a time that was ripe for theatrical exploitation, a golden age when vital strands of poetic and polemic could have been drawn together by an *homme de théâtre* of genius, preferably his own. Working as he did largely during and between the two world wars, such an enduring achievement proved unattainable – either he was not the man, or it was not the hour, or both. And Paris, 'that most fashionable of cities', as he called it, was certainly not the place. He was temperamentally ill-disposed to the kind of success which the city had to offer:

> The truth is that success, far from going to my head, contin-
> ually sobered me. That is because, as I was learning my craft,
> I became acquainted with its difficulties and its resources;
> the more I worked, the more I became dazzled by the possi-
> bilities of my art. New ideas filled my mind, discoveries
> enriched by imagination. And none of these things could
> have a place in our frenzied daily work which was slowly
> eroding my strength and taking me away from myself.
>
> (Rudlin and Paul 1990: 52)

The things that he could work on included such key concepts as sanctity of the text, scenic architecture (as opposed to individual production design), the renovation of classical theatre and the search for a contemporary style of playwrighting. However, the new ideas which created for him such an ever-receding horizon included, amongst others, the creation of a new improvised comedy and a new 'choric' tragedy, ensemble playing (in a 'brotherhood', as he called it) and a quest for a popular religious theatre. Copeau was the first to admit that his vision was apostolic. In 1919 he wrote to Jean Schlumberger, the first manager of his Parisian theatre the Vieux

32

Colombier: 'Some have already called me, derisively or insultingly, an apostle. If I am not that, I am nothing.' When the Vieux Colombier was scornfully referred to as a chapel, and its director as a theatrical Jansenist, Copeau retorted:

> These jibes do not frighten us. What is *religious* is everything which brings men together. Nothing great is ever accomplished without faith, and it is precisely that semi-religious consciousness of our art and our mission which constitutes the best in our ideal. What we want is to appeal to the public, to that public which needs something more than life can offer and comes to find it in the theatre.
>
> (Ibid.: 200)

He wanted his chapel, which he had stripped of all vestiges of nineteenth-century fourth-wall illusionism, to offer the possibility of communion between a small congregation and a catholic (with a small 'c') repertoire of past and modern classics and new plays. During the war he had written to one of his principal collaborators, Louis Jouvet, that he sought 'communion of the heart, and of the whole being, in a work which is as impassioned ... as sacred as that of the artisans of the Middle Ages (and like them in simplicity and in lack of pretension)' (Mignon 1993: 112). He wanted no part of the Little Theatre movement, but as a necessary first step in the re-development of the art of theatre, he was content with an auditorium of only 360 seats provided there was an audience 'composed partly of intelligent theatre-lovers, partly of people who no longer want to encourage the banality and insincerity of commercial theatre, and partly by a new cross-section of the public' (Rudlin and Paul 1990: 132). One such spectator, Rainer Maria Rilke, commented:

> What a pleasure to see well-intentioned forces on stage, seemly, decent, developing their thoughts in front of you, not wishing to win you over despite yourself by the use of tricks, but simply by being there as well-ordered humanity. What a beautiful, healthy and happy conception of theatre, and how much we all have need of it.
>
> (Mignon 1993: 90)

Copeau's vision of the Vieux Colombier was as a 'pure instrument' and unadulterated medium for the best dramatic poetry available; that was why, for its opening in 1913, he created what he called a *dispositif fixe*, an unchangeable architectural setting. He felt that texts were de-stabilised by changing décor, whereas 'a given stage architecture calls forth, demands and gives rise to a certain dramatic conception and style of presentation'(Rudlin and Paul 1990: 88). The stages of his masters, the Greeks, the Elizabethans, Molière and Noh, all had such an immutable quality. For its 1919 re-opening, the Vieux Colombier stage was re-cast in concrete with flights of stairs and ramps reminiscent of the designs of Adolphe Appia, inflexible, adamantine planes on which to act. During the summer closure in 1920, when looking at the stage one day 'in its natural state', he reflected 'I understood that everything that had happened to it last season – props, costumes, actors and lights – had only disfigured it. It is thus from the stage that we must proceed' (ibid.: 86).

In that dedicated space, Copeau placed the revered text: a play not worthy of such respect was, for Copeau, not worth interpreting. What he offered his audience were presentations rather than productions of such texts; production concepts were not imposed directorially, but discovered from within the lines themselves. He kept his actors seated round a table reading the play for as long as he was able to sustain their interest in analysing not only their own parts, but the meaning and rhythms of the text as a whole. Once on stage (he had no need of rehearsal rooms because a repertoire system enabled daytime use of the main stage, which was uncluttered by décor) he would sketch out his staging plan in terms of groupings and entrances and exits, and then rehearse '*sotto voce*, without any eloquence, careful not to force the text, just sketching tempo and rhythm without trying to achieve anything too early'.[1] The actors would then learn their lines and plunge into the actual interpretation. When they seemed to lose their initial grasp, Copeau encouraged his actors to maintain a physical sense of identity with their role and not to worry about the emotions they were supposed to be embodying. His function was to be the actor's 'guide and main-stay'. His main task was

> to keep the actor in line and within the limits of his part, not only to indicate to him when he is near the truth, not only to correct his mistake, but also to understand the difficulties confronting the actor and to show him how to solve those difficulties.[2]

His attitude was confidential, even confessional. So it was, too, with prop-makers, costumiers and technicians – seemingly every detail of a Copeau production had to have a difficulty, and that difficulty had to be resolved by him.

It was hardly surprising, therefore, that even after the 1919/20 season, the tension between Copeau's ideal and the actuality of what was possible began to wear him down. The last two years of the war had seen the company in New York performing a kind of 'weekly rep', a punishing schedule necessitated by the paucity of French speakers from which to form an audience. Now, no longer carrying the banner of French culture in exile, but greatly expected of by his home-town cultural elite, the daily grind did not cease and the modern affliction of artistic 'burn-out' began. By the end of the 1923/24 Vieux Colombier season, Copeau was no longer healthy and certainly not happy with either fixed stage, available texts or the quality of the actors. The concrete surface had re-affirmed the strengths of the classics, but had proved inhospitable to new dramatists. According to his friend André Gide, it was the authors who abandoned Copeau, but it would be truer to say that it was he who progressively abandoned the authors, since few of the plays presented had the poetic quality that he sought.

Furthermore, his own attempt to write the missing masterpiece, his long-awaited *La Maison natale*, had been a fiasco and was withdrawn after only a few performances. As to the actors, they needed more, not less, directorial correction or they lapsed into the old ways, reducing productions to 'their habits, their clichés, their affectations. They do not invent anything', Copeau protested, 'it is all sheer imitation of imitation' (Rudlin 1986: 45). Copeau locked the door of the Vieux Colombier and left the purging of Parisian theatre to his peer group, notably Louis Jouvet and Charles Dullin, in order to pursue some of his other new ideas. For five years he experimented with a company of young actors in a rural retreat in Burgundy. The 'brotherhood' of *Les Copiaux*, emergent from the acting school of the Vieux Colombier, now supplanted the latter. The text now took second place to the creativity of the actor, the actor to the ensemble, the ensemble, it has to be said, to its director.

Under Copeau's supervision, with his dramaturgical support and frequent participation as performer, the *Copiaux* took a few steps down a path along which he hoped others would later go further. The use of masks became as fundamental to their performance as to their training, the bare-boarded trestle stage of the *commedia dell'arte* their *dispostif fixe*. In 1929 Copeau moved away from the problems of day-to-day production work. When the little troupe created their first autonomous piece, *Les Jeunes fens et l'araignée*, he perceived it no longer embodied his ideas or how he felt they should be presented. *Les Copiaux*, in some relief, changed their name to *La Compagnie des quinze* and carried on without him.

It can be said that Copeau's theatrical quest was not only for communion, but also for Communion. (He had become a practising Catholic again in 1925.) In large-scale outdoor productions of religious texts – *Santa Uliva* (1933), *Savonarola* (1935) and *Le Miracle du pain doré* (1943) – and his play about St Francis of Assisi, *Le Petit pauvre* (never performed in his lifetime), he was able to create theatre of Faith even though he no longer had much faith in theatre. He perceived that the role of drama was no longer tied to the provision of nightly entertainment – that function could be left to the new media of cinema and radio – but had the possibility of creating mass spectacles for high days and holy days. In these productions, actual architecture replaced scenic architecture and the open air of the cloisters of Santa Croce in Venice and the Hospices de Beaune in Burgundy replaced the concrete of the Vieux, overtaken by enthusiasm for the role of the chorus and the choir in the search for the mysterious and the metaphysical. In a medieval mystery play, which he adapted for the celebration of the 500th anniversary of the founding of the Hospices de Beaune, and in which he played the role of the *meneur du jeu*, he was able to commune not only with an audience and fellow actors, but also with himself and with his conception of the divine.

Notes

1 Saint-Denis, Michel (1982) *Training for the Theatre*, New York and London: Heinemann: 30.
2 Jacques Copeau, quoted in Cole, Toby and Chinoy, Helen Krich (eds) (1963) *Directors on Directing: A Sourcebook of the Modern Theatre*, New York: Pearson Allyn & Bacon: 150.

Further reading

Mignon, Paul-Louis (1993) *Jacques Copeau*, Paris: Julliard.

Rudlin, John (1986) *Jacques Copeau*, Cambridge: Cambridge University Press.

Rudlin, John and Paul, Norman H. (eds and trans.) (1990) *Jacques Copeau: Texts on Theatre*, London: Routledge.

JOHN RUDLIN

ALEXANDER TAIROV (1885–1950)

The standard interpretation of twentieth-century Russian theatre still cautiously regards Alexander Tairov as a marginal figure. The fact that Tairov was alien to both of the mainstream traditions of Russian theatre – Stanislavskian psychologism and the more formal Meyerholdian approach – prompts scholars to view Tairov's art as a peculiar and extraneous offspring. The director's singularity thus impedes solid, objective approaches to the legacy of the Moscow Kamerny theatre which was founded by Tairov in 1914 and was, for the next thirty-five years, recognised as a major force in Russian theatre. The Kamerny was closed for alleged cosmopolitanism during one of the last Stalinist campaigns, a ruthless move which confirmed how alien the director's formal aesthetics were to officially approved socialist realism.

Tairov's contribution might be viewed in terms of four interrelated concepts that comprised the director's aesthetics: aesthetic theatre, synthetic production, the master actor and rhythm. All four aspects had deep roots in the modernist culture of the Russian Silver Age (1900–17). From this whirlpool of ideas, innovations and aspirations two major philosophical influences must be noted – that of the phenomenologist Gustav Schpet and that of the poet-theoretician Vyacheslav Ivanov. What Tairov derived from them was a modernist sensibility steeped in the crisis of the Christian humanist world-view that occurred when the previously indivisible ideal of Truth, Goodness and Beauty collapsed into three autonomous entities.

Choosing Beauty over Goodness and Truth early in his career, he interpreted it as an all-encompassing concept absorbing the other two. Beauty was evinced both in the overall form of his productions and as a female presence central to the plot. With respect to its visual aspect, the beauty of an image or movement turned out to be its own justification: it manifested itself on Tairov's stage in ever-mutating patterns of light, colour, movements and dynamic designs, as if the director complied with Kazimir Malevich's idea that one should 'make visual beauty self-sufficient.... Why may not beauty exist in non-comprehensible forms?'[1] Beauty as a female presence manifested itself in the tragic image created by Alisa Koonen, Tairov's leading lady and a great Russian tragedienne. This personification of Beauty was courageous enough to meet an inferior and hostile world face to face – despite her impending doom. The centripetal *mise-en-scène* in which Koonen stood wilfully centre-stage – towering over the world, detached from everyday life and immersed in the tragic sublime – turned out to be emblematic of the whole of Tairov's *œuvre*. As the raving world tried to destroy her, she was both grandiose and fragile, arrogant and helpless.

Although beautiful and enchanting, Tairov's productions often ignored everything that seemed to him too trivially human to be interesting. The everyday charms of domestic life were left to the Moscow Art Theatre to describe. Spirit rather than amity prevailed on Tairov's stage. Tairov's characters were of the heroic type and therefore had no chance of establishing a rapport with their peers. The notion of intimacy between the actors on stage and the audience in the stalls was also ruled out for the same reason. The primacy of the aesthetic principle led Tairov to perceive theatre as an end in itself. For him, a stage always remained a stage, a place for acting, with no need either to imitate life (naturalistic theatre) or to reflect the transcendental (symbolist theatre).

Schpet, who believed that theatre was an autonomous and not interpretative art form, helped Tairov shape his call for 'the theatricalisation of Theatre'.[2] The objective was to synthesise the elements of speaking, singing, dancing, pantomime and circus within a new type of stage production that was not drama, opera, ballet or pantomime but was related instead to the syncretic theatre of Ancient Greece. Tairov's theatre at its best – including such shows as *Princess Brambilla* (1920), *Phèdre* and *Giroflé-Girofla* (1922), *Desire under the Elms* and *Day and Night* (1926), *The Negro* (1929), *The Beggars' Opera* (1930) and *An Optimistic Tragedy* (1933) – never was, and was never meant to be, a purely dramatic theatre.

Synthesis in acting entailed the problem of genres. The fact that the elements of singing, speaking and dancing had to be blended together not only necessitated more universal content but also made it impossible for Tairov to put on psychological, realistic and documentary drama. Tairov came to identify two structures capable of accommodating such creations – namely, tragedy-mystery and comedy-harlequinade. Both genres were suitable for Tairov's movement-based blocking, larger-than-life gestures and rhythmic patterns of speech and action. Middle genres such as melodrama and tragicomedy were rigorously excluded until 1923 when, starting with *A Man Who Was Thursday*, various other combinations began to creep in. Harlequinade melted into revue and musical comedy with strong satirical overtones; tragedy lowered itself to the level of expressionist drama and, finally, to the politically correct play.

In addition to synthesis, Vyacheslav Ivanov introduced Tairov to the system of ideas expressed in Nietzsche's 'The Birth of Tragedy From the Spirit of Music'. The Apollonian/Dionysian dichotomy and the idea of music as an art form kindred to theatre became seminal to Tairov's practice. His tragic dramas began to display a complexity and diversity within the Apollonian/Dionysian paradigm in terms of both content and form: Tairov would either have an Apollonian character bringing harmony to a Dionysian world or a Dionysian creature revolting against the Apollonian pressure. An artist with a meticulous formal discipline, Tairov premiered exquisitely polished shows in which gestural and vocal components were executed with precision and harmony. The director renounced the vague imagery of symbolism, with its mystical truths and disengaged acting. Instead, he emphasised local colours, tangible, three-dimensional settings, ample gestures – the Apollonian principle of order and clarity. Tragedy moved forward armoured in ritual and harlequinade rolled on as a calculated counter-mechanism.

The concept of a synthetic production brought forward the third major component of Tairov's aesthetics, namely the master actor. Indeed, as the usually separate elements of speaking, singing, dancing and pantomime now constituted a unified means of expression for the actor, only an actor-virtuoso was able to realise their union on stage. Hence Tairov placed great emphasis on the actor's craftsmanship, on the versatility with which the actor's body and voice were used. In the acting school he founded as part of the Kamerny theatre, Tairov equipped physically fit and disciplined actors with a complete command of plasticity and rhythmic expression. Voice skills such as poetic declamation and singing were required as well. The director's pronouncement about an actor being 'the sole and sovereign bearer of the theatre art' (Tairov 1969: 90) was neither a truism nor a figure of speech. Tairov encouraged his actors to demonstrate their skills: for him, the essence of the theatrical act had nothing to do with the transformation of self into the character. The character's fictional stage existence did not supersede the real process of the actor's virtuoso flamboyance. During rehearsals the members of the Kamerny company never identified themselves with their parts: 'he'/'she' rather than 'I' was the pronoun used to denote character. In this respect, Tairov's actors were similar to *commedia dell'arte* performers with their joyful souls and jubilant spirit. The actor on the stage personified for Tairov a paragon of a human being fully consummated in the process of creative self-realisation.

While the actors created performances without ever losing a conscious awareness of the act of creation, the audience was cast as a passive recipient in Tairov's theatre. Spectators were supposed to admire a ready-made theatrical product rather than actively make connections using their own experience and imagination. The spectator's experience was limited to formal aesthetic pleasure: there was no question of emotional identification with the story-line. The pleasure the audience got from a performance was, in Tairov's view, a function of the formal combinations of the different rhythms he employed on stage.

Rhythm was the fourth major component of Tairov's aesthetics and always remained the foundation of his explorations. Following Nietzsche, Tairov believed that 'music is the closest to the art of theatre' (ibid.: 153). He sought a basic theatrical principle that was similar to a musical one. He strove to unveil the secret music of a play, hidden beneath its plot and topical message. Rhythm became a fundamental structural principle for the director's compositions. The architectural forms of a stage set – whether they were rendered as cubist or constructivist – were to reveal visual rhythms. Dark lines of stage make-up were to outline the rhythms of bodies and faces. Costumes helped to reveal the patterns of the actors' movements. The ever-changing rhythms of lights, colours and moving screens harmonised with the rhythms of speech, adding to the expressiveness of the director's theatrical composition.

Tairov's best productions were balletic in nature. In 1959, Erwin **Piscator**, recalling his impressions of the Russian avant-garde theatre, wrote of a specific 'Tairov' element that expressed itself in a 'particular virtuosity ... and integration of all [production elements] into movement and form'.[3] Piscator suggested something of a visual *gestalt* – a magnificent collective effort in which the integration of elements was attained by structuring everything on stage to the principle of a visual rhythm. The gestures, movements and relocations in space – like a grandiose dynamic painting that was executed by the actors' bodies – seem to have impressed Tairov's contemporaries more than any unfolding story-line. Supported by light and colour, these conflicts of pure movement – ascending versus descending, diagonal versus horizontal, centripetal versus centrifugal – rendered stage action in a larger-than-life, non-psychological way. They were not completely devoid of human emotions, however: as Andrei Levinson pointed out, Tairov 'discovered an entire inventory of indispensable, essential, and perfect gestures, poses, and groups capable of expressing the most deep and primal human feelings'.[4]

Notes

1   Malevich, K. (1999) 'Teatr <1>', *Eksperiment* 5: 98.

2   Tairov, A. (1970) *Zapiski rezhissera. Stat'i. Besedy. Rechi. Pis'ma*, Moskva: VTO: 192.
3   Piscator, E. (1959) 'Deutsche und Russische Theater: Gesprach mit G. Semmer, 10.6.1959', photocopied document in the Piscator Archive in the Akademie der Kunste, Berlin, cited in Kolyazin, Vladimir (1998) *Tairov, Meyerhold i Germaniya. Piskator, Brekht i Rossiya*, Moskva: GITIS: 62.
4   Rudnitsky, K. (1995) 'Strukturnyi realism Aleksandra Tairova (20–e gody)' in *Mir iskusstv: Al'manakh*, Moskva: RIK 'Kul'tura': 57.

Further reading

Tairov, A. (1969) *Notes of a Director*, trans. W. Kuhlke and C. Gables, Miami: University of Miami Press.

DASHA KRIJANSKAIA

ERWIN PISCATOR (1893–1966)

Erwin Piscator was an unlikely revolutionary. In the summer of 1914 he was a student of philosophy and theatre history at Munich. He was not terribly interested in politics and his only practical experience of the theatre was that of an amateur. The First World War changed all that:

> My calendar begins on August 4, 1914...
>
> 13 million dead
> 11 million maimed....
>
> The twenty-year-old was confronted by War. Destiny. It made every other teacher superfluous.
>
> (Piscator 1963: 7)

For Piscator, the scale of the havoc wrought by the war, together with the futility of its objectives, was clear evidence of the decadence and irresponsibility of bourgeois society. At the same time there was sufficient contact between communist Berlin and revolutionary Moscow for Piscator to have construed the revolution as the solution to all social ills. Just as the war alone incited him to action, so also the revolution alone rapidly became his objective.

One of the effects of Piscator's experience of the Front was that it made theatre – and art in general – seem decadent, a luxury that the

41

times could ill afford. As a result, Piscator viewed himself less as an artist than as a revolutionary who happened to chance upon the theatre as a convenient vehicle for his propaganda. A conspicuous feature of his book *The Political Theatre*, is its impatience with art in the face of the call to insurrection. 'Less art, more politics' (ibid.: 25) is an exclamation that runs through the book like a refrain. 'We banned the word *art* radically from our program', writes Piscator proudly, 'our "plays" were appeals and were intended to have an effect on current events, to be a form of "political activity" ' (ibid.: 45).

Piscator's early work reflects this exclusive concern with revolution and apparent disregard for the niceties of artistic endeavour. In 1920 Piscator started the Proletarisches Theater with a group of amateurs with strong communist credentials who put on simple but inflammatory political sketches in working-class bars. *Russia's Day* (1920), for instance, challenged its audience quite unambiguously: 'Either active solidarity with Soviet Russia in the course of the coming months', the programme read, '– or international Capital will succeed in annihilating the custodians of world revolution.'[1] The script was as lacking in finesse:

VOICE OF THE RUSSIAN PROLETARIAT: Proletarians, into the struggle.
WORLD CAPITALISM: Hell, devil, plague.
THE GERMAN WORKER: Struggle, struggle, struggle.
VOICES *FROM ALL DIRECTIONS*: Struggle, struggle, struggle.

(Willett 1978: 49)

Piscator was not in the least bit apologetic about the unsubtle nature of his text. 'Nothing was left unclear, or ambiguous and ... the connection with current political events was pointed out at every turn' (Piscator 1963: 83), he writes with satisfaction in *The Political Theatre*. His slogan was 'Subordination of all artistic aims to the revolutionary goal'[2] and he meant to stand by it uncompromisingly. A more complex drama would have diluted his political message and failed to reach his working-class audience.

The unease with which Piscator viewed 'plays, where the ponderous structure and problems tempt you to psychologize' (ibid.: 81) had the salutary effect of alerting him to the potential for direct action offered by alternative forms of theatre, such as those practised by **Meyerhold** in Moscow. Like Meyerhold, Piscator began to use flexible dramatic structures that would permit the interposition of music and dance, projections and film clips, statistics and captions. *The Red Revue* (1924), for instance, a montage depicting the triumph of communism, used everything from George Grosz caricatures on slide projections, to actors who would not only play characters such as Lenin and Rosa Luxemburg but would also comment on the action from various politically sensitive points of view. Unlike Meyerhold, however, Piscator was not interested in the formal aspect of these techniques. Piscator's concerns had entirely to do with impeaching the guilty and championing the victims:

> Thousands are learning this, you should too! Do you think it concerns only the others? No, it concerns you too! This is typical of the society in which you live, you cannot escape it – here it is again, and here again!
>
> (Ibid.: 82)

Piscator had been commissioned to produce plays by the German Communist Party and he would make good his assignment. He would put the establishment on trial and prove the need for revolution beyond a shadow of a doubt. The story of Piscator's theatre is the story of his struggle with the burden of this proof.

The two things a prosecuting lawyer requires to elicit a verdict of guilty are plausible evidence and a logical scheme that permits only a single rational deduction. Film gave Piscator access to both these features. Film was not only able to document the world in a manner that was incontrovertible but also permitted Piscator to structure his arguments such that mutually antithetical claims would, by failing to corroborate each other, provide a scathing commentary on the state of affairs Piscator wanted to attack: '*Film commentary* accompanies the action in the manner of a chorus.... It levels criticisms, makes accusations, provides important facts, indeed, at times it carries out direct agitation...' (ibid.: 239).

In *Rasputin* (1927), Piscator staged a discussion on the finer points of military strategy in front of a screen showing genuine film clips of a massacre on the Somme. Captions were used to similar effect: shots of corpses were inter-cut with projected quotations from the Tsar's letters to his wife extolling the healthy and invigorating life he was leading as head of his army.

A director seeking to use contradiction as a means of litigation needs a stage that is both capacious and flexible, providing a number of different spaces, each with its own medium and corresponding perspective. In 1924 Piscator welcomed the opportunity to work at the Völkesbuhne's Theater am Bulowplatz, an enormous arena equipped with a cyclorama, a revolving stage and adjustable rostra. However, neither this facility nor the Theater am Nollendorfplatz, where Piscator eventually set up the Piscator-Buhne, was technically as advanced as the theatre Piscator had designed but lacked the funds to realise. This so-called Total Theatre would have had 'variable performance areas and a series of seventeen slide or cine-projection booths, nine around the single-tiered auditorium, seven behind the cyclorama, and one in a turret that could be lowered from the roof'.[3] Within the less extravagant but perfectly serviceable confines of his existing quarters, Piscator used his ingenuity to create a theatre equal to the task of generating the multiplicity of perspective he required. If his theatre couldn't physically house the multi-storied structure he wanted, he used lighting to designate different playing areas. If Piscator's stage was not quite as compliantly elastic as he wanted, he designed a conveyer belt to carry his actors between scenes. If the conflict between scenes played simultaneously in different areas did not sufficiently unmask the hypocrisy that was Piscator's target, he planted actors in the audience who would air their opinions on various contentious issues so as to provide perspective on the action.

Piscator's first production at the Theater am Bulowplatz was Alfons Paquet's *Flags* (1924). The drama was played on a revolving stage divided by walls into segments, some of which were equipped with multiple levels so that action could take place simultaneously at different locations. Scenes 12 and 13, for instance, were played concurrently so that the courtroom verdict blended seamlessly into a celebration banquet. The judges attended the reception by shedding their robes in full view of the audience to reveal the white ties and tails they had on underneath all along – thereby making the point about the complicity between the bourgeoisie and the law. The action was hemmed in by two large screens on which were projected the titles of scenes, photographs of the various characters and a critical commentary on the action. For instance, a scene involving an unjust conviction was played in front of a caption that read 'The police threw the bombs themselves'. *Flags* was the first production to use projected captions in this way.

Piscator's first play at the Piscator-Buhne at the Theater am Nollendorfplatz was Toller's *Hoppla, Such is Life* (1928). Hugh Rorrison describes the set for the production:

A scaffolding 25 feet high, 35 feet wide and 10 feet deep was built on rails on the revolving stage. It was divided vertically into three sections, the outer ones having three cubicles one above the other, while the centre one was an individual shaft surmounted by a dome. External stairs at the sides and back afforded entrances at each level. A screen 25 feet by 35 feet could be lowered in front for film and black and white gauzes for projections....

(Ibid.: 202)

The drama began with a sequence of film depicting the war. Film was used again to show the passage of time, with clips depicting a series of historical events such as the uprising in the Soviet Union and the advent of Mussolini in Italy. The stage action was interspersed with songs and spotlights were used to pick out action in each of the cubicles in the scaffolding. In one scene dance was used to bizarre effect as a group of skeletons bathed in purple light performed the Charleston. Although the production received enthusiastic notices, Piscator was upset about the fact that the critics had chosen to emphasise the artistic excellence of the production at the cost of its political message. A decade into his political crusade, Piscator had not let his growing celebrity cloud the ultimately revolutionary nature of his project.

Productions such as *Flags* and *Hoppla* created a problem for Piscator's actors: in addition to presenting their characters, they had to 'clarify the historico-economic connections' (Willett 1978: 190), often by stepping out of character and mingling with the spectators or lecturing them on the relevance of the drama to the current political situation. Although Piscator intermittently ran a studio that coached his actors, he never systematically addressed this aspect of his art. As Piscator's self-confessed 'aim was to forget about "Art" and build an ensemble on the basis of common revolutionary convictions' (ibid.: 50), it seemed to him more important to indoctrinate his actors than to address the issue of the actor's technique: 'Since our view of the world is activistic, our actors must be educated in activism.... Political and literary lectures will be arranged to acquaint members with the political concept and the literary material of our theater' (Piscator 1963: 199–200). It was left to **Brecht** to evolve a methodical approach to training actors in non-naturalistic acting.

Enthusiastic as Piscator was with regard to the mechanical aspects of theatre production, these were hugely expensive to maintain. The concomitant irony was that Piscator was dependent on bourgeois funding for his revolutionary theatre. Although Piscator accepted the indignity of receiving financial support from the community he wished to displace, his critics were not quite so accommodating. Herbert Ihering, for instance, noted that to keep *The Adventures of the Good Soldier Schweik* (1928) running for an extended period merely because it was commercially successful was incompatible with what should have been the single-minded political agenda of a theatre collective. Thus Piscator was forced to take off lucrative hits in order not to renege on his undertaking to present a pre-arranged number of productions every season. The result, not surprisingly, was the financial collapse of his theatre. *Schweik* was taken off and a number of hastily assembled productions put on in its place. As these failed to attract an audience, Piscator could not raise the necessary funds to extend his lease at the Theater am Nollendorfplatz.

Piscator did manage to resurrect the Piscator-Buhne briefly but, when this project eventually folded, he left Germany. He worked as a film director in the Soviet Union before moving to the United States. Piscator returned to Germany only in 1951. And although he continued to work as a free-lance director – and later as the Intendant of the Theater der Freien Völksbuhne – his greatest work was behind him. After a run of poor reviews Piscator resolved, in a diary entry of 8 May 1956, to:

> get clear in my own mind
>
> 1. Whether my talent as such has declined...
> 2. Whether it is the audience that has changed....
>
> (Willett 1978: 172)

What had happened of course was that times had changed. Piscator was a revolutionary without a revolution. As he acknowledged bitterly, 'existentialists, degenerates and those who have given up hope' (ibid.: 173) had taken over. Europe was entering the age of Beckett and Ionesco.

Notes

1   Braun, E. (1982) *The Director and the Stage*, London: Methuen: 145.
2   Ibid.: 146.
3   Ibid.: 151.

Further reading

Piscator, E. (1963) *The Political Theatre*, trans. Hugh Rorrison, London: Eyre Methuen.

Willett, J. (1978) *The Theatre of Erwin Piscator*, London: Methuen.

SHOMIT MITTER

ANTONIN ARTAUD (1896–1948)

In 1936 the French actor, director, playwright and essayist Antonin Artaud was declared insane. An early member of the surrealist movement in Paris and a major influence on avant-garde European theatre, he was confined to an asylum for the better part of the reminder of his life.

A telling feature of Artaud's psychosis was the pleasure he took in being singled out for persecution. Whether it was his conviction that it was he who was crucified on Golgotha, or that Tibetan lamas were willing his death, Artaud rarely ceased to identify with the great martyrs of religious history. Like them, Artaud saw himself as the sole bastion of truth, holding out proudly against the unremitting onslaught of inauthenticity:

> And what is an authentic madman? It is a man who has preferred to go mad ... rather than be false to a certain superior idea of human honour.... [A] madman is also a man to whom society did not want to listen and whom it wanted to prevent from uttering unbearable truths.
>
> (Esslin 1976: 96)

Madness was Artaud's *raison d'être*, his religion, the source of his pride. Like the great martyrs of myth, Artaud felt it was his duty to shake society out of its crippling indifference to the higher truths to which, he believed, only he had divinely ordained access. Artaud felt he had to redeem his fallen tormentors, to orchestrate the salvation of mankind, to restore to human beings their capacity for transcendent experience.

It was through the theatre, Artaud believed, that he could do this. Theatre was for Artaud his surgery, his school, the vehicle of his revolution. It was through theatre that he would teach his fellow human beings what it was to live passionately. He would do this not by lecturing or haranguing them but by exposing them to experiences of such formidable fervour that they would see the light and be forever changed. As reason and language were powerless to change the deeply entrenched attitudes people had to life, theatre would enable Artaud to attack the deadness of his spectators through their senses. He would 'get hold of man's anatomy and through it heal' (ibid.: 76):

> Theatre is the only place in the world, the last group means we still possess of directly affecting the anatomy, and in neurotic, basely sensual periods like the one in which we are immersed, of attacking that base sensuality through physical means it cannot withstand.
>
> (Artaud 1981: 61)

The theatre could galvanise people like no other institution. It could shock and startle audiences. It could astonish and unsettle, jolt and stun. It could, if nothing else, unnerve people into accepting the moral upheaval Artaud was advocating.

Artaud was of course aware that contemporary forms of theatre were far too genteel to serve his compulsive and extravagant needs. The 'after-dinner theatre' (ibid.: 84) of Paris in the thirties was far too bound to language and the foibles of the conscious mind to generate the primeval energies Artaud had in mind. 'The damage wrought by psychological theatre', Artaud wrote in *The Theatre and its Double*, '...has rendered us unaccustomed to the direct, violent action theatre must have' (ibid.: 64). In place of mainstream traditions such as those of the Comédie Française, which, for Artaud, was 'a spurious theatre, facile and false' (Esslin 1976: 76), Artaud conceived of a theatre that would be ritualistic and ceremonial, that would assault the senses and tear into the nerves:

> Cries, lamentations, apparitions, surprises, dramatic virtuosities ... of all sorts, the magical beauty of costumes based on certain ritual models, splendrous lighting, the incantatory beauty of voices ... masks, mannequins several meters tall, and brusque changes in lighting....
>
> (Sellin 1975: 84)

Perhaps Artaud's greatest achievement was to have had the courage to forge out of his vision a project for the theatre which, however outrageous and impractical, was at least the beginning of a new way of viewing the function of the arts in our lives.

The cornerstone of Artaud's project was his conviction that the theatre could exist independently of language. Non-verbal communication in the theatre has recently become so much the vogue that one forgets how radical Artaud's revolt against the 'dictatorship of words' (Artaud 1981: 29) was in his time: '[W]e view theatre so much as just a physical reflection of the script that everything in theatre outside the script ... appears to us to be part of staging, and inferior to the script' (ibid.: 50).

The problem with this, for Artaud, was twofold. First, language, in his opinion, was just not equal to the formidable task of distilling a mysterious higher reality and communicating it to a sceptical and listless audience. When Artaud made his now famous declaration that one had to 'smash language in order to touch life' (Esslin 1976: 70), he located wellsprings of the human condition well outside the purview of grammar and vocabulary. Second, the theatre had, as a natural part of its visual and harmonic structure, precisely those elements that gave it access to these elusive orders of being. If theatre were able properly to develop the ideographic value of gestures, the theatre would lodge its appeal to the subconscious directly through the body. If, instead of language, one could use incantation and hieratic movement, then the obfuscating filter of reason would be circumvented and theatre would realise its limitless potential for transcendence.

In Artaud's conception, theatre would be most expressive if it were freed from the proscenium arch and let loose in a large space, such as a barn or a factory, which the performers would share with the audience. There would be no scenery and the audience would be surrounded by the action. The actors would appear splendidly dressed and would play upon ancient instruments, producing unendurable sounds to express the impact of uncontrollable forces. The lighting would be designed so as to engulf the audience 'in waves, or in sheets, or like a volley of flaming arrows' (Sellin 1975: 85).

It is an unfortunate characteristic of each of the scenarios Artaud sketched that they bear no indication of the manner in which the breathtaking spectacle they describe could actually be realised on stage. In Act 3 of *The Ghost Sonata*, for example, the lighting must be such that 'everything is distorted as though seen through a prism' (Artaud 1971: 103). In *The Conquest of Mexico*:

> The wall of the stage is crammed unevenly with heads, with throats.... Flying vessels cross a Pacific of purplish indigo....

> The space is stacked high with swirling gestures, horrible faces, glaring eyes, closed fists, plumes, armour, heads, bellies falling like hailstones pelting the earth with supernatural explosions.
>
> (Schumacher 1989: 82)

It is hard to imagine how one could persuade bellies to fall like hail – or indeed how effective such a contrivance would be even if it were possible – but the metaphor certainly conveys Artaud's passion. Artaud's use of metaphor is in fact consistently powerful: when, for example, he insists that the colour of light used in a scene should be 'as complex and as subtle as anguish' (Sellin 1975: 115), or when he wants sounds to 'splash out widely, forming arches' (ibid.: 117), he is expressing himself as a poet would. 'Silence comes and goes in gusts' (Artaud 1971: 108), writes Artaud in his production plan for *Le Coup de Trafalgar* and the direction has no trace at all of a technical requirement. Despite his contempt for language, it is the metaphor that attracts Artaud more than the stage-effect. Artaud argued that theatre should be tangible rather than cerebral; and yet his work, for all its visceral brutality, turns out to be more abstract than material.

Not surprisingly, Artaud's eloquent but fanciful notions of stagecraft remained largely unrealised. In the early 1920s Artaud acted in a number of plays directed by Dullin, Pitoeff and Komissarzhevsky. In the late 1920s he began to act in films, but also founded the Théâtre Alfred Jarry with Roger Vitrac and Robert Aron. Here he directed four productions, none of which could even remotely be said to embody his ideas. In the spring of 1935 Artaud produced *The Cenci*. It was his first attempt to realise his vision of the theatre. The production was slaughtered by the critics and had to close after a short run. For all Artaud's contempt for language, it was finally his language that had lasting appeal. In spite of Artaud's heartfelt conviction that only sound and movement would encapsulate his vision, his truest medium was language. Ironically of course, the message carried by that medium was a recipe for its own destruction. What Artaud's language proclaims most effectively is the need to break down the structures of language and replace them with non-verbal catalysts. For all his anti-semantic rhetoric, Artaud was, in the final analysis, helplessly reliant upon language to convey his vision of a theatre that would expand beyond the confines of the verbal.

To extend the expressive potential of a medium is commendable in the work of any artist. To conceive of extending it without actually following theory through into practice is less unambiguously admirable. So while most critics acclaim the manner in which Artaud supposedly broke theatre's dependence on language and invented a framework in which a new vocabulary of stimuli would operate, they also treat his failure to produce even a single instance of theatre that was true to his conception as a serious shortcoming. And yet, the more one reads of Artaud's writings, the more reluctant one becomes to condemn Artaud's implacably impractical spirit. Artaud clung to his failure like a widowed mother to her child. Although he was undoubtedly devastated by the demise of *The Cenci*, there was a sense in which success might have destroyed him even more comprehensively. It is almost as if a triumph would, in Artaud's view, have belittled his conception, grounded his transcendent vision by showing it up as being feasible. There is a deep sense in which Artaud needed to fail in order to preserve his self-esteem. Anything other than personal tragedy would have rendered him mortal, a part of the world he abhorred.

In a sense Artaud's work *did* have a practical dimension. He did follow his ideas through into practice – not on the stage but, far more admirably, in his life. Artaud once remarked that he could not 'conceive any work of art as having a separate existence from life itself' (Schumacher 1989: xxiv). And so he made his own life his medium and became himself an example of the principles he espoused. Artaud's appeal is, finally, a function not of what he did or wrote but of the manner in which he lived. The most significant aspect of Artaud's legacy is not the theatre that is now performed in his name; it is the desire to use theatre to inculcate a capacity for authentic living.

Further reading

Artaud, A. (1971) *Collected Works*, Vol. 2, trans. Victor Corti, London: Calder & Boyars.

—— (1981) *The Theatre and its Double*, trans. Victor Corti, London: John Calder.

Esslin, M. (1976) *Artaud*, Glasgow: Fontana/Collins.

Schumacher, C. (ed.) (1989) *Artaud on Theatre*, London: Methuen.

Sellin, E. (1975) *The Dramatic Concepts of Antonin Artaud*, Chicago: University of Chicago Press.

SHOMIT MITTER

BERTOLT BRECHT (1898–1956)

For the German dramatist, director and poet Bertolt Brecht, the theatre was an instrument of social change. 'I wanted to take the principle that it was not just a matter of interpreting the world but of changing it, and apply that to the theatre' (Brecht 1984: 248), he wrote. His forthright Marxism and revolutionary theatrical experiments made him a vital force in Berlin both in the 1920s and in the 1940s and 1950s where he directed for the most part at the state-supported Berliner Ensemble. Even in between, in what was essentially a period of exile in 'western' Scandanavia (1933–41) and later the United States (1941–47), Brecht held firmly to the belief that a theatre which merely interpreted the world was also one that accepted that world uncritically. When, for example, a Stanislavskian actor researched the 'given circumstances' of a role, there was the suggestion that those circumstances, being '*given*' were somehow not subject to change. When Stanislavskian actors sought to '*justify*' their actions, they unwittingly *vindicated* the situations they were presenting. The System actor's 'through-line' of motivation inadvertently generated the impression that the tight sequence of events presented was in some way inevitable: that, 'given' *a*, *b* was bound to follow. For Brecht the naturalistic theatre made it seem 'natural' that things were as they were. It accepted the world as it was. It militated against change.

This was anathema to Brecht, for whom social reality was a human construct and therefore eminently changeable: there was nothing absolute about a chain of events. In his theatre, therefore, he sought to break up sequences of action so as to demonstrate that, given *a*, it was *not* inevitable that *b* should follow. This would, he hoped, encourage his audiences to stop accepting that their lives were somehow predetermined and impossible to better. In an effort to dislocate what he saw as the crippling determinism of Stanislavskian theatre, Brecht evolved his so-called 'Epic theatre' in which adjacent segments of dramatic action were deliberately disassociated one from another: 'with an epic work, as opposed to a dramatic, one can as it were take a pair of scissors and cut it into individual pieces, which remain fully capable of life' (ibid.: 70).

Tightly structured narrative structures were broken up by songs, for example, which would frequently exhort audiences to question what they were seeing on stage. Often placards were used break up the story-line and offer a critical commentary on the action. This, Brecht hoped, would destroy the illusion that the characters in the drama were living rigidly determined lives. The audience would not be swept away by a supposedly inevitable chain of circumstances, but would have instead the opportunity to consider alternative courses of action.

The term for this effect of epic theatre is 'alienation'. Alienation occurs when familiar things are made to appear unfamiliar so that they may be analysed critically:

> The A-effect consists in turning the object of which one is to be made aware ... from something ordinary, familiar, immediately accessible, into something peculiar, striking and unexpected.... Before familiarity can turn into aware-ness the familiar must be stripped of its inconspicuousness; we must give up assuming that the object in question needs no explanation.
>
> (Ibid.: 143–144)

Thus Brecht would stage sequences of action against backdrops of projected titles which would comment critically on the events portrayed. At the Baden-Baden festival of *The Flight over the Ocean* (1929), for example, a large sign behind the actors urged spectators to follow the text in their programmes and to sing along loudly. In the Berlin production of *The Threepenny Opera* (1928), the title of the play was scribbled across the curtain and titles appeared on either side of the stage as the actors performed. In *The Measures Taken* (1930), a restraining rope cut the audience off from the action; in *Edward II* (1924) and *The Roundheads and the Pointed Heads* (1936), Brecht used a wire net to separate the audience from the actors. Through these devices Brecht hoped to 'alienate' the specta-tors from the action and encourage them to re-examine events with a view to finding alternative, possibly more constructive, courses of action than those portrayed on stage.

In order to generate alienation on the stage, the Brechtian actor must always be present in a dual capacity – as actor *and* character. Where **Stanislavsky** sought to bridge the gulf between the performer and the role, Brecht deliberately retained the rift so as to ensure that an unsettling internal inconsistency was possible:

> A definite distance between the actor and the role had to be built into the manner of playing. The actor had to be able to criticize. In addition to the action of the character, another action had to be there so that selection and criti-cism were possible.[1]

The example Brecht gives us is that of directors showing their actors how to play a scene: while they certainly portray the characters in question, they are also present as themselves, as directors commenting on what they are doing so that their actors may better understand what is required. In Brecht's *Short Organum*, there is a description of Charles Laughton playing Galileo in the Beverly Hills production of *The Life of Galileo* (1947):

> the actor appears on the stage in a double role, as Laughton and as Galileo.... Laughton is actually there, standing on the stage and showing us what he imagines Galileo to have been.... [W]e make him smoke a cigar and then imagine him laying it down now and again in order to show us some further characteristic attitude of the figure in the play.
>
> (Ibid.: 194)

The use of the cigar is a stroke of directorial genius. In so far as Laughton is required to put the cigar down every time he impersonates Galileo, the cigar becomes associated with the actor Laughton and the absence of it with the character Galileo. The result is the presence of both actor and character – which, as Brecht would have it, reminds the audience that what they are watching is not reality, but a play, a human construct that, like reality, is changeable.

Alienation in the theatre is effective in proportion to the ability of the actor first to empathise with the character and then to step away from the role. As Brecht once remarked to Giorgio **Strehler**, although his theatre depended upon the destruction of emotional empathy, that empathy had first to be created, since an atmosphere could never be destroyed until it first had been built up. It follows that, in rehearsal, Brecht's actors must first learn how to identify with their characters and only then go one step further and break the spell of that identification. This is reflected in the three-stage rehearsal programme Brecht once outlined for his company:

(1) Before you assimilate or lose yourself in your character you must first become acquainted with it....
(2) The second phase is that of empathy, the search for the character's truth in the subjective sense ... becoming one with it....
(3) And then there is the third phase in which you try to see the character from the outside, from the standpoint of society.[2]

The early stages of rehearsal draw heavily on Stanislavsky: Carl Weber recalls that 'paintings or other pictorial documents of the play's period were brought into rehearsal' in an effort to study what Stanislavsky would have called the 'given circumstances' of the play.[3] Scenes were worked out in terms of motivation: Mother Courage, for example, has to turn around towards Eilif before stepping up to the sergeant to let him draw his lot in order to frighten her son away from the war. Thus, Brecht's actors would initially use Stanislavskian techniques in their attempt to 'become' their characters.

Once these characters were established, however, Brecht's actors had to learn to draw back from their roles and view their parts with perspective. At this stage Brecht would ask his actors to speak their lines in the third person or in the past tense so that they were literally placed outside their roles. Actors were asked to exchange roles or parody one another's interpretations to the same end. Another way of dislocating actors from their roles was to have them play a scene either in slow motion or very quickly. As the 'natural' actions of the character become 'unnatural' as a result of being slowed down or speeded up, the actors were distanced from their roles and alienation was achieved. Having actors deliver tragic lines comically or speak in time with musical accompaniment was so effective that the device was often retained in performance. As the audience, accustomed to realistic speech, heard lines being sung or broken up, they were alienated from the action and led to question rather than accept what was being said.

As a result of these exercises the actors, who had begun by identifying with their characters, now learnt to distance themselves from their roles. However, what Brecht required in performance was not emotional distance in itself but the *transition* from identification to detachment, which is what creates alienation. There was therefore a further stage of rehearsal in which the actors had to learn the art of intermittently slipping into and out of character. One of the ways of doing this was to have the actors speak their lines together with the stage directions which applied to their characters. This required the actors to use two tones of voice – their own and that of the character – in turn – thus explicitly emphasising the provisional nature of reality.

In doing this, Brecht was not interested in merely underscoring the fact that a play is just a play. He wanted to use this awareness to explore the possibility of social change. The function of theatre in such a scheme was not to coerce the audience into adopting a particular point of view, but to use alienation as a way of encouraging spectators to think in terms of alternatives:

When he appears on stage, besides what he is actually doing he will at all essential points discover, specify, imply what he is not doing; that is to say he will act in such a way that the alternative emerges as clearly as possible, that his acting allows for other possibilities to be inferred.... The technical term for this procedure is 'fixing the "not ... but" '.

(Ibid.: 137)

'Not x but y' is an example of a sentence structure that comprises an alienation and offers an alternative. 'The car is not red but blue' alienates blue as being only one of a number of colours a car can be. Applied to the supposedly rigidly determined fabric of people's lives, alienation is designed to reveal that there is always an alternative to the way that things are.

Notes

1   Brecht, Bertolt (1964) 'Notes on Stanislavsky', *Tulane Drama Review* 9 (2): 156.
2   Ibid.: 159.
3   Weber, Carl (1967) 'Brecht as Director', *The Drama Review* 12 (1): 104.

Further reading

Brecht, B. (1984) *Brecht on Theatre*, London: Methuen.
Fuegi, J. (1987) *Bertolt Brecht: Chaos According to Plan*, Cambridge: Cambridge University Press.
Volker, K. (1978) *Brecht: A Biography*, trans. John Nowell, New York: Continuum Publishing Group.

SHOMIT MITTER

LEE STRASBERG (1901–82)

Strasberg is an odd choice for inclusion in a book about great directors. He directed very little and was not considered terribly accomplished when he did apply himself to the task. And yet Strasberg's contribution to the art of acting was so profound that it is impossible to exclude him. 'Along with **Stanislavsky** and **Brecht**, he was one of the major names in twentieth-century theatre' (Hirsch 1984: 150), says Viveca Lindfors of a director who was almost single-handedly responsible for the evolution of the most successful actor training system in history. He nurtured the talents of a galaxy of stars including Marlon Brando, James Dean, Paul Newman, Al Pacino, Shelly Winters, Marilyn Monroe, Anne Bancroft and Steve McQueen – both at the Group Theatre in New York which he co-founded in 1931 and at the Actor's Studio of which he became the director in 1950. Strasberg was the master's master, the seer into whose care the greatest actors of our age committed their skills.

Strasberg often referred to a talk by Richard Boleslavsky as having been instrumental in establishing for him the foundation upon which all his subsequent work would be based:

> Boleslavsky said in his first talk, 'There are two kinds of acting. One believes that the actor can actually experience on the stage. The other believes that the actor only indicates what the character experiences, but does not himself really experience. We posit a theatre of real experience. The essential thing in such experience is that the actor learns to know and to do, not through mental knowledge, but by sensory knowledge.' Suddenly I knew, 'That's it! That's it!' That was the answer I had been searching for.
>
> (Hethmon 1965: 145)

The interesting thing about Strasberg's method was that while it uncritically accepted the first premise – that the actor must really experience what the character experiences on stage – it failed to absorb the import of the second proposition – that the actor's most effective route to the world of real feelings was through the body rather than through the mind.

For Strasberg, emotion could only come from within, from the actor's existing stock of associations and responses. These alone could fuel genuine feeling on stage as these alone had the status of reality for the actor. The actor's task was less a matter of delving into the character's past than of exploring their own emotional experiences with a view to finding what could be used to bolster their sense of reality on stage. Once the appropriate emotional experiences were located, they had to be re-lived precisely – so that the resulting emotion, which would then be 'genuine', could be attributed to the character in the scene being played. This was what Strasberg called 'affective memory':

> Our experiences are literally engraved in the nervous system. They are woven into the fabric of our existence, and can be relived.... With affective memory work, you

choose an experience of your own that is parallel to a
particular moment in a scene....

When Kean in *Hamlet* picked up the skull of Yorick, he
cried, because he said he always thought of his uncle. The
ancient Greek actor Polis brought on the ashes of his own
recently deceased son when he delivered Electra's funeral
oration....

(Hirsch 1984: 141–142)

Under Strasberg, actors would seek to build up stocks of affective
memories that they could invoke as and when required. In performance, an experienced actor would know when to 'start' an affective
memory so as to produce the required emotional response at the
appropriate time in performance.

The skill of a director leading an exercise in affective memory is
to limit the actor to sense memories alone. Actors must not try to
remember emotions: they must try to recall only the sensual experiences associated with those emotions so that they may be recalled by
reliable and concrete means:

If you say, 'I remember standing in a room when that experience happened to me', that implies that your feet touched
something. What did they touch? Can you remember what
part of your foot touched what type of carpet? ... Is there a
light? Can you see where it is coming from? Can you see a
pattern that it throws on the wall?

(Hethmon 1965: 110)

Strasberg believed that if sensory stimuli are recalled with sufficient
vividness, the emotions associated with them infiltrate the actor's
being in performance automatically.

Foster Hirsch's history of the Actor's Studio contains a fascinating
behind-the-scenes look at Strasberg conducting an affective
memory exercise with the actor Pete Masterson:

'You have picked an experience you would like to
remember.... When you're ready, tell me where you are,
what you see and touch....'

'I'm in a room.... It's dark – brown – there's a lamp by
the couch. Brass. A plant in it. I see light green, light yellow.
I'm wearing rough cotton. I feel hot. Sticky heat. Throat
dry ... I'm touching the dog....'

'Do you want to make a sound? Go ahead, relax....'

Somewhere from deep inside, the actor emits a low, sustained groan....

(Hirsch 1984: 139–141)

What is interesting here is not just the attention to detail but the manner in which Strasberg is able to read the private landscape Masterson is exploring and intervene appropriately. It was this almost telepathic ability to read the actor's mind that made Strasberg so easy to trust. Without this trust, affective memory would not have worked. Powerful emotion is shy: it emerges only when the coast is clear. Strasberg's achievement was to have always kept that coast clear.

Trust alone cannot guarantee the success of an affective memory exercise. The actor must bring to the exercise a spectrum of highly sophisticated technical skills. In Strasberg's work there was therefore an elaborate programme of carefully orchestrated preliminary work, the first stage of which was to get the actors to relax physically. Relaxation, for Strasberg, was the most fundamental condition of all creative work: it was so important that he would often take all the allotted time in rehearsal just to achieve a properly relaxed state. 'Just relax', he would say, 'If you never get to the exercise, I don't care' (Hethmon 1965: 90). The exercises he used to achieve physical relaxation were fairly basic: his actors would work through each part of their bodies separately, trying to find a position in which they were relaxed enough to fall asleep. Mental tensions were located in specific parts of the body such as the temples and the bridge of the nose that were selected independently and relaxed.

The second stage of the work involved immersing the actors in an act of detailed imagining:

> Although you have put soap on your hands hundreds of times in life, here, when you have no actual soap, you have difficulty in creating the sensation.... You should say to yourself, 'Wait a minute. Do I have the weight of it at least? Do I have the shape of it?'
>
> (Ibid.: 96–97)

The important thing here is the attention to detail which, for Strasberg, was the actor's strongest ally. It is the detailed scrutiny to which the memory is subjected that makes it possible for the actor to recapture a body of familiar sensations when those sensations are in fact absent. The exercise is therefore an object lesson in the perils of making fiction real – which is of course the actor's task in its most general form. For Strasberg, 'that is the actor's job. He brings non-existent things alive on the stage. He first makes them real to himself in order to convey that reality to the audience' (ibid.: 101).

The exercise that most effectively bridges the gap between these preliminary attempts at making fiction real and the more difficult business of evoking complex emotional memories is Strasberg's 'private moment' exercise. This requires actors to act out intensely private situations in the glare of public scrutiny. For example, actresses may go through hygiene rituals that are normally performed only in the privacy of a bathroom. This may be embarrassing but it does open the way for them to take that further step which affective memory will eventually require – the revelation of a moment that is acutely painful, that cuts to the heart of their insecurity as human beings:

> the private moment exercise is a kind of therapy. It can rip through the actor's defences, release tensions that have built up over years, and help to free the actor physically and vocally.
>
> 'I remember a young actress who had trouble expressing what she felt,' Strasberg reminisces. 'She brought in a private moment where she was lying in bed listening to Turkish music. She started to dance. Hot dancing! In a way that was startling. From that point on, her voice on the stage started to change, she had more vocal colours, and we began to get a fullness of response...'
>
> (Hirsch 1984: 138)

The interesting thing here is the manner in which a psychological release triggers physical changes in the body that, one would think, were well beyond the purview of attitude and perception. The exercise embodies the essence of Strasberg's view of actor training: one trains the voice not by doing voice exercises but by freeing the self.

Although much of Strasberg's work was conducted outside the context of particular roles or scripts, he did direct on occasion and not without success. His 1933 production of *Men in White*, for instance, is now largely forgotten but was once regarded as 'one of the milestones in the American theatre' (ibid.: 85):

> Throughout the summer of 1933, Strasberg drilled his actors like a sergeant, taking them through exercises and improvisations on hospital routine. It was a historic case of

directorial overkill, but it paid off: the production gleamed with ensemble give-and-take, creating the illusion of a miniature world, a bustling microcosm. The comings and goings of patients and staff were rendered with exacting detail and with incidental natural sounds, background chatter, bells, sirens....

(Ibid.: 85–86)

A memorable characteristic of the staging employed by Strasberg was what is called 'deep focus' – a device whereby the action in the foreground is set against a carefully choreographed sequence of movements upstage which, read together, suggest that the action is part of a larger reality which lives on regardless of the drama.

Strasberg's method of working has over the years been subjected to two major lines of attack. First, it has been argued that Strasberg methods often reduced dramas to the orbit of the actors' experiences, which are inevitably more limited than those of the characters they are playing. As Sabra Jones observed: 'The technique is fascinating, but can destroy the play by promoting the narcissism of the actor at the expense of the playwright.... He's thinking about how his mother betrayed him at four instead of playing the scene' (ibid.: 212).

Second, actors often found it 'painful to dig back.... Lee crippled a lot of people' (ibid.: 77):

He had me going over and over a painful experience – my roommate had been killed the year before – until I thought I was going to crack.

(Ibid.: 77)

There were those for whom Strasberg was impossibly vicious and those for whom he was a rock, the foundation of all their creative work in the theatre. This polarity is inevitable given the sensitivity of the material Strasberg chose to use: the actor's inner self. What is important is that the vision he brought to the theatre had implications for the notion of authenticity generally. Strasberg's efforts to narrow the gap between the real and the affected had a significance that stretched well beyond the theatre: it became a way of being.

Further reading

Hethmon, R.H. (ed.) (1965) *Strasberg at the Actors Studio*, New York: Theatre Communications Group.

Hirsch, F. (1984) *A Method to Their Madness: The History of the Actors Studio*, New York: Da Capo.

SHOMIT MITTER

JEAN VILAR (1912–71)

Founder of the Avignon Festival in 1947 and the Théâtre National Populaire (TNP) in Paris in 1951, Vilar's mission was to create new audiences commensurate with his idea of 'popular theatre'. The theatre had been a middle-class institution. Its new audiences were to come not only from the industrial working class, but from all the *classes laborieuses*: clerical and other small-scale employees, artisans and shopkeepers, and rural workers as well as the traditional peasantry (Vilar 1975: 189, 355). In this, Vilar went against the Marxist thought that had made such a great impact on French artists and intellectuals from the 1940s to the 1960s, via **Brecht**. He insisted against his left-wing critics, notably Jean-Paul Sartre, that since 'popular' did not simply mean 'proletarian', he was not obliged to produce a militant theatre tailored to a canonically defined working class: 'the theatre must be open to everybody' (ibid.: 188–191, 348).

Vilar's terms re-activated the principle of universal access to education and culture that was integral to the politics of national unification of the Third Republic (1875–1940). They also linked him to Firmin Gémier, who was appointed in 1920 by the government to form a popular theatre company at the Palais de Chaillot, the very place assigned to Vilar by a later government for his TNP.

Republicanism was not the only influence on Vilar's notion of the 'popular'. He was deeply affected by the Resistance, whose aim of national liberation from below inspired the grass-roots associations *Peuple et Culture* and *Travail et Culture*, founded at the end of 1944. The first of these was devoted to education for the 'masses', the second to 'art for everybody'. Both spawned the Youth Movements among whose varied activities was the co-operative organised by Vilar with fellow actor-directors Jean-Louis Barrault, Roger Blin and Hélène-Marie Dasté to provide acting workshops for future cultural facilitators in deprived areas, especially in the countryside. Vilar believed that widespread distribution was necessary, since the theatre was a repository of 'knowledge and culture' and the yardstick by which the 'greatness of a civilization could be judged' (ibid.: 356, 503).

These activities were part of the drive towards 'decentralisation' by which the goods, opportunities and benefits concentrated in Paris were to be devolved to the provinces. Vilar created the Avignon Festival in the spirit of decentralisation, and it was one of the first examples of democratised theatre in France, with its easier social and geographic availability, greater intake of spectators, lower ticket prices and egalitarian seating. All of this palliated against the idea of theatre as privilege and coterie. The Festival took place in the summer, and its open-air performances generated a feeling of celebration. It was supported financially and in other material ways by the municipality, but it had national rather than local significance and some of that unifying purpose ascribed by Vilar to popular theatre. Although the larger part of its audience was regionally based, the Festival attracted spectators from all over France, and, increasingly, from abroad.

The Festival was especially solicitous towards young people in the 18–25 age bracket. Schools were converted into Centres, which provided housing and meals at very reasonable prices, procured tickets to performances, organised discussions and debates and arranged excursions into the region. Vilar supported their efforts by organising meetings throughout the Festival between directors, performers, writers and the public. In this whole network is to be found one of Vilar's greatest achievements, that of mobilising new audiences to become artistically sensitive, well-informed, alert and articulate – indispensable criteria, in his view, for what subsequent generations were to describe as 'empowerment'.

Under Vilar's direction until his death in 1971, the Festival expanded its horizons to include music, film and dance. It had also surmounted the financial difficulties that had prevented Vilar in the 1950s from developing artists and audiences by bringing innovative international companies to Avignon. With this goal in mind, he invited the Living Theatre to perform *Paradise Now* and *Antigone* at the 1968 Festival. The event was caught up in the aftermath of May '68, when extremists calling themselves *enragés* descended on Avignon from Paris and accused Vilar of creating a 'supermarket of culture' (Bardot 1991: 497–522). The Living Theatre's Julian **Beck** joined the fray, pitting his own brand of anarcho-radicalism against Vilar. Today, the Festival still embodies Vilar's immense contribution, as actor, director *and* manager to the debate central to the twentieth century on who makes theatre for whom in society, and why it matters.

Avignon was Vilar's invention. The TNP, on the other hand, was offered to him by Jeanne Laurent, a fervent supporter of decentralisation, who was to hold a key post in the future Ministry of Culture. The TNP at the Chaillot was to be Vilar's 'winter Avignon', and Avignon was to be the TNP's summer residence. The Chaillot's auditorium could seat 4000 spectators, which, on the face of it, corresponded with Vilar's image of mass theatre, as exemplified by the Palais des Papes in Avignon, transformed by him into an amphitheatre. Nevertheless, the glacial Chaillot, with its huge spaces and inhospitable corridors and stairways, was a 'poisoned gift' (Vilar 1975: 396). Its architectural idiosyncrasies made the choice of an appropriate repertoire exceedingly difficult. The same was true of staging and performance.

Furthermore, the terms set by the government for its operation were unfavourable. This theatre was 'national' from the government's point of view because it was state-subsidised; 'national' from Vilar's point of view because it brought together the nation, irrespective of class distinctions. Its subsidies, however, were risible: a mere 50 million francs annually (old currency) compared with the 450 million received by the Comédie Française and one billion by the Opéra (ibid.: 181). All the office equipment, costumes and props bought by the TNP out of its allowance belonged to the state. The theatre had to pay its way from box-office receipts. Deficits were the responsibility of the director and were to be met exclusively by him (although the state covered deficits of the Comédie and the Opéra) (ibid.: 244). So much for the government's support of its flagship popular theatre company!

Vilar eliminated all external signs of privilege. Ticket prices were brought down and kept low. The auditorium, which Vilar refurbished to hold 2700 seats, was not divided according to social category in the manner of the Italian-style theatres in Paris. Tipping ushers, an obligatory part of theatregoing, was stopped, as was payment for cloakrooms. The starting time of performances was changed from 9.00 p.m. to 8.00 p.m. so that working people from the suburbs could return home before midnight. Food was made available at the theatre. Every one of Vilar's reforms was designed to help medium- and low-income earners in a practical way and to change perceptions regarding the theatre as such. What is taken for granted today as a normal part of theatre-going was, in Vilar's 1950s, nothing short of revolutionary.

Vilar's most daring innovation was his system of group tariffs for trade unions and other work-based organisations such as the *comités d'entreprise* – shop-floor committees that involved workers in cultural outings or in in-house educative or leisure events. Group bookings with reduced ticket prices and special previews were arranged for the *comités* and a whole range of *associations populaires*, including youth associations like the ones involved with the Avignon Festival. Buses were hired to bring these spectators to and from the theatre. Discussions with Vilar and the actors about the productions were arranged in their workplace, clubs or at the Chaillot. Nothing was thought too insignificant to open up the TNP to new audiences, among whom were the 'hard' proletariat championed by Sartre. Nor was anything spared to make it a veritable *service public* since theatre was as necessary as 'gas, water, electricity' and 'as indispensable to life as bread and wine' (ibid.: 103, 109, 173).

The process of social integration initiated by Vilar called for additional action. He took his company to working-class suburbs, notably, Suresnes and Gennevilliers, so that 'this Paris which is larger than Paris' would not forever remain neglected by the capital (ibid.: 199). Halls, here, served community purposes, but were usually unsuitable for theatre performances. They posed problems for rigging lights, adjusting play to small stages or to none at all, and battling with acoustics, cold, makeshift dressing rooms and impro-vised seating arrangements for the audience. Yet Vilar was determined to present the company exactly as it was at the Chaillot and Avignon, with the same repertoire, style and stars, Gérard Philipe and Maria Casarès among them. Vilar refused to level the TNP's quality downwards on the false assumption that the popular classes could not understand what cultivated Paris took for granted.

The TNP's programme of suburban performances, with talks and discussions, lasted eight years. Meanwhile, the company was expected to provide an international showcase for French theatre, rather like the Comédie Française, despite the fact that it had nothing like the latter's resources. This meant touring Europe as well as visiting the Soviet Union, Canada (Québec), Argentina and Chile, culture being used by France to gain political influence. Vilar, who had consistently negotiated with the government for better financial and working conditions for his company, finally resigned in 1963.

Much was also accomplished during Vilar's directorship of the TNP from an artistic point of view. Curtains disappeared from the Chaillot. The traditional three knocks on the floor to announce the beginning of a performance were replaced by a trumpet call – a prac-tice Vilar had established at Avignon. Brightly coloured oriflammes flew outside the theatre to create a sense of ceremony, as they did at the Palais des Papes, Vilar arguing that an everyday service to the public should not be doomed to shabbiness. He did away with the footlights, tore down the rails that hemmed in the stage and extended it into the auditorium to facilitate 'dialogue with audiences' when intimacy was not possible because of the sheer size of the Chaillot. Space free of décor became his trademark. He skilfully appropriated the huge stages at his disposal in Paris and Avignon to this aesthetic principle by creating different playing areas in them to signal changes of focus or scene and by using swathes of light to valorise action, time and place. Light virtually replaced décor. Occasional props – a chair, a stair, a seat, a stylised rather than natural tree or a huge mobile by Alexander Caldor – were used for play rather than effect.

Rich, beautiful costumes and expressive make-up were Vilar's only indulgences on the stage. Costumes historicised the characters, guiding spectators to situate them appropriately which, Vilar believed, was necessary for a repertoire filled with French classics. *Le Cid* (1951) and *Lorenzaccio* (1952) became the company's signature works. Vilar's attachment to national classics was closely bound up with pragmatic and ideational factors. On the pragmatic side, Vilar acknowledged the *national* dimension of his task: he was responsible for the Théâtre National Populaire, which, he reminded his critics, obliged him to show French works abroad (ibid.: 210). On the ideational side, he insisted on the importance of French classics for *popular* theatre, since classics of whatever country provided the best of knowledge and culture. As such, they belonged as much to the *classes laborieuses* as to anybody else.

Vilar's many innovations succeeded in giving pride of place to the actor. He sought an 'internal' quality in their acting, that is, a capacity for projecting emotions, thoughts and actions without histrionic display. In this, his project was close to that of **Copeau** at the Vieux Colombier and the TNP developed a sober, restrained performing style that gave Vilar's productions an air of poise and harmony.

The TNP 'style', Vilar noted, had a natural distancing effect which enabled the company to deal well with Brecht (ibid.: 250). He was the first major director to stage Brecht in France, starting with *Mother Courage* in Suresnes (1951), followed by the Chaillot premieres of *The Resistable Rise of Arturo Ui* (1960), *The Good Person of Szechwan* (1960) and *The Life of Galileo* (1963). To his chagrin, his detractors found his Brecht too moral and not political enough, due to his inadequate understanding of the purpose of awakening the curiosity and critical faculties of the lower social classes.[1] However, where Brecht propagated the idea of revolutionary consciousness, Vilar aimed for what is best defined as civic awareness.

Vilar vigorously challenged the status that had been conferred on the director since Copeau, arguing that actors and their relationship with audiences were considerably more important. He even went so far as to call the director an 'egocentric miracle-worker' and declare that the *mise-en-scène* 'ought to be ousted, assassinated' (ibid.: 295, 255); he preferred to speak of himself as a *régisseur* (stage manager), and of his production work as *régie*. His attack on the high claims of directors for direction stemmed from the value Vilar ascribed to texts. The aim of productions was to respect the text they performed. Ultimately, for Vilar, 'the author is the creator in the theatre', while *régisseurs* and actors are really only the interpreters of the author's Word (Vilar 1955: 65).[2] The *mise-en-scène*, then, could not claim to be an act of creation in its own right. At the very most, it was a triple act of interpretation carried out, on the author, by the *régisseur*, actors and audiences (ibid.: 96).

Vilar's preferred texts, whether national or foreign, were those from which he could draw themes that he believed addressed, or corresponded with, the pressing issues of his day. The themes of greatest significance for him in the classics were: war, tyranny and power, as in Corneille's *Cinna* (1954), Kleist's *Prince of Homburg* (1952) or Büchner's *Danton's Death* (1953), which, as staged by Vilar, was taken to be about Stalinism; the impact of corruption (*Lorenzaccio*); and the all-pervasive ideology of money (Balzac's *Schemer [le Faiseur]*, 1957). The 'heroic' classics of his repertoire, which ranged from *Le Cid* to Sophocles' *Antigone* (1960), explored the struggles of individual conscience against authority, usually that of the state. Vilar rediscovered this issue in modern plays such as *Murder in the Cathedral* (1952), Brecht's *Galileo* and Robert Bolt's *Man for all Seasons* (renamed *Thomas More*, 1963).

Vilar's choice of contemporary plays reflected similar concerns, focusing more openly on current problematics: Nazism (Brecht), Gaullism and the Algerian war, (*The Toad – Buffalo*, Armand Gatti, 1959), and atomic warfare (Henri Pichette's *Nucléa*, 1952). Vilar staged a number of works by contemporary French writers at the Récamier theatre, which he had rented as an experimental space. If the venture was short-lived and unsuccessful, it is to Vilar's credit that he wished to expose Gatti, Vinaver, Vian, Pinget and Obaldia to a wider public. He lamented the lack of contemporary texts suitable for his needs and believed that the 'Theatre of the Absurd' was not civic in its concerns, although he staged Beckett's *Krapp's Last Tape* at the Récamier in 1960.

Notes

1 See, especially, Copfermann, Emile (1969) 'Et si ce n'était pas Vilar?' in *Le Théâtre populaire, pourquoi?*, Paris: Maspéro: 199–206.
2 The capitalised 'Word' is mine.

Further reading

Bardot, Jean-Claude (1991) *Jean Vilar*, Paris: Armand Colin.

Leclerc, Guy (1971) *Le TNP de Jean Vilar*, Paris: Union Générale de l'Edition.

Vilar, Jean (1955) *De la Tradition théâtrale*, Paris: Gallimard.

—— (1975) *Le Théâtre, service public et d'autres textes*, presented and notes by Armand Delcampe, Paris: Gallimard.

Wehle, Philippa (1974) *Model for an Open Stage: a Study of Jean Vilar's Theater for the People*, Columbia University, unpublished dissertation.

MARIA SHEVTSOVA

TADEUSZ KANTOR (1915–90)

Tadeusz Kantor, Polish visual artist, theorist, and theatre director and founder (with Maria Jarema) of CRICOT 2 theatre company (1955), was born in Wielopole, Poland. He was educated in Tarnów and Kraków. While studying painting and stage design at the Academy of Fine Arts in Kraków (1933–39), Kantor was introduced to symbolism, constructivism and the Bauhaus. In 1938, he founded the Ephemeric (Mechanic) Theatre, where he presented Maurice Maeterlinck's *Death of Tintagiles*. In 1942, with a group of young painters, Kantor organised the underground, experimental Independent Theatre in Kraków during the Nazi occupation for which he directed Juliusz Slowacki's *Balladyna* (1942) and Stanislaw Wyspianski's *The Return of Odysseus* (1944). As noted by Kantor in his 'Lesson 1' of 'The Milano Lessons' (Kantor 1993), this production was instrumental in the creation of his concepts of an object, reality of the lowest rank, and autonomous space. These concepts were carefully dealt with in the period from 1944 until 1990 when Kantor questioned the official historical narratives that had found a successful way of glossing over Adorno's haunting question of what it means to represent after Auschwitz and queried the extant conventions of creating or displaying art.[1]

Thus:

> 1944. KRAKÓW. CLANDESTINE THEATRE. THE
> RETURN OF ODYSSEUS FROM THE SIEGE OF
> STALINGRAD.
> **Abstraction, which existed in Poland until the**

outbreak of World War II, disappeared in the period of mass genocide. [...]
The work of art lost its power.
Aesthetic re-production lost its power.
The anger of a human being trapped by other human beasts cursed A R T. We had only the strength to grab the nearest thing.
THE REAL OBJECT
and to call it a work of art!
Yet,
it was a P O O R object, unable to perform any functions in life, an object about to be discarded.
An object which was bereft of a life function that would save it.
An object which was stripped, functionless, a r t i s t i c! [...]
A kitchen chair....
An object, which was void of any life function, emerged for the first time in history.
This object was empty.

(Kantor 1993: 211–12)

Considering the significance and the direction of transformations in twentieth-century art in general, and in Dada, surrealism, abstract art and informel art in particular, Kantor emphasised here his departure from geometric or abstract forms, which were to obliterate or transcend historical events such as the First and Second World Wars, towards degraded reality filled with objects stripped of their asignifying features by the events of war. It was not only the object which lost its artistic function. More importantly, according to Kantor, Odysseus, in the 1944 production of *The Return of Odysseus*, 'refused categorically to be only an image, a representation. [...] In times of madness created by men, in times of war, death and its frightening troupes, which refused to be shackled by Reason and Human Senses, burst into and merged with the sphere of life' (ibid.: 274). The pathos of drama and its mythological characters were thrown into and merged with everyday life – here, the war. The play was staged not in a theatre building, but in a room which 'was destroyed':

bare bricks stared from behind a coat of paint, plaster was hanging from the ceiling, boards were missing in the floor, abandoned parcels were covered with dust, debris was scattered around, plain boards reminiscent of the deck of a

69

sailing ship were discarded at the horizon of this decayed decor, a gun barrel rested on a heap of iron scrap, a military loudspeaker was hanging from a rusty metal rope. The bent figure of a helmeted soldier wearing a faded overcoat [of a German soldier] stood against the wall. On this day, June 6, 1944, he became a part of this room.

(Ibid.: 272)

Whereas in 1944, Kantor focused his attention on an object, which lost its pre-assigned functions because of the war activities, in 1963, the objects exhibited in the Popular Exhibition made irrelevant any classification by which they were located in space or time sequences that unified them. Instead, the objects re-articulated their functions in relationships which were accidentally formed and which could not be anticipated according to any pre-given norms. The Popular Exhibition, also known as the Anti-Exhibition, comprised the objects which were usually removed to the margins of creative activity, glossed over by the traditional conventions and discarded as irrelevant: 'It was an inventory [of facts, theatrical objects, drawings, sketches, prescriptions, letters, stamps, tram and bus tickets, etc.] without any chronology, hierarchy, and locality.'[2] Thus, the focus was on their inherent structure rather than on the totality of their effects; on a manual process of signification rather than the visual sovereignty of the eye which produces the representational image in a classical, three-dimensional space; on non-figurative, and non-illustrative processes; on that which 'refuses the consolation of correct forms, refuses the consensus of taste permitting a common experience of nostalgia for the impossible, and inquires into new presentations'.[3]

In order to accomplish this, Kantor incorporated ready-made elements – objects, events and environment – into artistic activity. This reality was not subjugated to artistic moulding, nor did it correspond to any representational conventions. As observed by Kantor:

Reality can only be
'u s e d.' [...]
Making use of reality
in a r t
signifies
an annexation of reality. [...]
During this process,
reality
t r a n s g r e s s e s

its own b o u n d a r y
and moves in the direction of the
'i m p o s s i b l e.'
The annexed reality contains in itself
real objects,
situations,
and an environment described
by time and place.

(Ibid.: 96–97)

The strategy of annexing reality signified the process of exploring the functioning of objects in relation to other elements positioned in space. It allowed the artist to be 'surprised, accidentally and unexpectedly, by the unknown and ignored sphere of reality which intervenes in art' (Borowski 1982: 76). In Kantor's production of Stanislaw Ignacy Witkiewicz's *The Cuttlefish* (1956), the environment, objects and actors were engaged in an intricate process of constituting diverse spatial formations, shocks and tensions in order to unblock the imagination and to crush the impregnable shell of the drama. This exploration was different at different times during the 1960s. In 'The Informel Theatre' (1961), Kantor explored matter:

[an unknown aspect of REALITY or of its elementary state],
which is
freed from abiding by the laws of reality,
is always changing and fluid;
it escapes the bondage of rational definitions;
it makes all attempts to compress it into a solid form ridiculous,
helpless, and vain;
it is perennially destructive to all forms,
and nothing more than a manifestation;
it is accessible only through
the forces of destruction,
by whim and risk of COINCIDENCE,
by fast and violent action.

(Kantor 1993: 51)

In 'The Zero Theatre' (1963; see ibid.), Kantor radically repositioned the representation of actors' emotional states and their relationship with a dramatic text. In the *Madman and the Nun* (1963), he used a construction made of folding chairs: 'the death machine'.

71

While operating on stage, the machine destroyed the possibility of presenting a dramatic text and its characters – the actors – pushed aside, had to fight for acting space and struggle not to be thrown off the stage. The actions on stage could not illustrate the plot any more than the actors could create the illusion of characters, since the action on stage was constructed by references to other events taking place in the stage environment; the actors could only represent themselves and their own emotions. Thus, 'The Zero Theatre' was a detour from instant gratification: it teased the audience with the lack of synchronisation between the text and the stage action and between expected emotions and the actors' expression of their own emotional conditions.

In 'Theatre-Happening' (1967; see ibid.), Kantor drew attention to everyday realness and its potential for being a non-conceptual medium or a 'ready-made' object 'which [had] been found; an object whose structure [was] dense and its identity [was] delineated by its own fiction, illusion, and psychophysical dimension' (ibid.: 85). Using objects, matter, marginalised objects, degraded objects, which were positioned within the dynamic, fluid and open fabric of reality, Kantor challenged a model of culture or artistic activity which was based on the artistic representation of the image/object, or a text. (Kantor's theatre experiments, which from 1965 to 1969 took the form of Happenings, further developed these ideas.)[4]

'The Theatre of Death' Manifesto (1975; see ibid.) articulated a shift in Kantor's theatre experiments. The productions following it explored the notions of memory, history, myth, artistic creation and the function of the artist as chronicler of the twentieth century. In *The Dead Class* (1975), his exploration of memories took place in a space behind an impassable barrier. The audience, which entered the performance space, encountered a frozen group of Old People waiting for a sign from Kantor to engage in the process of the construction and deconstruction of memories, historical narratives, as well as to bring to life the forgotten fragments of their own individual lives. *Wielopole, Wielopole* (1980) introduced the concept of the room of memory, which was inhabited by the members of Kantor's family who brought to the fore the dubious process of reconstructing one's private and public memories. *Wielopole, Wielopole* was Kantor's attempt to give a material shape to his visual memories staged in a three-dimensional theatrical space. *Let the Artists Die* (1985) continued his 'memory' project. This time, however, his theory of negatives modified the notion of the room of memory – now called a 'storeroom of memory'. A performance space was a place where memories no longer unfolded in a linear fashion, but were superimposed one upon the other. Nothing encapsulates this process better than the following statement made by Kantor:

> I consist of a multiple series of characters embracing all
> possibilities from childhood up to the present moment –
> all marching from the DEPTHS OF TIME.
> They are all me.
> I am sitting on stage: I, THE REAL ONE.
> On the bed lies one the twins:
> I, THE DYING ONE….
> In a moment A LITTLE SOLDIER will show up –
> I AT THE AGE OF SIX
> IN A PRAM.
>
> (Ibid.: 342)

In *I Shall Never Return* (1988), Kantor explored the concept of the 'inn of memory', which existed beyond the confines of time and space, where Kantor, the Self, could finally encounter his own past creations, the Others. As he noted, until now:

> When I wanted to die,
> someone else was dying for me.
> He was playing the part of me dying. […]
> When […] I kept returning to the memories
> of my School Class,
> it was not I, but the others (the actors)
> who returned to the school desks.
>
> (Ibid.: 353)

In the inn of memory, Kantor destroyed the dichotomy between the Self and the objects of his creation by being fully integrated into the stage action, which unfolded as a collage of items from his past productions and unexpected encounters with the objects of his creation.

Today is My Birthday (1990) was filled with objects and people from Kantor's room of imagination/memory: his paintings, objects, characters from past productions, people, and so on. All of them participated in the process of exploring the relationship between the world of Illusion and the world of Reality.[5] This production continued the process initiated in *I Shall Never Return*, while, at the same time, it fully demolished the impassable barrier that Kantor first established in 1975 by placing school benches in the corner of a performance space separated from the audience by two ropes. Now, the space of art and the space of life converged, overlapped and coalesced 'sharing their fate and destiny' (ibid.: 383).

Kantor's theatre experiments and his chronicling of the official and unofficial history of the twentieth century are a testimony to his belief that theatre is an answer to reality rather than a representation of it – any reality, whether the Second World War, post-war Europe or Socialist Poland. Theatre, as he insisted:

> is an activity that occurs if life is pushed to its final limits, where all categories and concepts lose their meaning and right to exist; where madness, fever, hysteria, and hallucination are the last barricades of life before the approaching TROUPES OF DEATH and death's GRAND THEATRE.
>
> (Ibid.: 149)

Notes

1 See Adorno, Theodor (1978) 'Commitment' in Arato, Andrew and Gebhardt, Eike (eds) *The Essential Frankfurt School Reader*, Oxford: Basil Blackwell: 300–318.
2 Kantor, Tadeusz (1976) 'Zero' in *Ambalaze*, Warsaw: Galeria Foksal: 21.
3 Lyotard, Jean-François (1993) *The Postmodern Explained*, trans. Don Barry, Bernadette Maher, Julian Pefanis, Virginia Spate and Morgan Thomas, Minneapolis: University of Minnesota Press: 15.
4 Kobialka, Michal (2002) 'Tadeusz Kantor's Happenings: Reality, Mediality, and History', *Theatre Survey* 43 (1): 59–79.
5 See Kantor (1993): Part 2, 'The Quest for the Self/Other: A Critical Study of Tadeusz Kantor's Theatre' for a detailed discussion of the concept of memory in Kantor's productions from the period between 1975 and 1990.

Further reading

Bablet, Dennis (1983) *Tadeusz Kantor*, Paris: CNRS Editions.
Banu, Georges (ed.) (1990) *Kantor, l'artiste à la fin du XXé siécle*, Paris: Actes Sud-Papiers.
Borowski, Wieslaw (1982) *Tadeusz Kantor*, Warszawa: Wydawnictwo Artystyczne i Filmowe.
Kantor, Tadeusz (1993) *A Journey Through Other Spaces: Essays and Manifestos: 1944–1990*, ed. and trans. Michal Kobialka, Berkeley: University of California Press.
Plesniarowicz, Krzysztof (ed.) (1999) *Hommage à Tadeusz Kantor*, Kraków: Cricoteka.

—— (2000) *The Dead Memory Machine: Tadeusz Kantor's Theatre of Death*, Aberystwyth: Black Mountain Press.

MICHAL KOBIALKA

JOAN LITTLEWOOD (1914–2002)

Described by one of her collaborators, Murray Melvin, as 'our Galileo: she opened up new worlds for us' (*Independent*, 26 March 1994), Joan Littlewood pioneered a theatre practice fuelled by creative enquiry, formal experimentation, political urgency and a deep respect for, and celebration of, humanity in all its complexity, vibrancy, beauty, failure and humour. Rejecting the sterile, middle-class manners of mainstream British theatre she encountered at RADA in the early 1930s, Littlewood fled to Manchester where she became involved in the Workers' Theatre Movement. Here, she met Ewan MacColl with whom she co-founded Theatre Union in 1936, a nucleus of actors, designers and technicians committed to generating theatre that confronted contemporary political and social forces, including the ongoing class war, the burgeoning Pacifist Movement, the Spanish Civil War and the rise of fascism. Forced to disband during the Second World War, several members of Theatre Union reformed as Theatre Workshop in 1945 and began touring European classics and new works by MacColl to the industrial north of England, Scotland and Wales.

In 1952, Theatre Workshop reached a contentious decision to secure a permanent base at the Theatre Royal, Stratford East in London, a move to the metropolitan centre that prompted the departure of MacColl, who feared the threat posed to the company's philosophical basis and working methods. In the following decade, radical interpretations of classics, vibrant new writing, popular theatre forms, avant-garde experiment, theatrical inventiveness and ground-breaking representations of working-class life earned Theatre Workshop a reputation for invigorating the British stage. The company also established itself as one of Europe's most critically acclaimed and influential companies. None the less, throughout her career Littlewood endured an endless battle with hostile funding bodies that refused to acknowledge her originality and theatrical influence with adequate financial backing.[1] Forced to court West End managements keen to cash in on the successful Theatre Workshop formula, Littlewood retreated from directing following her seminal production *Oh What a Lovely War!* (1963) and finally retired from professional theatre after the death of Gerry Raffles, her long-term partner and General Manager of Theatre Workshop, in 1975.

She famously wrote 'I do not believe in the supremacy of the director, designer, actor or even of the writer. It is through collaboration that this knockabout art of theatre survives and kicks',[2] and maintained faith in the centrality of the ensemble, the composite mind engaged in a co-operative sharing of ideas, skills and creativity. Above all, she refused to adopt an autocratic directorial presence by predetermining the outcome of a performance before rehearsals commenced. Littlewood insisted:

> No one mind or imagination can foresee what a play will become until all the physical and intellectual stimuli, which are crystallized in the poetry of the author, have been understood by a company, and then tried out in terms of mime, discussion, and the precise music of grammar; words and movement allied and integrated.[3]

Keen to foster an ensemble that could exhibit physical, emotional and creative intelligence, Littlewood sought ways to facilitate these qualities through research, training and dynamic rehearsal processes. She championed regular voice and movement training to encourage skilled, dextrous actors, and a common embodied knowledge and performance vocabulary. Having first encountered Laban's work at RADA, Littlewood embraced his theory and analysis of kinesics and invited Jean Newlove, who had studied and worked with Laban, to join Theatre Workshop in 1948. Company members transposed Laban's ideas on the interrelationship between time, space and energy to physical characterisation, rhythm and spatial dynamics to counteract 'an inbuilt resistance we all have to using our bodies in a different way' (Goorney 1981: 159).

In a radical departure from the text-bound British acting tradition of the period, this formal training coincided with games and improvisation 'to develop initiative, excite curiosity, exercise the imagination' (Littlewood 1994: 199), with a view to creating the conditions for theatrical invention, an unspoken 'process of thought' (ibid.: 372) that enabled actors to be original, intuitive, responsive and *real* in rehearsal and performance. Extended improvisations aimed to capture the authentic human minutiae of everyday interaction, the shifting moods, silences, physical detail, rhythms, textures, antagonisms, demotic speech patterns and complex spatial relations so that actors could *live* rather than *act* on stage, complementing and counter-pointing each other's actions like a jazz ensemble. Working on classical plays, actors would research the social background to the text, analyse objectives, experiment with every part and replace dialogue with colloquial speech, gibberish or action to unearth collectively the most effective timing, delivery and tone. New plays were starting points for improvisations, and Littlewood developed a reputation for cutting, reconfiguring and adding material as she responded to the enacted, live event and the creative interaction between text and performance. This was a tendency that ensured Theatre Workshop's engagement in the campaign against theatrical censorship, particularly following its high-profile prosecution for Henry Chapman's *You Won't Always Be On Top* in 1957.

One of Littlewood's remarkable attributes as a director was her ability to maintain the centrality of exploration, experimentation and improvisation until the last possible moment in the rehearsal process. With an opening night snapping at her heels, she would sculpt and choreograph material to generate the appropriate spatial relations and a dynamic sequence of pictorial images, group formations, shifting tempos, rhythms, tones, energy, text, music, movement and action. Even then, Littlewood refused to court closure, fixity and the nightly resurrection of slickly packaged corpses. Any sign of complacency, cosiness, milking an easy laugh or 'bloody acting'[4] was denounced in coruscating notes on dressing room walls, derided in an acerbic turn of phrase and rooted out in ongoing rehearsals. The success of these rigorous and unconventional practices was reliant on the trust built up between long-standing collaborators. Over the years, however, Theatre Workshop became an increasingly loose alliance of regular and irregular participants as established members left for more lucrative work elsewhere or were embroiled in West End transfers. This dispersal meant Littlewood increasingly worked with actors unfamiliar with improvisatory techniques and the generational possibilities of her unpredictable methods.

Aesthetically, Littlewood drew on an eclectic range of sources. Like a magpie, she devoured, stole and reconstituted ideas from the great popular traditions of Greek, *commedia dell'arte* and Renaissance theatre, alongside contemporary ideas on staging, compositional strategies, performance devices and acting styles from **Stanislavsky**, Laban, **Meyerhold**, Appia, **Piscator** and **Brecht**. She assimilated useful ideas, discarded the rest and, in the process, established her own unique approach, one flexible enough to adapt to each given text and which enabled her to engage the creative and critical agency of the spectator in different ways. From the days with Theatre Union, Littlewood experimented with stagecraft to animate every horizontal and vertical axis of the playing space to create multi-textured theatre that drew on the technological possibilities of design, lighting and sound. Working closely with the designer John Bury, Littlewood rejected representational settings in favour of striking, atmospheric networks of levels, ramps, revolves and scaffolding, and illuminated areas with shafts and pools of light that cast stark geometric shadows. Each production brought a new integration and layering of space, narrative, image, sound, song and choreography. A constructivist set, synchronised sound sequences, rhythmic lighting and stylised movement emerged in *John Bullion* (1934). *The Good Soldier Schweik* (1938) introduced back projection and a silent movie aesthetic. In 1945 Theatre Workshop's double-bill of Molière's *The Flying Doctor* and MacColl's *Johnny Noble* drew on the grotesque comedy and caricature of the Marx Brothers' and *commedia dell'arte* in the former. The latter, 'a ballad opera', used amplified sound, a cappella singing, dance and naturalistic sequences.

In the 1950s, Littlewood developed an international reputation for starkly economical, modern productions of classics such as *Arden of Faversham* and *Volpone*, alongside exhilarating depictions of working-class life that conjured with the rumbustious spirit of the popular music hall. Brendan Behan's *The Quare Fellow* (1956) initiated the trend for combining robust demotic speech, gallows humour and a wry look at the darker recesses of humanity as a prison population prepares for the execution of one of its members. As usual, Littlewood concentrated on authentic action: 'day to day routines were improvised, cleaning out cells, the quick smoke, the furtive conversation, trading tobacco and the boredom and meanness of prison life' (Goorney 1981: 105). Authenticity similarly infused Shelagh Delaney's social realist depiction of a grotty Salford bed-sit in *A Taste of Honey* (1958) that Littlewood theatricalised by having direct address, variety-style banter and a live jazz trio burst through the fourth wall.

For many critics, the technical inventiveness, end-of-pier format and rousing popular entertainment of *Oh What a Lovely War!* marked the high point of Theatre Workshop's achievements. Inspired by Charles Chilton's radio programme, *A Long Long Trail*, Littlewood created a framework of exuberant, parodic, comic and poignant First World War songs on which she hung a collage of antithetical styles that revealed the absurd brutality of war and a defiant celebration of resistance and survival. Projected images, running the width of the stage, displayed recruiting posters, followed by photographic evidence of war casualties. Meanwhile, a 'ticker-tape' newspanel flashed contextual information, official death tolls and statistics of battles fought, won and lost. These living newspaper techniques functioned in dynamic interplay with multi-faceted live action: a Master of Ceremonies' jocular interjections and actors, as seaside pierrots, enacting satirical sketches, vaudevillian acts and realistic scenes of trench life.

Alongside her process-oriented and aesthetic concerns, Littlewood returned consistently to material that raised urgent questions about human responsibility, political action and ethical accountability. In 1936, civil war in Spain prompted a staging of Lope de Vega's *Fuenteovejuna*, a story of revolt against tyrannous feudal overlords, to promote solidarity with the International Brigade's struggle against fascism and the forces of Franco. The implications and widespread anxieties generated by the discovery of atomic energy and events in Hiroshima and Nagasaki fuelled *Uranium 235* (1946). *The Other Animals* (1948) presented a philosophical meditation on the nature of truth and conscience told from the perspective of a political prisoner. Behan's vaudevillian *The Hostage* (1958) indiscriminately attacked British colonial rule, the IRA and the Catholic church, amongst other institutions, also maintaining humanitarian concerns at its core when an eighteen-year-old soldier is accidentally killed after being taken hostage in retaliation against the British army's plan to execute an IRA revolutionary. Even when Littlewood tackled classic texts, she stripped away their usual reverential treatment to uncover topical, political resonance, even if this meant drastically cutting and re-situating scenes. Justifying her 1957 modern-dress version of *Macbeth*, which cast Macbeth as a dictator facing a firing squad for his crimes against humanity, Littlewood explained:

> The poetry of Shakespeare's day was a muscular, active, forward-moving poetry, in that it was like the people to whom it belonged. If Shakespeare has any significance today, a production of his work must not be regarded as a historical reconstruction, but as an instrument still sharp enough to provoke thought, to extend man's awareness of his problems, and to strengthen his belief in his kind.
>
> (Cited in Goorney 1981: 154)

Oh What a Lovely War! cemented this tradition of socio-political critique with a satirical dissection of the capitalist imperatives, power-brokerings, class relations and devastating human conse-quences of the Great War, a 'War To End All Wars', re-interpreted in the long shadow of the Second World War and the widespread political fall-out of the very present Cold War.

As her engagement with professional theatre waned during the 1960s, Littlewood increasingly directed her energies towards localised projects that emphasised cultural democracy. In particular, she initiated the unrealised Fun Palace project. Described as a 'university of the streets',[5] Littlewood re-conceptualised what entertainment could encompass in the technological age by proposing a combination of high art, popular culture and education in one vast arts complex for the East End of London. Together with the architect Cedric Price, Littlewood envisaged a flexible network of multiple activities that eroded the borders between everyday life and theatre, education and entertainment, observation and participation, pleasure and intellectual pursuit, the attainment of new skills and the joy of doing nothing. Above all, Littlewood strove to encourage active participation in a public, communal space with a view to animating the humanist preoccupations with the social transformation and community-based values that resurface in all her best work. From her clinical Living Newspapers, revitalised classics, vibrant 'slice of life' tragi-comedies, to her ambitious plans for 'a laboratory of pleasure',[6] she sought to defy the stultifying, polite tradition of English theatre and to celebrate and affirm the creative agency and social potential of cultural intervention, collaboration and shared collective imaginings.

Notes

1   Holdsworth, Nadine (1999) 'They'd Have Pissed on My Grave: the Arts Council and Theatre Workshop', *New Theatre Quarterly* 15 (57): 3–16.
2   Littlewood, Joan (1965) 'Goodbye Note from Joan' in Marowitz, Charles, Milne, Tom and Hale, Owen (eds) *The Encore Reader*, London: Methuen: 133.
3   Ibid.: 133.
4   Faxing permission for Clwyd Theatr Cymru's 2003 revival of *Oh What a Lovely War!*, Littlewood reiterated her antipathy towards 'bloody acting'. See Paget, Derek (2003) ' "The War Game is Continuous": Productions and Receptions of Theatre Workshop's *Oh What a Lovely War!*', *Studies in Theatre and Performance* 23 (2): 71–85.
5   Littlewood, Joan (1964) 'A Laboratory of Fun', *New Scientist* 22, 14 May: 432.
6   Ibid.: 432.

Further reading

Barker, Clive (2000) 'Joan Littlewood' in Hodge, Alison (ed.) *Twentieth Century Actor Training*, London: Routledge: 113–128.

Goorney, Howard (1981) *The Theatre Workshop Story*, London: Methuen.

Goorney, Howard and MacColl, Ewan (eds) (1986) *Agit-Prop to Theatre Workshop*, Manchester: Manchester University Press.

Littlewood, Joan (1994) *Joan's Book: Joan Littlewood's Peculiar History as She Tells It*, London: Methuen.

NADINE HOLDSWORTH

YURY LYUBIMOV (1917–)

Born in the year of the October Revolution, a child of the new Soviet state, Lyubimov would nevertheless remain in constant opposition to the latter, although this opposition does not make his theatre political. For some forty years he inspired both his actors and his audience to feel self-esteem and uphold a value system that places human beings above politics.

Lyubimov embarked on his career as a director by rejecting the aesthetics imposed from above upon the Soviet theatre of the 1950s: the make-believe approach legitimised by **Stanislavsky**'s 'method', or rather its distortion; the Moscow Art Theatre's concepts of *perezhivanie* (emotional experience) and psychological realism, which lulled spectators emotionally rather than inviting them to think; the illusion of political stability represented in socialist realist plays. Instead, he turned to **Brecht**'s epic theatre, which favoured a demonstrative, rational and blatantly theatrical approach.

Lyubimov's break away from the Stanislavsky 'system' was initiated by his abhorrence for the pompous sets and costumes demanded by stage realism:

> The coarsely daubed backdrops, all the stage properties such as goblets, beards, wigs; all decor which imitates real life such as bushes, clouds, hammocks, lawns, … are as irritating as the general belief in the necessity of make-up, the use of paint and powder on one's face, which is most often nonsensical, and quite repulsive on men.[1]

All this merely served to create a cheap imitation of reality. With his students at the Vakhtangov Theatre's Shchukin School, Lyubimov staged in 1963 Brecht's *The Good Person of Szechwan*, which established him as a director. In the last days of Khrushchev's 'thaw', he was appointed to the post of Artistic Director of the Theatre of Drama and Comedy on Taganka Square. The Taganka was exposed, as were all Soviet theatres, to the control of both state and Party organs, with whom Lyubimov would fight over his artistic programme for the next twenty-five years. The constant tension between him and the authorities informed his approach to rehearsals, where Lyubimov often cited episodes from debates with officials to explain certain actions of a character to an actor. This fuelled his reputation as a dissident, avant-garde director.

At the Taganka, Lyubimov formed a new ensemble and created his own repertoire, eventually consisting of more than thirty productions. They included not only plays, but adaptations of classical and contemporary prose and poetry, and encompassed light, design, music, choreography, mime, song and dance. His is an *auteur* theatre where the director manipulates the material for the production according to his own vision. Theatre is a place where the fourth wall between the stage and the auditorium is broken down. The actor communicates with the audience and steps beside the role he plays so that his own personality is evident in the performance.

The portraits of four great directors of this century – Stanislavsky, **Meyerhold**, Vakhtangov and Brecht – dominate not only the foyer of the Taganka theatre, but also Lyubimov's work. Yet Lyubimov's approach is not an amalgam of these four directors. It is idiosyncratic. He proceeds from the exterior to the interior, from the form of a dramatic text to its content, from movement and action to the right feeling or sub-text for the actor's performance. An essential feature of all his productions is their fragmentary structure. Such a structure can be found in the plays of Brecht, but it can also be created by using prose of an episodic nature or by collating poems. Lyubimov has classified many of his productions as 'montage', 'collage' or 'spectacle', where he collates several works by one author (Mayakovsky's poetry in *Listen!*, 1977), or combines the works of different authors (war poetry in *The Fallen and the Living*, 1965).

The need for episodic material is also connected to the pace of contemporary life, which plays a vital role in Lyubimov's work. Historical and social developments, as well as technical progress, have changed the pace for people, obliging them to grasp information at greater speed, and this requires a different rhythm for the events on stage. Fragmentation and simultaneity of action are also introduced with this change of pace.

Lyubimov destroys the illusion of the stage world as a separate reality and, like Brecht, he wishes to foster in spectators their awareness of being in the theatre:

> We must not forget for a minute that we are in the theatre,
> we must not try to act with untheatrical means, we must

not imitate reality; then, the feeling of truth and of life on stage will be stronger, and the spectator will believe us.[2]

The actor, then, need not pretend to identify completely with his role or to evoke emotions in himself artificially. He/she brings his/her own personality into the role, not to play-*act*, but to re*act* with his/her personality both to the role and to the reaction of the audience:

> The link of the actor with everything that surrounds him on stage, plus the constant awareness of the auditorium as a living partner imposes special requirements on the range of the actor's capabilities. [...] The actor at the Taganka ... is able to shift his stance and ... define it anew at any moment in the performance; the character, the personality of the actor and their reception by the spectator meet and merge in this stance.[3]

This approach means that the lines spoken always sound meaningful in respect of the current situation in the country. For example, during performances in 1990 of *Ten Days that Shook the World* (1965), the actors said of a scene played with music-hall singers: 'This is what our people need'. They thus commented not only on the interest in music-hall entertainment in the United States in the 1920s, but also on the increasingly commercialised culture of post-perestroika Moscow. Reflections on the revolutionary period were thus extended to the present.

The stage design prevents hypocrisy and 'false' acting, since it ensures sincerity by using only authentic properties and costumes: 'The natural item taken from everyday life set by the designer into interaction with the actors makes any falsehood in acting impossible.'[4] Lyubimov's designer, David Borovsky, also provides a central metaphor which concentrates both the contents of the literary material in a formal image and the guiding concept of the production.

Lyubimov assumes the responsibilities of an *auteur* by writing, adapting or assembling texts to form a play. He directs the production with the right to impose his personal interpretation on the material chosen. In this theatre, the actor becomes an executor. According to Lyubimov:

> Theatre is a collective art, but it is naive to think that actor and director work on an equal footing in the process of the

creation of a production. They have different jobs. The director thinks up the concept, while the profession of the actor is an executive profession.[5]

In rehearsal, Lyubimov manoeuvres his actors like puppets, asking them to repeat the intonations and gestures he demonstrates for them. During each performance, he controls, like a conductor, the rhythm of the action with the help of a torch. His approach to acting relies on the personality of the actor rather than on professional training, and he drew to the Taganka, especially in its early years, actors who would later develop in other artistic spheres as well. Among them are the bard and poet Vladimir Vysotsky, the writer Leonid Filatov and the film directors Nikolai Gubenko and Ivan Dykhovichny. He developed the device of several actors playing one complex character to enhance the character's multi-layered personality.

Lyubimov's ideas changed with social and cultural change, which he reflected in his productions. His work at the Taganka falls into three broad phases: the socio-political agitation of the 1960s, when he encouraged audiences to take life and politics into their own hands; the tragic mode of the 1970s, when people appeared threatened by society and politics; the religious visions of the 1980s, where faith is presented as the sole bearer of a moral value system. This last phase had largely been prepared by Lyubimov's work abroad in opera.

Lyubimov is first and foremost an innovator of theatrical form, but his major innovation is his creation of a new theatrical genre, the poetic theatre, in which all evolves around one metaphor expressed in the set design. It is not the literary work that stands at the centre of a production, but the *idea* that Lyubimov develops from a contemporary reading of this work. The rhythm of movement and word, and the pace and tempo of the production, help to sustain this idea. Lyubimov's concern has always been with the individual and people's predicament under particular historical, social or personal conditions. If theatre is political simply because it appeals to audiences, whether to improve society or to preserve their dignity and behave in good conscience, or simply to accept their fate, then Lyubimov may be called political. In all this, he remained a convinced socialist, except that his view of socialism and equality comprised principles of democratic participation, which clashed with the Soviet distortion of the socialist ideal. Lyubimov always recognised the danger of any idea, political or otherwise, and believed that an idea could wreak destruction when it dominated human behaviour.

Aesthetics rather than ideas gradually assumed prime importance in his work. It was still strongly visual, but its musical element became stronger as the Taganka moved into the post-Soviet era. In a synthetic theatre, emphasis on the visual proved too intellectual an approach to generate spiritual rebirth. The focus was therefore shifted to music, which might reach the audience on a different and higher plane than images or words.

The Taganka had occupied a special place in society. Its audience was composed of dissidents and members of the liberal intelligentsia, former prisoners and workers, teenagers and pensioners, party and state officials, and foreign visitors. Encouraged by the intelligentsia, which was under constant pressure from the authorities and struggling to exist in a totalitarian state, the Taganka played a powerful role in social and cultural life before Lyubimov was exiled in 1984.

Lyubimov returned after the collapse of the Soviet Union, but the Taganka ensemble split into two. With his half of the theatre, he tried to restore the Taganka's function as a place where people could find moral and spiritual support. Yet he did not take account of the social and political changes that had taken place during his absence, and lost contact with reality and with contemporary audiences. People could now turn to the Church for spiritual support, and political views were discussed in the open and debated in the new parliament.

Lyubimov's work after his return to Russia shows that his theatrical approach cripples actors, reducing them to puppets, whilst the director continues to fight an invisible and imaginary political enemy. He continues to work in the aesthetics of the 1960s, unable to connect to contemporary society or theatre. A thought Lyubimov repeated over the years has become true: 'Theatres are like people; they pass through different phases: they are born and they die. A theatre does not have a second life' (unpublished interview with the author, Berlin, 8 August 1988).

Notes

1   Lyubimov, Yury (1974) 'Algebra garmonii', *Avrora* 10: 60.
2   Lyubimov (1975) *Khudozhnik, stsena, ekran*: 20.
3   Krechetova, Rimma (1977) 'Lyubimov' in *Portrety rezhisserov*, Moscow: Iskusstvo: 138, 140.
4   Berezkin (1972) 'Stsenograf i veshch', *Dekorativnoe iskusstvo* 11: 31.
5   Lyubimov (1974: 64).

Further reading

Beumers, Birgit (1997) *Yury Lyubimov: Thirty Years at the Taganka Theatre (1964–1994)*, Amsterdam: Harwood.

Gershkovich, Alexander (1989) *The Theatre of Yury Lyubimov*, trans. Michael Yurieff, New York: Paragon House.

Lioubimov, Youri (1985) *Le Feu sacré*, Paris: Fayard.

Maltseva, Olga (1999) *Poeticheskii teatr Yuriya Lyubimova*, St Petersburg: Rossiiskii institut istorii iskusstv.

Picon-Vallin, Beatrice (ed.) (1997) *Iouri Lioubimov, Les Voies de la Création Théâtrale XX*, Paris: CNRS Editions.

BIRGIT BEUMERS

GIORGIO STREHLER (1921–97)

Strehler's name is indissociable from the Piccolo Teatro di Milano, which he founded in 1946 with Paolo Grassi, his manager-associate until the 1970s. The Piccolo was the first permanent repertory company in the country along the lines of the Moscow Art Theatre, breaking with Italy's *mattatore* tradition of theatre led by a star-actor/manager. Strehler and Grassi's belief in the social role of the theatre was also new for Italy and they shared with **Vilar** the idea that high-quality art theatre was for everybody and was a 'public service' rather than a privilege (Strehler 1974: 36).[1] Their convergence of perspectives was largely due to the post-war circumstances in which these three men defined their anti-fascist, democratic positions, Strehler and Grassi showing a far more pronounced socialist profile than Vilar.

The Piccolo was guided by Strehler's vision of what he was to describe in 1972 as a 'supranational', that is, European, theatre (ibid.: 95). Accordingly, in the 1970s he signed up the Piccolo for a series of performances from its recent repertoire at the Odéon in Paris: *King Lear* (1972), *The Cherry Orchard* (1974), and Goldoni's *Il Campiello* (*The Little Square*, 1975) and *Arlecchino servitore di due padrone* (*Arlecchino, the Servant of Two Masters*, 1977). The Piccolo already had a major reputation across Europe, but its impact in Paris was immense. Strehler staged Goldoni's *Villeggiatura* trilogy (1978) for the Comédie Française, which played it at the Odéon in French.

His supranational aspirations grew with the progressive unification of Europe and the support he had received from powerful pro-Europeans, notably, Jack Lang, founder of the avant-garde

Nancy Festival of Young Theatre who became the Minister of Culture in François Mitterrand's government in 1981. In 1983 Lang turned the Odéon into the Odéon-Théâtre de l'Europe, its new identity announcing his intentions for it; he appointed Strehler to be its first director. For the rest of the 1980s Strehler virtually divided his time between Paris and Milan. In 1990 he became the first president of the Union des Théâtres de l'Europe, an agency based at the Odéon-Théâtre de l'Europe to promote exchange and facilitate protection for theatres at risk, including ex-Eastern European companies.

Strehler's inaugural production at the Odéon-Théâtre de l'Europe in 1983 was with the Piccolo and his acclaimed production of Shakespeare's *The Tempest* (Milan premiere in 1978). But his inaugural production for the theatre in French came one year later with *L'Illusion*, Strehler reverting to Corneille's 1660 revised title of *L'Illusion comique* (*The Theatrical Illusion*) to signal his change of emphasis. The production stressed not the illusory nature of the theatre as such, but the interconnections between the illusions of life and those of the theatre, a theme running through Strehler's work. Like *The Tempest*, it also reflected upon the theatre's powerful relationship to people in that visually refined and emotionally subtle, yet deeply moving, manner characteristic of all his productions.

L'Illusion projects its cluster of ideas through subverted images. Alcandre, the magician, shows Pridamant the death of his son Clindor whom he has exiled – only to turn this picture upside down by showing that Clindor is really an actor playing a part. Pridamant is in the auditorium, unable to join his son when he discovers that his son's death was merely a sleight of hand. He is thus left with his hopes of reconciliation shattered, the point being that desires are nothing but fantasies, as conjured up by the theatre and magic. Strehler's innovative positioning of Pridamant among the spectators is reinforced by a casting innovation by which actors double each other so as physically to create the idea of mirror reflections explored thematically. The scenography by Ezio Frigerio – a lifelong collaborator, as was stage and costume designer Luciano Damiani – merges perfectly with the production's intentions. A panorama of pastoral, Watteau-like scenes traverses a transparent screen, the whole bathed in chiaroscuro. A flickering black marble floor suggests Alcandre's cave and alludes to Plato's cave of shadows which deceive.

In *The Tempest*, the play of illusions occurs on multiple levels simultaneously: visually, by such details as billowing silk waves for the sea on which a small ship is tossed to indicate that the tempest was a magic trick; physically, by Ariel's balletic and acrobatic feats in the air, clown's clothes and make-up whimsically deflating Prospero's magic; gesturally, by Caliban's ambiguity, who at one moment is a 'savage' roughly carrying out archaic rituals and, at another, has the mannerisms of a handsome, urbane man. Caliban represents the servitude imposed by colonialism and by the actor's profession, since Prospero is an emblematic director figure. At the end of the production, Prospero lifts his wand and snaps it in two, a signal for the whole stage to collapse. Flies and drapes tumble to the floor; the orchestra pit, on which the blue silk of the sea had been draped, collapses. The power of the theatre to pretend and convince is revealed, as is its capacity to influence people and help them to reconstruct their lives. During Prospero's monologue, the stage is reassembled before the spectators' eyes – the power of magic to build, to restore, to inspire. The production indicates, as well, that political power (configured in Prospero), is not immutable, but can be brought down.

This *Tempest* is Strehler's second production of the play (the first in 1948) and follows his practice of returning to texts that have key meaning for him. *Arlecchino*, for example, saw six different versions, from the first in 1947, for the Piccolo's first season, to the last in 1987. All reflected Strehler's different relationship to the changing times. The first celebrated his revival of *commedia dell'arte*, which had fallen into oblivion in Italy, and gave *commedia* aesthetic stature while sharpening its potential for social commentary (as Dario Fo was to do, particularly in the 1960s). It also celebrated the presence of politics in the theatre, Arlecchino becoming Strehler's prototype for popular political intervention.

Arlecchino went through several variations on the idea of empowerment (1952, 1956, 1963), Strehler developing improvisation with each one. His penultimate *Arlecchino* (1977) was a brooding production in which he appears to question the viability of popular power in the current climate in Italy of anarcho-terrorism and growing authoritarian backlash. His ultimate *Arlecchino* (1987) was far more optimistic, confirming the socio-political role of the theatre and offering a synthesis of forty years of research on corporeal principles for the theatre. Two extraordinary Arlecchinos have played the character – Marcello Moretti and Ferrucio Soleri (from 1961, after Moretti's death) – enabling Strehler and his actors to become veritable pioneers of *commedia* for the world.[2] The *commedia* is woven in to Strehler's work everywhere, whether in full-blown form

(Stephano and Trinculo in *The Tempest*), allusively (*The Cherry Orchard*) or elusively (*La Villeggiatura*). Its laughter blends in with the myriad of tones that make Strehler's such delicately nuanced compositions.

Strehler's revitalisation of *commedia* accompanied his recovery of Goldoni as a spirited social observer and an advocate of the people contra Goldoni's reputation for parochial Venetian interest. Strehler rediscovered other regional dramatists: Bertolazzi (*El nost Milan* – Our Milan – performed in the Milanese dialect in 1955 and revived several times) and Pirandello in whose allegedly Sicilian quirkiness and purely formal structures he found a seductive lyricism treating such serious themes as human fragility and oppression. His Pirandello cycle began with *The Mountain Giants* in 1947, which saw a Düsseldorf version in 1958 and a return Milanese version in 1966 reputed to be 'among the finest of all his stagings' (Hirst 1993: 13). It ended with *As You Desire Me* in 1988.

Strehler introduced Salacrou, Gorky, Büchner and Toller to Italian spectators, but his greatest revelations were Shakespeare (starting with a 1948 *Richard II*, followed by *Richard III* in 1950), and **Brecht** (starting with *The Threepenny Opera* in 1956). He increasingly interpreted Shakespeare through Brecht, highlighting in the former the political struggles analysed by the latter; and, by understating the 'Englishness' of Shakespeare, he stressed how the power play of rulers affected all citizens in contemporary Europe. This slant was evident in *Richard II*, *Richard III* and *Macbeth* (1952), but was unmistakable in his 1965 *Henry* trilogy, renamed *Il Gioco dei potenti* (literally, 'The Game of the Powerful'). His explicitly Brechtian perspective on the challenge to the power of rulers by the ruled appeared in *Coriolanus* (1956) with the 'epic rigour' Strehler admired in Brecht (Strehler 1974: 99).

Nowhere do Shakespeare's dialectics of power appear more forcefully than in *King Lear*, where, in a muffled prologue suggesting the distance of the action, Tino Carraro, Strehler's celebrated Prospero, tears a semi-transparent veil in two. Metaphors for the division of Lear's kingdom, these two pieces become sheets hung on a line, which, when busily shaken and folded by Goneril and Regan, become metaphors for the intrusion of the power of state into personal life. The interplay between history and domesticity continues throughout as the torn sheets stand for familial disintegration, sexual passion, civil war, destitution and madness, the whole played out in black leather costumes recalling fascist/Nazi Europe and the world of skin-heads and punks (Goneril, for instance, sports a green Afro hair-do). It alludes, as well, to 1930s cabarets and 1970s discos.

The production is set in a circus ring (scenography by Frigerio) where the Fool, dressed like a modern clown, doubles as a clown-like Cordelia to indicate that clownerie is the satirical reverse of repression and control. Narrative is conveyed through an economy of means typical of Strehler. When Gloucester is blinded, for example, his head is pushed beneath a trap door in an innocuous-looking wooden contraption and dragged back up to reveal large black spots. This contraption 'tells' of multiple situations and events in a condensed space that continually redefines its identity. It is a drawbridge, a cage, Edgar's cave and the cliffs of Dover over which Gloucester intends to throw himself.

Brecht's dialectics of power, on the other hand, took Strehler through several variations of *The Threepenny Opera*, the last performed in Paris in 1986. The first (1955), rehearsals for which Brecht attended at the Piccolo, was, according to Brecht, superior to his own production (Hirst 1993: 96). It led to Strehler's being viewed as Brecht's heir, and he was offered the directorship (declined) of the Berliner Ensemble after Brecht's death. After *The Good Person of Setzuan* (1958, revised in 1977 and 1981), practically not a year went by in the 1960s and 1970s without a Brecht production, most notably, *Schweyk in the Second World War* (1961), *The Exception and the Rule* (1962), *Galileo* (1963), *Mahagonny* (1964), and performances of poetry and song, among them *Io Bertolt Brecht*, a series of three of which the last part appeared in 1979. All of them filtered Strehler's insights into Brecht through aspects of Italian culture. Italian cabaret was the touchstone for *The Threepenny Opera* and the evenings of poetry and song; the visual harmony of the Italian Renaissance (scenography and costumes by Damiani) contra-dicted the brutality of the *raison d'état* exposed in *Galileo*.

Although profoundly influenced by Brecht, Strehler repeatedly acknowledged his debt to **Stanislavsky** for the importance of ensemble acting, close textual and sub-textual reading, and the idea of creating characters with biographies and psycho-emotional moti-vations. In all his works he achieved the allegedly impossible: binding together the dramatic and the epic theatres – Stanislavsky *and* Brecht – contrary to Brecht's theory of their antithesis. This was particularly striking in Strehler's 1970s productions, not least in the diaphanous *The Cherry Orchard* and *The Little Square*, both composi-tions in white. Whiteness, in the first, signifies life and memory in conflict with encroaching history.[3] In the second, it is the colour of dreams, aspirations and everyday struggle. *The Cherry Orchard* has a vast white veil dipping, like a canopy, from the top of the front of the stage to the back, and covered in autumn leaves that continually fall in the 'breeze'. Below are several child-size tables and chairs (Damiani's design), recalling the past. In *The Little Square* a white wall, small windows and a small puddle (also Damiani) narrow space so that action frequently occurs at the windows. Stories about the people of the square are inward-looking as well as extroverted, played as well as told.

Strehler's comparison of his theatre to interlocking Chinese boxes is relevant to all of his productions. The first box contains the immediate reality of story and people. The second contextualises them socio-historically and politically. The third concerns particular instances, but attributes universal values to them. The fourth box contains the other three and might be said to crystallise everything sedimented through them (Strehler 1974: 260–263). Yet Strehler's box imagery cannot hope to convey the fluidity of his work, which is intimately bound up with his musicality. No other director in the twentieth century has his ear for rhythm, intonation, cadence, accent and beat, nor for semi-tones, overtones, measure, harmony, melodic line and polyphony. These qualities essentially turn his productions into scores whose orchestral richness and finesse move synchronically and diachronically simultaneously.

His musicality has made Strehler an incomparable director of over thirty operas at the Teatro alla Scala in Milan and elsewhere by composers as different as Verdi, Prokofiev and his beloved Mozart. His last opera and final work was *Così fan tutte* (1997), which inaugurated the Nuovo Piccolo Teatro, the new theatre for which he had fought the Milanese authorities for decades. He died before its opening night, but it was opera as he had fashioned it for fifty years: not grand or exhibitionistic, but opera sung for meaning whose singers mould their voices to their characters. Opera aspiring to the condition of the theatre, and, particularly, to chamber theatre – this was Strehler's revolution for the opera of the second half of the twentieth century. *Così fan tutte* encapsulates Strehler's life's work. It has the translucence, grace, purity of form and lightness of touch unique to his theatre, and its emotional depth.

Notes

1   My translation. Strehler explains: 'We were a generation without teachers, without leaders.... We were young ... in human and theatrical

experience. And we were the ones who were going to have to guide "the others". These "others" lived apart in a world of their own in which their way of working and their whole approach to the theatre had become decadent. They were profoundly cut off from reality in every sense. They knew neither the words to speak, nor the way to speak them. They were trying to keep alive a theatre which both from a historical and a human point of view was at least fifty years out of date.' Strehler (ed.) (1953) *1947–58 Piccolo Teatro*, Milan: Moneta: 13, quoted in English in Hirst (1993: 9).

2   Moretti initially refused to wear the uncomfortable *commedia* mask and painted one on his face instead. When Moretti gradually came to 'accept the tyranny of the mask', he 'was the first to discover the endless mobility of the mask: he realised the full expressive force of its mouth and gradually discovered how to externalise a whole range of emotions when he let himself be "conquered" by the mask; he found liberty in the restriction, and the most rigid of conventions released his imaginative capacity, allowing him to realise the most vital part of himself' (Strehler quoted in Hirst 1993: 42–43). This step was possible because the stiff cardboard and lint masks used for Strehler's first *Arlecchino* were replaced by the flexible leather masks designed by Amleto Sartori for his second. It was only then that Moretti understood how the mask trained the actor to use his entire body for expressive purposes.

3   See Shevtsova, Maria (1983) 'Chekhov in France, 1976–9: Productions by Strehler, Miquel and Pintilié' in Donaldson, Ian (ed.) *Transformations in Modern European Drama*, London: Macmillan: 85–89.

Further reading

Guazzotti, Giorgio (1965) *Teoria e realtà del Piccolo Teatro di Milano*, Turin: Einaudi.

Hirst, David L. (1993) *Giorgio Strehler*, Cambridge: Cambridge University Press.

Ronfani, Ugo (1986) *Io, Strehler: Conversazioni con Ugo Ronfani*, Milan: Rusconi.

Strehler, Giorgio (1974) *Per un teatro umano*, Milan: Feltrinelli.

MARIA SHEVTSOVA

JULIAN BECK (1925–85)

The title of the third chapter of John Tytell's book on Julian Beck's avant-garde New York theatre group, *The Living Theatre*, is 'Accomplishments'. The heading of the first section of the chapter is 'Prison'. It is almost as if Julian Beck and his partner and long-time associate Judith Malina willed incarceration upon themselves so as to deem the American 'system' evil enough to support the extravagant protests that fuelled much of their theatre. Virtually every page of Beck's *The Life of the Theatre* is a clarion call to revolution that, however impractical politically, was nevertheless the life-blood of the undeniably vibrant theatre he created. Beck's conviction that only a 'Non-violent Anarchist Revolution' could 'feed all the people ... stop all the wars ... open the doors of all the jails [and] ... undo early death' (Beck 1972: 24–25) may seem simplistic; but it did fuel *Paradise Now* (1968), a production which changed forever our perception of what it was possible to achieve in terms of audience participation in the theatre.

Living Theatre devotees would perhaps resent the suggestion that Beck and Malina's achievements in the theatre were more important than the lives they led. Beck often claimed that he was 'not interested in theatre' (ibid.: 4): 'I do not choose to work in the theatre but in the world' (ibid.: 5), he wrote; 'We don't need plays, we need action' (ibid.: 38). Beck and Malina were first and foremost revolutionaries who, to their credit, lived even the most private aspects of their lives in a manner that was consistent with their convictions. They were not just public figures who burnt draft cards to challenge the government's position on the Vietnam war; they also embraced joyfully the inconvenience of having fifteen others sharing their cramped New York apartment as a way of practising socialism. Their theatre merely reflected what they were trying to do in their lives – which was to realise their 'dreams of a free society' (ibid.: 10). Given the seriousness in which Beck and Malina held the notion of liberty, the United States of the 1950s, of the McCarthy hearings and the Eisenhower years of conformity and jingoism, represented a betrayal of the American dream. As they took to the streets to voice their disapproval, they involuntarily instigated a vicious circle whereby imprisonment merely confirmed their convictions, which led in turn to further protests.

Given their talent for reckless immoderation, many of their demonstrations took on the character of theatrical events. For example, when the Inland Revenue Service seized their theatre in 1963, Beck and Malina decided to resist the eviction order by staying behind in the quarantined building and living off food supplied by neighbouring restaurants in baskets which were hauled through windows on hastily improvised pulleys. Outside, a group of demonstrators began to chant 'Free the Living Theatre' and marched with signs declaring the seizure unfair. Richard Schechner conducted an interview with Beck, shouting up his questions from the street. The orchestration of the actors, who appeared periodically at windows to cry 'Help', was of course deliberately theatrical, a shrewdly calculated means of exciting the interest of the growing numbers of journalists and television crews that had gathered on the street below. By acting with habitual preposterousness, Beck and Malina had managed to convert a routine dispossession into a drama about freedom and imprisonment. When Robert Brustein spoke of The Living Theatre production of Jack Gelber's *The Connection* (1959) as an attempt to 'break down barriers between what was going on onstage and what was going on in life' (Tytell 1997: 158), he could scarcely have imagined how much truer this would be of Beck and Malina's lives than of their theatre.

If Beck and Malina's lives often took on a theatrical aspect, their theatre also began systematically to resemble real life. Beck had long railed against Broadway where the 'tone of voice is false, the mannerisms are false, the sex is false' (Beck 1972: 7). He had declared that he 'wanted to change the whole method of acting' (Biner 1972: 27) and, as changing whole methods was the *raison d'être* of the Living Theatre, the art of acting was not immune to the universal sweep of their reforms. Beck and Malina opposed the artificiality of Broadway not with a more realistic style of acting but rather with the complete absence of style. In what eventually came to be called 'nonfictional acting', the actors were required to appear not under the cover of their characters but as themselves.

The beginnings of this change were detectable in *The Connection* where the jazz musicians, who appeared simply as musicians, became models of authenticity for the actors:

> When a jazz musician plays his music, he enters into *personal* contact with the public; when he goes home ... there is no difference between the way he is now and the way he was on stage.... *The Connection* represented a very important advance for us in this respect: from then on, the actors began *to play themselves.*
>
> (ibid.: 48)

By playing their drug-dependent characters as themselves, the actors made the point that the addicts' need for a 'fix' was not an isolated evil that people could complacently condemn but was symptomatic of a problem that pervaded society as a whole.

This was carried forward in the Living Theatre's next major production, Kenneth Brown's *The Brig* (1963), a play set in a brutally run Marine Corps prison which, for Beck, provided a vivid distillation of the duress he believed characterised life as a whole. In *The Brig* the amalgamation of theatre and real life was achieved by compelling the actors who played the prisoners genuinely to suffer the sadism of the prison guards. Rehearsals were conducted in accordance with unreasonably strict rules which, if broken, were punished with soul-destroying work details. If the tension during the deliberately barbarous seven-hour sessions of actor training became too great, the actors could 'cry for mercy' whereupon they were given a five-minute break:

> The brig had become a reality that was being tested by the actors day after day. Their behaviour was becoming the behaviour of victims and tormentors....
>
> Judith did not want to substitute; she wanted the actors to experience directly. By this means too, the public would be able to feel immediately and directly the horror of the brig.... *The Brig* turned into a monstrous creation; the actors had never felt more defenceless in their lives.... Their physical well-being was being threatened during any given performance.
>
> (Ibid.: 67–71)

If **Grotowski** had insisted that his actors genuinely suffer in the manner of the great martyrs of myth so as to inspire his audience, Beck and Malina required that their actors convey to their spectators the humiliation of the human condition so completely as to goad them into rebellion.

By the time they were performing *Mysteries* (1964), Beck and Malina had dispensed with the artificiality of stage sets and costumes. The actors had begun to appear in whatever they happened to be wearing on the day so as to emphasise the singular nature of their presence:

> Instead of saying, as a traditional actor: 'I am the embodiment of Richard III,' or as a Brechtian actor: 'I am Mother Courage, but I'm also Helen Weigel playing Courage,' the actor in the Living Theatre says: 'I am Julian Beck and I play Julian Beck.'
>
> (Ibid.: 170)

It followed from these attempts to create a performance environment in which the actors ceased to be actors that the audience too would eventually come under pressure to relinquish their conventional passivity and engage more actively with the drama. The motivation for this was political: audiences had to 'discover that they are no longer the "privileged class" to whom the play is "presented" but are needed by the actors for the very accomplishment of the play' (ibid.: 173). To this end *Mysteries* began with a single actor standing silently to attention on a bare stage, waiting for some sort of audience reaction to begin the play. In the first performance of *Mysteries* in Paris, a member of the public responded to the actors' provocation by piling seats one on top of the other to make a mountain that he then climbed, screaming obscenities. In Brussels, almost fifty members of the public 'died' with the actors in the distinctly Artaudian plague scene with which the performance ended. In Trieste, *Mysteries* was banned because the audience refused to leave the theatre despite being ordered to do so by the police. As the action of a Living Theatre performance became more ritual than narrative, acting became less a matter of making believe than of living intensely in the present.

Encouraged by the extent to which audiences had readily participated in *Mysteries*, the Living Theatre went on to design *Paradise Now* as an event that would rely almost entirely on the audience for its momentum. *Paradise Now* was put together collectively by the company as a structured meditation on the manner in which a shackled society could achieve Elysian liberation. The purpose of the drama was to ensure that the audience would experience rather than merely bear witness to the evolution of emancipation. The drama, comprising a series of stages or 'rungs' that spanned the whole gamut of human experience from bondage to deliverance, was designed such that progress from one level to the next was dependent on the impetus the actors received from the audience:

> The moments where the audience is invited to go to the next rung are entirely open to suggestions. The company does not at this point shift its role from that of guide to that of leader, but tries to develop the audience's ideas to their full potential.
>
> (Ibid.: 174)

Paradise Now began with a catalogue of prohibitions ('I am not allowed to smoke marijuana', 'I am not allowed to travel without a passport') that were gradually overcome through the course of the drama, level by level, at the instigation of the audience. 'I am not allowed to take my clothes off', for instance, was a restriction that was tackled in the so-called 'Rite of Universal Intercourse' which had the audience join the actors in a pile of naked bodies, all humming and caressing one other. The drama ended with the actors, some of whom were still undressed, leading the spectators out on to the street in a celebration of the death of authority.

In *Paradise Now* the audience danced with an ecstasy little known in the theatre since the bacchanalian rites of ancient Greece. They sought the sublime with the fervour of an oriental congregation chanting mantras in the knowledge that God is near. In the West such feelings have long been absent. Their restitution was a formidable achievement. Politically however the Living Theatre was less successful. Not only were they unable significantly to change society, they were not even able to make their ideals viable within the closed world of the community in which they lived. The pressure to work on the basis of democratic consensus, a model of the egalitarian ideal to which the members of the group aspired, proved to be the group's undoing. At midnight, September 1969, on board a ship, Beck and Malina announced that they were leaving the company they had formed. The company had lived together in exile, they had eaten and slept together, they had even been to prison together. But finally they disbanded, unable to make politically viable the indomitable vision that had fuelled so much of their redoubtable artistic success.

Further reading

Beck, J. (1972) *The Life of the Theatre*, San Francisco: Limelight Editions.
Biner, P. (1972) *The Living Theatre*, New York: Horizon Press.
Neff, R. (1970) *The Living Theatre: USA*, New York: Bobbs-Merrill.
Tytell, J. (1997) *The Living Theatre: Art, Exile and Outrage*, London: Methuen.

SHOMIT MITTER

PETER BROOK (1925–)

Of all the directors discussed in this book, Peter Brook is perhaps the most elusive, the most multifaceted, the most difficult to characterise in a few pages. Whereas it is possible to locate the work of most directors within the orbit of certain pet pre-occupations, Brook has deliberately embarked upon a series of radically dissimilar projects through the course of his long career. He has worked on everything from West End musicals, Shakespearean drama and opera to improvised scenarios built around pairs of shoes in the depths of the Sahara. Indeed, if there is a single principle that encapsulates this formidable range of work, it is that the moment a certain mode of working is successful, it must be abandoned lest it ossify into a habit. Yet it is not as if Brook has re-invented himself with startling originality. The areas he has explored are almost without exception those mapped previously by others. Brook has rummaged about in other people's backyards, often to emerge, it must be admitted, with more telling contributions than those of his mentors. Yet he remains a director who, for all his obvious brilliance, will be remembered as a consolidator rather than a creator, a man without a definable bequest or legacy.

In 1962, Brook rehearsed a Royal Shakespeare Company (RSC) production of *King Lear* with Paul Scofield in the title role. The parameters of the production were broadly Stanislavskian: Brook was concerned principally with the truthfulness of the emotions. The early readings were devoted to the analysis of objectives and improvisations concentrated on developing the background information actors are thought to require in order to play their characters with authenticity. So, for example, the Fool and Cordelia were asked to improvise a scene in which Cordelia is preparing for what is in effect the first scene of the play. The thinking here is that actors gain confidence by giving their characters a 'real' identity that exists in the corridors and rooms adjacent to those featured in the play. Even the crowd scenes were anchored in improvised fictions which established what **Stanislavsky** would have called the 'given circumstances' of the drama. The knights were all given names and their past was sketched in.

In 1966 Brook created *US* in response to the crisis in Vietnam. There was no script: the performance was put together collectively by members of the RSC using methods that derived principally from **Brecht**. Like Brecht, Brook at this point believed that 'society needs changing – urgently' (Brook 1987: 54). And, like Brecht, Brook knew that 'For an idea to stick it is not enough to state it' (ibid.): the theatre must work by 'breaking open a series of habits' (ibid.: 107) using 'a multitude of contradictory techniques to change direction and to change levels' (ibid.: 63). However, Brook, more mindful of mendacity than Brecht, insisted that it was not sufficient merely to present the audience with contradictions that made them think. If audiences were to be made not merely to think, but to act, they had to be presented both with the situation that demanded action and with a sketch of *their own* irresponsibly passive reaction to it. *US* was a compound title: it stood both for the United States and *us*.

Like Brecht, Brook initially required Stanislavskian authenticity in order to build up a number of portraits that would, at a later stage, be set up so as to contradict one another. In the early stages of rehearsal, the Fulbright Committee Hearings were unearthed and a Buddhist monk was invited to speak to the cast. The actors played at being American film stars and learnt to cook rice and sweep huts as though they were Vietnamese villagers. The object was eventually to make thematic links between these different worlds. This could only be done by actors trained to move rapidly between different styles of acting. In an effort to achieve this Brook had his actors spend several hours on a Brecht exercise: they went through *Good King Wenceslas*, singing alternate lines – each moving quickly from Sinatra to Caruso and then to Mick Jagger. As the actors moved between these radically different impersonations they learnt the very Brechtian art of rapidly embodying and relinquishing character. A similar 'alienation' effect was achieved by having a monk's suicide played out in front of a number of actors who were coached to respond to the improvisation by making statements prefaced by their name, the place and date.

In 1970 Brook chose to direct a provocative and compelling production of *A Midsummer Night's Dream* at Stratford for no other reason but that 'it was such a contrast with everything I had been doing since 1964' (Hunt and Reeves 1995: 143). In marked contrast to the largely analytical manner in which Brook had worked on *King Lear* in 1962, characterisation was now sought through a decidedly anti-intellectual series of physical exercises such as passing batons around in a circle and making sounds to search out the impulses behind the words of Shakespeare's play. The actors were told that 'listening to the rhythms of the words, rather than attending to their literal meaning will take one towards a deeper understanding' (Selbourne 1982: 11):

> Brook taps on a drum two differentiated rhythms, which he wants respectively from the mechanicals and the courtiers. As a result, Theseus' 'The wall, methinks, being sensible, should curse again' has the heightened arrogance of a swift and (as if) princely wit, while Pyramus' reply 'No, in truth, sir, he should not', with its heavy round vocables, has more than ever the pedestrian gait of the sturdy Bottom.
>
> (Ibid.: 201)

In order to search out the rhythms in which the deep structures of meaning were encoded, Brook had the actress playing Helena sing her 'O weary night' speech; he had the lovers recite their lines while climbing up and down various sets of ladders; and the Bottom/Pyramus 'Death' speech was broken up and read simultaneously by three actors. By giving up the direct pursuit of meaning, Brook achieved a performance that was, in the opinion of some, better spoken than most people had known. The production becomes one of the Royal Shakespeare Company's greatest successes.

Brook responded to his success, typically, by leaving. He left the RSC and went to Paris where he set up his own company, the Centre International de Créations Théâtrales. With a newly assembled international cast Brook produced a number of experimental productions including *Orghast* (1971), a performance loosely based on the Prometheus myth. The performance extended the work on sound and rhythm in *A Midsummer Night's Dream* by abandoning conventional language altogether. The actors expressed themselves through a combination of chants, cries and guttural howls, the product of Ted Hughes' attempt to fashion a universal language that would communicate by using the relationship between sound and emotion rather than words and meaning. The assumption was that human beings have a common sensitivity to tone and pitch and that sounds contain within them the seeds of emotional conditions which they can invoke in anyone, regardless of the language in which they speak.

The test of so extreme a claim is of course to play to an audience that is, in social terms, as unlike the members of the group as possible. To this end, Brook took his company to Africa the following year, where his actors improvised shows on a carpet using a minimum of props – some boxes, some sticks, a pair of old boots:

> [Marthouret] was on the carpet, struggling with a cardboard box. The crowd fixed on the box with total attentiveness. There was a stillness about the people, an expectancy. What's in the box....
>
> Helen Mirren went on the carpet, blowing on a slide whistle. She talks with the whistle to Miriam Goldschmidt who replies with a flute....
>
> What next? Nobody knew. Brook wasn't saying anything either. Enter a void! No actor was moving. Until Katsulas

suddenly took off his huge army boots and placed them in
the centre of the carpet....

(Heilpern 1977: 65–66)

This was theatre shorn of all sophistication, devoid of custom and
tradition. The actors faced their bemused audiences defencelessly –
and were able to forge out of their minimal resources something
that had the simplicity and clarity of a shared event. This, for Brook,
was the essence of theatre. This was the core that had, in the West,
been obscured by formality and affectation.

In 1985 Brook staged a nine-hour version of the Indian epic, *Le
Mahabharata*. The performance was in some ways the product of a
lifetime's work in the theatre for it contained elements that derived
from each of the various stages of Brook's career. The manner in
which Cieslak played Dhritirashtra, for instance, was realistic in the
best Stanislavskian tradition; in contrast, Dussasana's death was played
with grotesque exaggeration – and then undercut with a perfectly
Brechtian speech which addressed the audience directly, pointing
out that what they were watching was only theatre. The miracle of
the production was that it allowed these supposedly contradictory
playing styles to operate in conjunction with one another without
mutually neutralising one another. The death of Ganga's child was
played in mime, a musical instrument doubled as an elephant's
trunk, a wheel suggested a chariot in one scene, a wooden board
was chariot in another. Actors wore trousers in some scenes and
dhotis in others. The flight of arrows was played realistically in one
scene and mimed in another. This was Brook at his flamboyant best.
He had had the courage to ignore the rules of stylistic consistency
and was duly rewarded with a complexity of expression which
alone, Brook believed, could do justice to the heterogeneity of the
material, deriving as it did from an epic that is eight times the length
of *The Odyssey* and *The Iliad* put together.

Le Mahabharata was very much the high point of Brook's work,
the masterpiece that defined everything that went before and after.
Since then Brook has produced a number of notable productions,
including *The Tempest* (1990), which featured a black Prospero and
white Caliban, *Qui est là* (1996), a version of *Hamlet* which was
interspersed with quotations from **Artaud**, and *Le Costume* (1999), a
story set in Sophiatown and played with all the profound simplicity
that had informed the 1975 *Les Iks* which also had a small cast, used
no scenery and had very few props. If Brook has finally settled on a
style it is this: to tell a story with detachment and clarity.

Further reading

Brook, P. (1968) *The Empty Space*, London: Penguin Books.

—— (1987) *The Shifting Point*, New York: Harper & Row.

—— (1998) *Threads of Time: a Memoir*, London: Methuen Drama.

Heilpern, J. (1977) *Conference of the Birds*, London: Penguin Books.

Hunt, A. and Reeves, G. (eds) (1995) *Peter Brook*, Cambridge: Cambridge University Press.

Selbourne, D. (1982) *The Making of A Midsummer Night's Dream*, London: Methuen.

Williams, D. (compiled) (1988) *Peter Brook: A Theatrical Casebook*, London: Methuen.

SHOMIT MITTER

AUGUSTO BOAL (1931–)

Not many directors have explored the question as to how theatre can change society with as much innovative pragmatism as the Brazilian Augusto Boal. Not many directors have had as much reason: Boal lived through the 1960 elections, the coup of 1964 and the repression that followed the infamous AI-5 legislation of 1968. In 1971 he was arrested, tortured and exiled. The interest of Boal's theatre is the link that exists between his work and his changing political status: as the situation around him altered, so too did the form of his theatre, which had to adapt to the varying restrictions imposed by the government. '[T]heatre is a weapon' (Boal 1979: ix) Boal once observed, and he meant this quite literally: his intention was not merely to discuss oppression or to voice his protest but to use theatre to combat oppression actively. Just as weapons have to be deployed strategically so as to glean the best possible advantage from confrontations, so Boal's theatre was not just an abstract vehicle for intellectual indignation. It was a means of waging guerrilla warfare, with all the guile and shrewdness that such a term implies. Boal's is a career littered with wily adaptations to circumstances. Each new constraint is the seed of a creative response that is as politically astute as it is formally ingenious. The result is a body of work that unites artistic inventiveness and political commitment in a manner that is quite unparalleled.

In the early 1960s Boal toured Brazil extensively with the Arena Theatre of São Paulo, playing extravagant, activist agit-prop to the poor. These were flamboyant, proselytising missions that targeted the downtrodden and urged them to rise up against oppression. Boal selected his audiences carefully: he chose shanties in the inner-city areas of São Paulo, where an enormous gulf divided rich and poor, and remote rural areas where forlorn peasants had lost land to rapacious landlords. Fired by his indignation, Boal staged heroic tales of bloody insurrections and valiant triumphs over adversity. Performances ended with calls to revolution – although at that point the group had little or no idea as to what precisely revolution would mean for the various audiences to whom they played. Boal was genuinely angered by injustice and felt that the veracity of his emotions somehow guaranteed the political success of his methods. That this was not so came home to him quite abruptly when a peasant, who was clearly moved by the troupe's revolutionary fervour, offered Boal some guns and asked him to join in the fight against a murderous local landlord. In his introduction to *The Rainbow of Desire*, Boal recalls the lessons he learnt from that startling challenge:

> Agit-prop is fine; what was not fine was that we were incapable of following our own advice. We white men from the big city, there was very little we could teach black women of the country ... Since that first encounter – an encounter with a real peasant, in flesh and blood, rather than an abstract 'peasantry' – an encounter which traumatised but enlightened, I have never again written plays that give advice, nor have I ever sent 'messages' again.
>
> (Boal 1995: 3)

To sing 'Let us spill our blood for freedom' was not just glib. It was irresponsible.

Boal responded to the problem by radically overhauling the form in which he presented his plays. Instead of protesting against oppression generally, he would henceforth address only the specific problems of his spectators. Instead of offering premeditated solutions, he would help spectators reach their own conclusions. Theatre, in Boal's hands, now became dramatised discussion. The group continued to tour as it had done – but they no longer carried a show. They would arrive at the scene of a conflict – a factory on strike, for example, – and study the situation. They would then dramatise the crux of the conflict and play it through to the point of crisis that needed to be resolved. The actors would then stop and ask the spectators, whose situation was being dramatised, for suggestions as to how best to proceed. The spectators would recommend certain courses of action around which the actors would improvise a scene. So as to ensure that such events retained some semblance of order, the conduct of both spectators and actors would be overseen by a master of ceremonies, the so-called 'joker' of Boal's pack.

The difficulty with this form of 'simultaneous dramaturgy' was that Boal's actors had to improvise the reactions of characters who were better known to the audience than to them. On one occasion a woman remained dissatisfied with the manner in which the group had rendered the scenario she had sketched. Frustrated by the woman's hostility, Boal asked her if she would like to come up on to the stage and demonstrate to the actors what precisely she had in mind. To Boal's surprise the woman not only accepted but turned in a performance which the actors, for all their professionalism, could never have equalled. As Boal recalls,

> this truth dawned on me: when the spectator herself comes on stage and carries out the action she has in mind, she does it in a manner which is personal, unique and non-transferable, as she alone can do it, and as no artist can do it in her place. On stage the actor is an interpreter who, in the act of translating, plays false.
>
> (Ibid.: 7)

And so, 'simultaneous dramaturgy' became 'forum theatre'. The actors continued to research and sketch scenes, but now the specta-tors took it in turns to play the role of the oppressed protagonist and attempt, by their own theatrical exertions, to arrive at solutions:

> he [the spectator] himself assumes the protagonic role, changes the dramatic action, tries out solutions, discusses plans for change – in short, trains himself for real action. In this case, perhaps the theater is not revolutionary in itself, but it is surely a rehearsal for the revolution. The liberated spectator, as a whole person, launches into action.
>
> (Boal 1979: 122)

The spectators now became what Boal called 'spect-actors': they were no longer passive recipients of alien intervention but partici-pants in the quest to be masters of their fate.

In the mid-1970s the political repression to which Boal was subjected became so intense that he felt it was dangerous to continue practising his particularly volatile brand of forum theatre. Rather than court imprisonment by continuing fruitlessly to defy the government ban on inflammatory performances, Boal invented what he called 'invisible theatre'. Invisible theatre involved a group of actors performing a rehearsed scene in a public space, such as a market or a town square, while pretending to be members of the public participating in a normal, everyday situation. The 'audience' were passers-by who chanced upon the 'incident', unaware that it was in fact a drama seeking surreptitiously to supply information or stimulate debate at a time when political activity was banned. For example, while Boal was in Argentina he discovered that, although there was a law that permitted the poor to receive free meals at restaurants, no attempt was made to make the existence of this law known to the public. So Boal's actors entered a large restaurant separately and sat at different tables. The 'protagonist' ordered a meal, ate it appreciatively and then announced loudly that he was not going to pay the bill: the law permitted it. When he was challenged, another actor, playing the part of a lawyer, went up to the manager and explained that there was indeed such a law. Eventually a number of the people at the restaurant joined in the debate. Thus invisible theatre met the needs of forum theatre – to stimulate public discussion and help overcome oppression – while shielding Boal from the sinister consequences of being overtly activist.

As Boal's reputation spread so too did the network of secret police determined to engineer his arrest. Boal moved to Europe but found that, in the less threatening political climate of countries such as France and Britain, his passion for combating explicitly malevolent oppression seemed almost irrelevant. Europe was not teeming with farmers who had been evicted from their lands by murderous landowners. Here people were terrified not of the secret police but of loneliness. At first the dread of existential emptiness seemed to Boal something of a luxury in comparison with the threat of torture. Gradually however he realised that it exercised as tyrannical an influence on the psyche and was no less traumatic for the individual:

> In Latin America the major killer is hunger; in Europe, it is drug overdose. But, whatever form it comes in, death is still death.... I decided to work with these new oppressions....
>
> (Boal 1995: 8)

'Cop in the Head' was the name of a series of forum-theatre type workshops Boal headed up in Paris in the early 1980s which

105

addressed the repressive effects of media, education and politics which, Boal felt, encouraged needless passivity in the face of redundant moral dictates.

If 'Cop in the Head' was a term that derived from Boal's view of the psychosis at the heart of Western culture, then 'Rainbow of Desires', an alternative term for the same body of work, derived from Boal's determination to overcome it. 'Three Wishes' is an example of a 'Rainbow of Desires' improvisation that encourages the protagonist to transform a scene from something oppressive to something acceptable:

> The director gets the participants to transform the scene into a frozen image. He gives the protagonist the right to make three wishes come true.... On each wish, the protagonist is allowed to modify the image of the scene.... [T]he protagonist sculpts her wishes herself, by manipulating the image, by physically changing it and, by the same token, changing herself.
>
> (Ibid.: 65)

'Rainbow of Desires' is not just about society 'as it is' but society 'as it could be'.

In 1986 Boal returned to Brazil. In the new political climate he found himself elected as a member of the Rio City Council. Boal now used forum theatre to solicit suggestions for new laws from members of his constituency. This was 'legislative theatre', a means by which under-privileged sections of the community could voice their views on how their lot could be bettered. Boal wanted 'the electors to give their opinions, to discuss the issues, to put counter-arguments, we want them to share the responsibility for what their parliamentarian does' (Boal 1998: 20). By getting the man in the street to play at being a member of the council he not only empowered the weak; he also restored to theatre its capacity to treat reality as malleable through the vehicle of a suspended fiction.

Whereas theatre normally implies a division between those who perform and those who bear witness, Boal works with just one category: those who take responsibility for the continuance or cessation of a certain course of action. The success or failure of a revolutionary course of action is not the issue. What is important is the decision on the part of an individual to go on stage and make something happen, to change the way things are. Although theatrical scenarios are a far cry from reality, they do help us make some 'real' changes. We become active. We trade in our habitual acceptance of the way things are and emerge better able to take responsibility for our futures.

Further reading

Boal, A. (1979) *Theatre of the Oppressed*, trans. Charles A. and Maria-Odilia Leal McBride, London: Pluto Press.

—— (1995) *The Rainbow of Desire*, trans. Adrian Jackson, London: Routledge.

—— (1998) *Legislative Theatre*, trans. Adrian Jackson, London: Routledge.

Schutzman, M. and Cohen-Cruz, J. (eds) (1994) *Playing Boal*, London: Routledge.

SHOMIT MITTER

JERZY GROTOWSKI (1933–99)

In 1959, the Polish director and theatre theorist Jerzy Grotowski founded a small experimental theatre in Opole, a town near Wroclaw in Southern Poland. Over the years this Laboratory Theatre grew in reputation and stature, but never lost touch with the almost monastic austerity that lay at its heart. Grotowski's was to be a 'poor theatre', a theatre that would ruthlessly eliminate everything that could possibly be eliminated from the theatre so as to lay bare its essence. This was to be a theatre without costumes, a theatre without make-up, a theatre without lighting and sound effects. This was to be a theatre in which the art of performance would be reduced to its core – the task of being deeply and intensely human. The first item on Grotowski's list of the aims for his theatre read: 'To stimulate a process of self-revelation' (Grotowski 1969: 96). 'It is the act of laying oneself bare', Grotowski explained, 'of tearing off the mask of daily life' (ibid.: 178).

Under the terms of such a conception of theatre, the actor was required to be less concerned with playing a character than with using the process of characterisation as a way of exploring the self:

> To play a part does not mean to identify with the character. The actor neither lives his part nor portrays it from the outside. He uses the character as a means to grapple with his own self, the tool to reach secret layers of his personality.... We are dealing here with the painful, merciless process of self-discovery.[1]

107

The purpose of rehearsal was not to learn about a character but to learn about oneself through the act of playing a character. The purpose of performance was not to play a role but to lay bare one's self in the presence of the audience. As Zbigniew Osinski, a long-time commentator on Grotowski's work, observes, 'this is neither a story nor the creation of an illusion; it is the present moment. The actor exposes himself and ... he discovers himself.... This is no longer acting' (Osinski 1986: 85). Grotowski's actor was placed *literally* in the situation of the character and asked to measure up. In *The Constant Prince* (1965), the actor Ryszard Cieslak *really* suffered the torment inflicted on the protagonist of Calderon's drama: he left the stage with red welts on his back.

It is no coincidence that Grotowski should have abandoned the idea of theatre as illusion and embraced the idea of theatre as reality in the course of his work on a play that demanded so much by way of sacrifice from his actors. Grotowski believed that the inner self was most explicitly revealed only when confronted with pain in this way. Only by facing situations of immense physical and psychic difficulty do human beings generate the self-respect required to shed social masks and genuinely be themselves.

> What did the work do?
> It gave each actor a series of shocks.
> The shock of confronting himself in the face of simple irrefutable challenges.
> The shock of catching sight of his own evasions, tricks and cliches.
> The shock of sensing something of his own vast and untapped resources.
>
> (Peter Brook in Grotowski 1969: 11)

In workshop, the idea was distilled into a number of practical exercises. 'Use your voice to make a hole in the wall', Grotowski would demand, 'to overturn a chair, ... to make a picture fall' (Grotowski 1969: 134). In his book *Towards a Poor Theatre* there is an exercise called 'Flight' which literally requires the actors to take off and land like birds as they learn to 'compel the body to go beyond its natural, biological limitations'.[2] The demands are deliberately outrageous: like the scapegoat of the ancient Greeks, like Christ who died on the cross so as to redeem society, Grotowski's actors seek to cleanse society by their suffering. For Grotowski, the 'violation of the living organism ... returns us to a concrete mythical situation, an experience of common human truth' (ibid.: 23).

As Grotowski's actors became more and more technically proficient as a result of the intense training regime to which they had to adhere, two problems began to emerge. First, the sheer physical virtuosity of their performances alienated audiences by giving them an example they had no means of following. Second, virtuosity gradually became an end in itself, a mask behind which actors began to hide. Looking back on the work he had done in the early 1960s, Grotowski realised that the self-revelation he had sought through the transcendence of physical barriers would be achieved not by arming actors with techniques, but by persuading them to *shed* what they had learnt.

> The education of an actor in our theatre is not a matter of teaching him something; we attempt to eliminate his organism's resistance to this psychic process.... Ours then is a via negativa — not a collection of skills but an eradication of blocks.
>
> (Ibid.: 16–17)

Grotowski's work on the voice now involved encouraging the actor 'to think not of adding technical elements (resonators, etc.), but ... at eliminating the concrete obstacles he comes up against (e.g. resistance in his voice).... [T]he decisive factor in this process is humility, a spiritual predisposition: not to do something, but to refrain from doing something' (ibid.: 36–37, bold in original). The *via negativa* is the application of the principle of Poor Theatre to the art of the actor. Just as Grotowski's stage was bereft of sets and props, so also his actors had to shed their arsenal of skills and tricks so as to lay themselves bare in all humility — as simple human beings.

Through the course of the 1970s, Grotowski began to work on ways of transferring the fruits of these exercises to the spectator. The problem he faced was that theatre audiences were typically passive and therefore unable to benefit from processes that were essentially active. Grotowski had attempted to combat this in his productions by forcing audiences to be active. In *Kordian* (1962) the spectators were designated as inmates of an asylum as they sat on hospital beds and had actors dressed as doctors forcing them to sing. In *Dr Faustus* (1963) the spectators sat along the length of two long tables at a refectory while Faustus sat at a smaller top table at one end, greeting each member of the audience as though they were invited guests. Grotowski eventually rejected these experiments in audience participation as it became apparent that, by placing spectators physically in the midst of a drama, he inhibited their capacity to participate in the action. He realised that, by manipulating the audience into assuming an active role, he was less likely than ever to achieve the revelation of self that was central to his purposes.

Grotowski therefore decided to drop the notion of performance altogether in favour of workshop-type events which allowed his actors to work on equal terms with their audiences. As it turned out, these meetings facilitated the states of self-revelation Grotowski favoured by virtue of nothing more or less than the act of meeting itself, by the 'utter opening to another person ... a total acceptance of one human being by another' (ibid.: 25).

> A man arrives then at the point, which has been called 'humility', at the moment in which he simply is and in which he ... accepts someone, together with his acceptance of someone – he accepts himself ... without the differentiation between outer and inner, between the body and the soul.
>
> (Kumeiga 1987: 228)

Notice that the terms in which authenticity is discussed are the same as before: sincerity is still a matter of symbiosis between the man that *is* and the man that is *shown*. The only difference is that human contact now supersedes technical virtuosity and monastic dispossession as the most viable medium of authenticity. The unaffected simplicity of Grotowski's idealism inspires trust on the basis of which individuals meet one another defencelessly, devoid of their social masks. They can *be* without acting; they can *be themselves*.

In the early stages of the work with outsider participants, the model followed was that of rehearsal. Someone would beat a rhythm on a simple percussion instrument. Someone else would respond with a different rhythm. They would try and find each other. Someone else would help them by humming – and so on, until a meeting was achieved through the medium of music. At other times Grotowski would ask the participants to use simple domestic activities such as clearing spaces, baking bread and walking in the woods as vehicles for the orchestration of contact. As more and more of this work took place out of doors, a new imperative emerged: a preoccupation with contact with Nature.

[W]e disperse in the forest. I stand face to face with a tree. It is strong – I can climb it, support myself delicately on its branches. On its crown a strong wind blows on us both, on the tree and myself. With my whole body I feel the movements of branches, the circulation of fluids, I hear the inner murmurs. I nestle into the tree.[3]

Some of this may seem to be a far cry from Grotowski's earlier work, but the motivation is remarkably consistent. When we have Richard Mennen digging in the wet earth 'asking the roots who I was',[4] we have the same concern with self-knowledge that informed Grotowski's work in the 1960s. When Steven Weinstein speaks of overcoming his resistance to being slapped with wet branches till he 'transcended personal pain',[5] we have an experience not dissimilar to that of Ryszard Cieslak having to bear real pain as the Constant Prince.

In time, Grotowski came to realise that experiments of this kind were prone to degenerate into what he called an 'emotive soup' (Richards 1993: 120), lacking the discipline of his earlier work. Much of his subsequent work at the University of California, Irvine, and at the Workcentre he founded in 1986 in Pontedera, Italy, was directed at recovering the precision that characterised the work of the Laboratory Theatre. This was not a return to performance: workshop exercises were now treated purely as vehicles for the actors, means by which they gained access to states of being that were encoded into the actions they performed. The so-called 'Objective Drama' project was concerned with the manner in which dances, songs and incantations from various parts of the world impacted the human body and generated states of self-awareness. Improvisation was now discarded in favour of learning how precisely to execute certain actions that belonged in various oriental or tribal systems of performance. This, Grotowski believed, would yield access to states of being that interested him by virtue of their ancient lineage:

Grotowski emphasises the affective potential of traditional songs as a means of accomplishing this act of *anamnesis*, this journey back to origins. He suggests that traditional songs from various cultures yield an extremely potent form of yantra, one which exerts a discernible impact on the physical and energetic state of the doer through precise patterns of vocal vibration.... Grotowski speaks of vibration in connection with the Hindu science of mantra, suggesting that specific sounds affect an individual's psychoenergetic state in physically objective ways.

(Wolford 1996: 119)

If the work with Nature was an attempt to find oneself in epiphanic contact with the elements, the work with ancient traditions of performance was an attempt to find oneself in terms of one's participation in the wisdom of antiquity. Writing about Grotowski's production of *Apocalypsis Cum Figuris* (1968), Jennifer Kumeiga remarked that Grotowski's intention was 'to bring us momentarily into contact with the deepest levels within ourselves' (Kumeiga 1987: 97). Almost three decades later, the ambition of Grotowski's work was much the same: to encourage actors to discover that, within the mortal confines of their bodies, there exists a pure pulse of selfhood that beats across both continents and centuries.

Notes

1   Barba, Eugenio and Flaszen, Ludwik (1965) 'A Theatre of Magic and Sacrilege', *Tulane Drama Review* 9 (3): 173.
2   Barba, Eugenio (1965) 'Theatre Laboratory 13 Rzedow', *Tulane Drama Review* 9 (3): 155.
3   Kolankiewicz, Leszek (1978) 'On the Road to Active Culture', trans. Boleslaw Taborski, Wroclaw, unpublished document: 22.
4   Ibid.: 76.
5   Ibid.: 81.

Further reading

Grotowski, J. (1969) *Towards a Poor Theatre*, London: Eyre Methuen.

Kumeiga, J. (1987) *The Theatre of Grotowski*, London: Methuen.

Osinski, Z. (1986) *Grotowski and his Laboratory*, trans. Lillian Vale and Robert Findlay, New York: PAJ Publications.

Richards, T. (1993) *At Work with Grotowski on Physical Actions*, London: Routledge.

Schechner, R. and Wolford, L. (eds) (1977) *The Grotowski Sourcebook*, London: Routledge.

Wolford, L. (1996) *Grotowski's Objective Drama Research (Performance Studies)*, Jackson: University Press of Mississippi.

SHOMIT MITTER

LUCA RONCONI (1933–)

Orlando furioso, which played nationally and internationally to great acclaim after its first performance at the 1969 Spoleto Festival, proved to be seminal to Ronconi's work. For all his eclecticism, he continued to explore this production's novel use of place and architecture, space and perspective, audience–performance interaction, its combination of performance genres, machinery and speech. Throughout his career, Ronconi was to describe his experiments with recitation as a commitment to a representational rather than an interpretative style of delivery, that is, to what amounts to a declamatory mode rather than a realistic approach to character construction. His script with Edoardo Sanguineti of Ariosto's sixteenth-century poem, whose extravagant heroes are personified by the chivalrous-absurd and allegedly 'mad' Orlando, initiated the practice he was to pursue vigorously in later years of staging non-theatre texts. This notably includes *Lolita-sceneggiatura* (2001), based on Vladimir Nabokov's script for the film by Stanley Kubrick (which Kubrick had only partly used) and *Quel che sapeva Maisie* (*What Maisie Knew*, 2002), which Ronconi adapted from Henry James' novel.

Relatively short at 90 minutes, *Orlando furioso* transferred Ariosto's third-person narratives to the first person, thereby deploying narration as action with actors directly engaged in their own stories. Ariosto's intricacies were reduced to the narrative spine of his three main tales – Orlando's love for cruel Angelica, Bradamante's for Ruggero, the battle between the Saracens and the Christians outside Paris – which Ronconi fragmented and dislocated temporally and spatially. These principles of montage and aleatory effect were particularly well suited to a structure of concurrent events performed on platforms wheeled by actors among the crowd. Two stages, whose curtains opened and closed to mock this theatre convention, faced each other from a great distance, marking the limits of the playing space. Epic episodes took place on the rolling platforms. This was theatre on a vast scale in unconventional venues – a de-consecrated church in Spoleto, the squares of Italian cities (Bologna's central square accommodated 3000 spectators, while Milan's Piazza del Duomo held 8000), the disused markets of Paris (Les Halles) in 1970 and, among other found spaces, a skating rink at the Edinburgh Festival in that same year.

It was also promenade theatre in which audiences were spectator-participants, free to select one narrative or to roam in the polyphonic organisation of mobile performances led by some forty heavily made-up actors, many of them on horses of metal and wood. All were in outlandish costumes combining medieval dress, fantasy haute couture and the garb of science fiction. Thrills were to be had galore as the actors ran at great speed among the spectator-participants and the platforms threatened to roll over their feet. An enormous shining hippogriff hoisted up on a large crane swept above their heads. Marvels abounded: a magic castle, a magic island, a wizard, a witch, a mythological deep-sea monster, a gigantic labyrinth of chicken-wire cages into which people crowded, only to be trapped with the actors in paladins' armour inside. The battle of Paris was on a platform, spectacular in perspectives recalling the paintings of Paolo Uccello. At the end of the performance, the hippogriff flew Astolfo to the moon in search of a key to humanity's problems in Orlando's idealistic 'mad' brain.

A mixture of Sicilian puppetry, fairground entertainment, tournament, athletics, traditional storytelling, fable and ritual, the production inspired questions as to whether it was a 'people's' theatre. *La Stampa* (6 July 1969) declared it was 'essentially an intellectualistic operation', albeit destined for a 'popular' public in good faith. The consensus that *Orlando furioso* was 'a brilliant demonstration of how to make "new" theatre' (*Il Mattino*, 6 July 1969) was invoked when Ronconi used another medium, television, to create a 'popular' spectacle in another sense of the word. This highly publicised version of *Orlando*, closer to a fantasia on technology than to a communal festivity, was shown in five one-hour episodes in 1975.

Ronconi returned to immense spaces and promenade productions in 1990 at the Fiat factory in Lingotto, a neighbourhood of Turin, then, in 2003, at La Scala's abandoned workshops and warehouses in Bovisa, Milan. The Lingotto production, *Gli ultimi giorni dell' umanità* (*The Last Days of Humanity*), was based on the notoriously 'unplayable' 800–page drama completed in 1926 by the Austrian, Karl Kraus. Ronconi deftly turned Kraus' war themes into emblematic scenes, filling them with ironic, bizarre, grotesque or indefinably startling images whose strangeness was highlighted by the surrounding heavy machinery used to produce the chassis of motor cars. It was not Ronconi's intention to offer a critique of the industrial world, although critical meaning could be attributed to his juxtaposition of image and space. Rather, his point was to construct an industrial piece according to what is surely best described as his ornate, baroque theatricality.

The Bovisa production, *Infinities*, used a text by the English mathematician John D. Barrow. Women stared from recumbent positions on the floor or sat under, or beside, contraptions looking like space-age hair-dryers. Their mannequin-like faces, half-masked or covered with thick make-up, looked as if they had undergone plastic surgery. Similar faces were to be seen on decapitated heads here and there. Mummy-like figures in wheelchairs on different planes and at different heights recalled Casanova in Ronconi's *Phoenix* (2001) by Marina Tsvetayeva. Men in flesh-coloured masks, dressed in suits and holding up open umbrellas, walked on blocks of stone in narrow corridors. Or else they lay above each other on shelves in these corridors, Ronconi consistently moulding scene and movement to the building's architectural and interior design. Elsewhere they stood or sat, wrapped in outsize bandages, or hung upside down in open vistas, where costumes were once hung, their white garments suggesting space suits.

The actors performed a myriad of non-logically assembled actions as they recited theories of numbers, time and space (hence 'infinities') by renowned mathematicians across the ages, most of it incomprehensible and all of it declaimed in the artificial style – accentuated syllables, wrongly placed stresses, over-extended intonations – that Ronconi had, by now, made his own. He played with the idea of mathematical progression by using five platforms, each sequence on each platform lasting fifteen minutes. Groups of spectators entered consecutively at twenty-minute intervals, one group following the next until it completed the circuit. The show for each group lasted seventy-five minutes. The whole show lasted five hours. Spectators could repeat the circuit, finding that each sequence was modified in every round.

Ronconi returned to outdoor space in 2002 with Euripides' *Prometheus Bound* in the ruins of a Greek amphitheatre in Syracuse, Sicily. The protagonist performed in the palm of the hand of a gigantic white statue bending forwards. Below him, nymphs danced in water. Above him, in the distance, the cranes of a construction site were visible – a fortuitous recollection of the crane in *Orlando furioso* (not available for *Prometheus* in Lyon's well-preserved amphitheatre later in 2002, where, according to his usual principle, Ronconi let the new space influence the production's character). The water recalled the flooded stage for Monteverdi's *L'Orfeo e Il ritorno di Ulisse in patria* (1998), one of several baroque operas among more than fifty directed by Ronconi since the 1970s. His Rossini series in the 1990s was set in the imposing architectural structures typical of his dramatic theatre.

The late 1970s was a period of experimentation for Ronconi, working with his Prato Laboratory on such texts as *Calderón* by Pier

Paolo Pasolini. In the 1980s he experimented with architectural surface and depth, and planes of light and colour for the 'naturalist' drama Ronconi thought was normally denied such a designer aesthetic. He staged *John Gabriel Borkman* (1982), *St Joan of the Stockyards* (1984) and *The Three Sisters* (1989) accordingly. However, the artificial speech (mannered shouting in *The Three Sisters*), arguably appropriate for his epic productions, appeared to be no more than rhetorical posturing in the confines of the proscenium arch.

The 1990s was Ronconi's period as director of the *teatri stabili* (municipal- and state- subsidised theatres). He ran the Teatro Stabile di Torino (1989–94), during which time, apart from *Gli ultimi giorni*, he deconstructed such 'standard' texts as *Measure for Measure* (1990) and O'Neil's *Strange Interlude* (1990), and founded an acting school. At the Teatro di Roma (1994–98), he explored new possibilities for staging through play-texts scripted from novels (for example, *The Brothers Karamazov*, 1998). In 1999, he assumed the direction of the Piccolo Teatro di Milano, leading **Strehler**'s theatre away from its hitherto social concerns towards his own focus on developing a 'theatre language'. This, Ronconi believes, is incumbent on what he defines as the 'director-dramatist' whose formal innovations, scenic as well as textual (including scripting from novels), are the only way forward in the 'crisis of contemporary playwriting' (Ronconi 2000: 16–17).[1]

Ronconi's inaugural productions at the Piccolo were a diptych on the idea of the dream: *Life is a Dream* by Calderón de la Barca in the Nuovo Piccolo, now known as the Teatro Strehler, and Strindberg's *The Dream Play* in the Studio of the Piccolo complex. They also explored two different kinds of spaces. The first has an unusually long stage, which allowed Ronconi to work it as a cinema screen. He split visual frames and ran diverse actions, times and places at various eye levels simultaneously, – a demonstration of his faith in 'the positive influence of cinema and television on the evolution of theatre language' (ibid.: 19). This influence was equally evident in Ronconi's arsenal of mechanical devices, among them a mechanism on which a hippogriff slides diagonally upwards on a crane (clearly a cross-reference to *Orlando furioso* and its theatrical exploits). The Studio, a round space, allowed him to operate on axes of the circle in an extremely stylised, if not robot-like, rendition of Strindberg.

He continued his quasi-cinematographic research in *Lolita* and *Maisie*, projecting complementary pictures of Lolita as an abusive girl and Maisie as an abused one. *Lolita* is possibly the most complicated production, technologically and visually speaking, mounted by

Ronconi in a 'traditional' theatre. His words on how the cinema has re-educated the spectator's gaze succinctly describe the thrust of these two productions, and that of his work since the 1980s.

> My frequent recourse to moving spatial structures could be explained, for instance, by the exigency of reproducing theatrically the 'logic' of contemporary optical perception which, formed by the filmic paradigm of the play of fields [of vision], counterfields, long-range views, close-ups and very close shots, tends to pick out significant items and details from the general visual space, cancelling out whatever is superfluous to it.
>
> (Ibid.: 18)

Ronconi's formal experiments frequently yield glacial productions. On the occasion of his experiment with dual vision in *'Tis Pity She's a Whore*, one version with a mixed-gender cast, the other solely male, the critic Franco Quadri, Ronconi's earliest and greatest supporter, observed that it was 'time he took his feelings out of the freezer' (*La Repubblica*, 28 June 2003).

Notes

1   Lecture delivered by Ronconi when he was admitted to the degree of Doctor of Arts, Music and Performance *honoris causa* at the University of Bologna, 29 April 1999. I wish to thank Franco Vespiero, archivist at the Piccolo Teatro, for drawing my attention to this lecture. All translations are mine.

Further reading

Innamorati, Isabella (ed.) (1996) *Luca Ronconi e il suo teatro*, Milan: Bulzoni Editore.
Quadri, Franco (1973) *Il rito perduto. Saggio su Luca Ronconi*, Turin: Einaudi.
Ronconi, Luca (2000) *Lezioni di teatro*, Milan: Edizioni Piccolo Teatro di Milano.

MARIA SHEVTSOVA

PETER SCHUMANN (1934–)

When, age twenty-seven, a penniless Peter Schumann looked at the world through the filter of New York's lower East side, he saw a city as drab and soulless as his native Germany, confirming his suspicion that mankind's attraction to the conveniences of modern life was deeply dehumanising. Sensing that humanity had somehow lost touch with the wellsprings of meaningful living, Schumann resolved in his art to re-establish the link between's man's material and meta-physical existence: his theatre was to achieve 'the spiritual regeneration of mankind' (Brecht 1988a: 14):

> The art was to be not just indulgence, nor just entertain-ment, but means of salvation: for the artist and for his fellow men.
>
> (Ibid.: 40)

If the false god of technology had induced indolence and lethargy with regard to mankind's 'higher calling', Schumann would use his art to bring people into contact once again with a transcendent reality. Schumann's theatre would take over the function that reli-gion had abrogated: it would restore to humanity its mislaid sense of the sublime.

Schumann's theatre spans the full range of theatrical conventions from agit-prop type street shows to more formal indoor perfor-mances. He has worked indoors and outdoors, in churches and in fields. He has performed for children and for adults, for the intelli-gentsia and for the underprivileged. His theatre has included the audience and excluded it, he has used language and rejected it. Yet, for all this variety, Schumann's theatre has never lost its undisputed virtuosity. Schumann's theatre is grand without being pretentious, ceremonial without being self-consciously hieratic. Using slow motion to generate a sense of otherness and awe, Schumann carves out of inexpensive materials and simple gestures a vision of breath-taking intensity. Man's destiny lies not in the unremarkable debris of faddish living but in the blazing glory of redemption and resurrec-tion.

Schumann called his theatre The Bread and Puppet Theatre. For Schumann, bread was a means by which he could instil in his audi-ences a sense of a community and sharing. Schumann baked bread himself and served it to the spectators, passing it around in what became a simple, ritualistic invocation of the values he wanted so much to see in society. The bread became a way of drawing the audience into his world in a ceremony that was as pure as it was artless, as effortless as it was dignified and seeped in the spirit of communion. The association with the communion was important: it made it possible to engage with the issues of good and evil without invoking the knee-jerk scepticism that one would expect in the largely godless universe of modern, materialistic America.

The puppets Schumann has used are of so many different kinds that it is difficult to generalise about them. He has used puppets that are operated from behind a curtain and puppets that are operated without a curtain. He has used puppets that are operated invisibly from inside and puppets that are operated visibly from the outside. He has used small puppets that are operated by rods and life-size puppets that are strapped to the actors' bodies. For all their variety, what Schumann's many puppets have in common is that they resemble works of sculpture more than dramatic artefacts. They express archetypes more than characters, ethical abstractions more than plausible personalities:

> One becomes aware only slowly of their power and beauty. They are touched by the consciousness we imagine hovers anxiously over boundaries of sleep and death…. The lips are variously opened, closed, half-closed, fixed in transitional positions between smiling, grimacing, speaking, drinking. The faces seem to have been struck a blow, though there is no evidence of wounds, only awareness recoiling upon itself….[1]

Schumann's figures are not common cardboard cut-outs, simplistically communicating a pre-selected range of moral imperatives. They are imbued with a wisdom that speaks the language of essences from a region beyond the purview of individuality and time.

In so far as Schumann uses puppets rather than actors, his performers have a more passive role than we are accustomed to seeing in the theatre. In fact, Schumann does not really regard the performers with whom he works as actors in the traditional sense at all: he calls them 'operators' – a word that emphasises the primacy of the puppet at the cost of any creativity one may habitually expect from an actor in a performance. Many of the operators Schumann uses are non-professional – which suits him both financially and artistically. He likes the rough edge his inexperienced cast gives to his performances:

> Crouching on the floor, he tells us through a hand-mike the simple story of the play as it unfolds. When necessary,

he takes part in the action, or accompanies the players on the violin. Literally, he stage-manages the show before our eyes and no attempt is made to conceal by conventional stagecraft the untidy seams or unfinished joins. What he is trying to communicate – his essential vision of man and God – is more important than the superficialities of stage-craft.[2]

The passivity of the performer permits Schumann to create images that constitute perhaps the most memorable aspect of his theatre. Anyone who has seen the swarm of pigs' heads in *The Cry of the People for Meat* (1969) or the imprisoned Vietnamese woman covered in rolls of bright red tape in *Fire* (1962) will testify to the enduring directness of Schumann's visual vocabulary. It is a language made possible by the fact that Schumann's actors execute his instructions without imposing upon his poetry their own vision of the world. Schumann's actors do not perform in a play as much as make that play possible by refraining from performing.

Schumann's sense of the importance of sharing extends to the process of constructing the show, of making the puppets, of selecting themes. In *The Bread and Puppet Theatre*, Stefan Brecht discusses the making of *A Monument for Ishi* (1975):

> Everyone was encouraged to bring as many friends as possible....
>
> Several people were put to work inking these printing blocks and printing them on bed sheets. Others constructed top hats for the Butchers from corrugated cardboard. Still others began making masks ... [from] negative plaster moulds which had been made over the clay models sculpted by Peter....
>
> (Brecht 1988b: 295–298)

The bond the group thus forms with the local community has the effect of making his audiences more willing to participate in the show when it is eventually performed. This for Schumann is vital. He believes that art never affects spectators as much as its practitioners: if his message is to spread, it can only happen through direct action on the part of the spectator.

Initially Schumann saw his theatre as a protest against the evil rampant in the world around him. His intention was not so much to try and induce change as to help people work out their own position with regard to certain issues. In 1966 Schumann set about denouncing the Vietnam war by placing puppets in sequence in a parade so as to make a simple allegory:

> Giant puppet heads of Vietnamese women chained together, their stark white faces bound by black blindfolds. A mock wooden aeroplane, with shark's teeth, diving out of the March sky. A band of skullheads, blowing an unearthly tune on horns improvised from washing machine agitators and rattling a dirge on old gasoline cans.
>
> (Brecht 1988a: 520)

Among the skullmen (who represented war) and the women (who represented suffering and goodness), Schumann included puppets depicting Christ and his disciples. Schumann's purposes were as pious as they were astutely political: he knew that a religious image is harder to marginalise than an overtly factional street march. The suffering of Christ elevated the level of the debate about Vietnam from a conflict between national and selfish interests to an issue involving an opposition between moral and degenerate imperatives. Rather than call for withdrawals, Schumann decided to make it impossible for his spectators both to pray in a church and defend the American position. War was to be abandoned not out of concern for the suffering of the Vietcong, but because it was evil.

In 1970 Schumann left New York and took up a position at Goddard College in Plainfield, Vermont. In March 1971 he directed a production of *The Domestic Resurrection Circus* in a large hall in Providence, Rhode Island. The production was built around a number of sketches tracing the history of the world from Creation to Judgement Day when the damned fall into Hell (dolls falling from a great height into the centre of the hall) and the Saved sit in a gallery up on high looking down at the earth. After a sequence depicting the wrath of War, the lights were switched off and the audience waited in the dark listening to a single note played on a pipe organ. White praying figures gathered in the hall, linked to one another by a rope. And then suddenly the organ sounded, the lights blazed, an aeroplane appeared overhead and Schumann himself joined his puppets in a gigantic pile of bodies in a corner. Finally the audience was led out of the hall singing while a group of about twenty actors formed the outline of a boat, unfurled a sail and floated across a meadow. Some spectators parted like water to let the Ark pass. Others jumped on board to find a new way, to make a new start.

In the early 1970s Schumann began to use the 'circus format' that permitted him to present a diversity of material under the umbrella of a single show. After Schumann disbanded The Bread and Puppet Theatre in 1974, these became annual outdoor celebrations to which anyone who cared to attend was invited. The idea was to form a community around an event set in nature that would avail of what Schumann saw as 'the consoling perspective of nature's ever-lasting bounty, natural life's self-regenerative – resurrective – power' (Brecht 1988b: 276). On a weekend in August 1975, Schumann put on the first outdoor *Domestic Resurrection Circus* at Dopp Farm in northern Vermont. The performance was divided into three parts, the first two of which were played in a grassy open-air amphitheatre. The first part, a spoof on the circus that is history, was presided over by a ringmaster with a whistle who introduced a motley bunch of characters including a pink-headed Christopher Columbus and a Vietnamese angel who gets shot by a gigantic GI figure. The second part bore some resemblance to the traditional circus, with its animals and acrobats: dragons danced, pretty girls played leapfrog, a group of clowns got into a mess pretending to be firemen.

The third part, a radical departure from the first two parts in terms of both form and content, was played in the meadows and pine forest above the improvised theatre. It was into these hills that a small white puppet fled, set upon by a flock of menacing black birds. It was over the brow of these hills that a herd of white deer appeared, to the sound of a hymn sung by a choir, only to die in a heap on stage. It was over these hills that the birds arrived in the deepening dusk, swooping over an ox cart that bore the body of a veiled white woman. And so the drama was played out amid a chorus of beating drums and shrieking birds, the story of man's relationship with the elements. It was a story that sought to place death, and even slaughter, in the context of the view that life goes on. The rebellious Schumann of the protest marches had by now learnt the wisdom of accepting the inevitable as natural, of celebrating it even. Resignation was not surrender: it was an awakening. It was a movement from darkness to light, from death to resurrection. It was a recognition of the fact that evil is a part of the world and that the world as a whole is self-rejuvenating.

Notes

1 George Dennison on Schumann's *Fire*, in Sainer, A. (1975) *The Radical Theatre Notebook*, New York: Avon: 117.
2 Evans, J.R. (1989) *Experimental Theatre*, London: Routledge: 125.

Further reading

Brecht, S. (1988a) *The Bread and Puppet Theatre*, Vol. One, London: Methuen.

—— (1988b) *The Bread and Puppet Theatre*, Vol. Two, London: Methuen.

SHOMIT MITTER

JOSEPH CHAIKIN (1935–2003)

Although Joseph Chaikin started the Open Theatre in New York City in 1963 as a forum for experimental theatre without having any premeditated agenda, the group, from its inception, had an inclination to work with non-naturalistic material. This was a reaction to both the timorous commercialism of Broadway musicals and the dominance of Method acting in the serious American drama of the 1950s. Chaikin's attempts to break this mould included the use of sound rather than language as a vehicle for communication and the use of spatial arrangements and movement to discover centres of emotion in the body. The implications of this shift from speech-oriented theatre to movement-oriented performance constitute a vital facet of Chaikin's enduring legacy.

Chaikin's work on *The Serpent* (1968) was based on *Genesis* and began as a series of images of the garden of Eden assembled collectively by members of the group:

> One actor will get up and do his garden and if another actor is sensitive to it, he will join him so that they make a little world…. Then it's over and somebody else tries it…. Roy London arranged several actors, including himself, into a single creature with five flicking tongues and ten undulating arms and hands. Immediately, the workshop recognised its serpent…. Then someone tried putting apples into the creature's hands. And it became a bizarre, stunning amalgam of serpent and tree.
>
> (Blumenthal 1984: 110–112)

The ability of this image to yoke together separate dimensions of significance is entirely a function of its visual appeal. It is the quintessential product of improvisation and demonstrates how powerful theatre can be when action rather than language is made the medium in which drama is constructed. It is significant that the actors 'recognise' their serpent *after* it has been assembled. The mind plays no part in determining what the body will create.

The Serpent drew heavily on Chaikin's work between 1963 and 1966 when the Open Theatre was able to work in rehearsal situations without formally committing to theatrical performances. 'My real interest is in investigating things', observed Chaikin, '[f]orming an exercise is one of the most important things a theater person can do' (Chaikin in ibid.: 69). In her book *Joseph Chaikin*, Eileen Blumenthal describes some of the exercises that were invented in this period and have subsequently become the stock in trade of theatre workshops all over the world:

> Chaikin also had the actors simply 'try on' different bodies to discover the emotions to which those physical states corresponded. The Open Theatre experimented with various walks ... to connect actors with characters through their bodies rather than through words or emotions. He had the actors move as if they were flying or floating, as if the air were changing density or temperature around them ... [T]hey let physical images of inanimate objects (such as weapons) inform their movement in order to discover emotional states.
>
> (Ibid.: 86)

The exercises encouraged the actors to build up a repertoire of correspondences between externally imposed sounds and movement patterns and the internal states of feeling they generated. Just as language uses rhythm and metaphor to link ideas, so also posture and sound now set up a lattice of associations that connected different areas of significance. The interest of Chaikin's theatre is that it created a world quite unlike any that is reachable through language, for action distils reality in a way that is markedly different to the way in which language structures reality.

In time, the actors learnt to manipulate these associations and to transmit them physically from one person to another:

> One actor would begin a simple, repeatable gesture using both body and voice, not selecting in advance what the action should express, but playing with it until it touched on a clear condition; that actor then approached a second, who tried to copy the forms exactly, thereby being led to their emotional content.... Using kinetic impulses to locate

inner states, actors were able to discover emotions that had not been in their experience before.

(Ibid.: 83)

Notice that the patterns of sound and movement are engaged independently of conceptual thought. The purpose of the exercise is not to use the body to express what has already been envisaged, but to allow the muscles to lead the mind into new regions of experience that cannot be entered into intellectually. As the actors alter the physical impulses they receive, they sculpt their emotions. They play palpably with what is incorporeal.

In spite of Chaikin's aversion to institutionalised performance, he did require spectators, if only because the relationship between the performer and the audience formed a vital part of the area he was investigating. Observers were therefore invited to attend workshops from time to time. These rapidly took on the air of experimental variety shows with a number of different items making up the programme. Some of the short plays that were used in this way were put together as *America Hurrah!* (1966). This was the beginning of the 'second phase' of the Open Theatre's work. The 'pure' work of the first three years now gave way to a period during which the group put together a number of theatre pieces of which *Terminal* (1969), *The Mutation Show* (1971) and *Nightwalk* (1973) are the best known. Each of these was created by the group in workshop rather than scripted in advance by a playwright.

However, the group did on each occasion have on hand a resident playwright whose job it was to give shape to the material generated in workshop. Susan Yankowitz, the playwright involved with the final version of *Terminal*, describes the process:

> I learned to leave space for the actor to supply meanings through his own instruments: pitch, inflection, gesture, body.... Paul Zimet, who performed the part, had worked out vocal and physical rhythms; I wrote the speech from a list of single lines and thoughts which seemed to me consistent with the character and with the rhythms which Paul had already established. This was later compressed into a coherent monologue.[1]

Rhythm was to precede language as the actors took their cue from an externally imposed condition and used it to work inwards into emotion or character. The director provided a discipline – a rhythm tapped on a drum, a set of objects or musical instruments, a stance or a movement pattern – which generated an image or a state of being. The skill of the director consisted in knowing which actions were most likely to be productive. If the exercises were fertile, the actor had a way of creating a character that was immune to self-consciousness.

The result of this work was a series of dramatic performances in which 'the text cannot be fully understood apart from the production. Visual and verbal patterns are interwoven; word, sound and image reinforce and elucidate one another'.[2] *Terminal* was played on a stage with a proscenium arch on which five slabs of wood depicted a number of different settings: hospital beds in one scene, stretchers or graves in others. The lighting rigs were visible to the audience and occasionally became props in the drama when, for instance, they were used as instruments of torture. The actors were always present on stage, stepping into their roles simply by entering the pool of light that delineated the playing area. They wore simple white garments that suggested hospital uniforms in some scenes and the cloth in which Egyptian mummies were wrapped in others. They used tambourines, drums, chants and incantations to create a 'pure' structure in which '[m]eaning does not accompany the music, but is contained within it'.[3] The actors spoke in a manner that did not just communicate the idea of a word but bore testimony to the complete experience of it. By emphasising the visceral qualities of sound such as rhythm, tone and timbre, the actors sought to make their voices more 'present'.

'Presence' was a loaded word for Chaikin. It appeared in the title of his book and referred to the quality of being utterly and abundantly alive. This animation was seen as an antidote to the apathy that seemed to Chaikin to dog the world and render people unable to respond compassionately to one another. Theatre's affirmation of the quality of being alive therefore had a political aspect: it made people sensitive to the little appreciated miracle of unquenched vitality. Chaikin often spoke of the need 'to understand the stage as a weapon' (ibid.: 42); he often said he wanted actors who were 'politically oriented' (ibid.: 42). Chaikin was in this sense very typical of a growing group of anti-establishment artists who had become prominent in New York in the late 1950s and early 1960s. This was a period in which the United States saw a lot of civil rights activism. Chaikin had himself been involved in civil disobedience demonstrations and much of his early work, with both the Living Theatre and the Open Theatre, was markedly activist. Even the non-naturalistic forms of theatre that Chaikin subsequently developed had a covert political aspect. For Chaikin, the problem with naturalism was that it insisted on actors limiting themselves to a repertoire of actions that conformed to what was socially acceptable. This seemed to Chaikin coercive: naturalism restricted freedom and bound people to the inauthentic facade that it was the responsibility of theatre to combat.

Even the notion of collective creation was in some ways a function of Chaikin's politics. Ensemble work at the Open Theatre was a product of the principle that members of a group must be jointly responsible for determining the nature of the work produced. Always an actor at heart, Chaikin remained wary of the ascendancy customarily accorded to the director in most traditional theatre groups. This led to a somewhat misguided reluctance to 'lead' in the conventional sense of the term. As a result, the actors were often left groping for feedback and the group as a whole stumbled in their search for a sense of direction. This led to the eventual dissolution of the group.

Through the course of the 1960s, Chaikin broke the group down into a number of workshops, each of which had its own leader. By the early 1970s some of these units had begun to perform independently and Chaikin was left without a stable group of actors with whom to work. In 1976 he once again assembled a group under the disconcertingly provisional title 'Winter Project' but led it somewhat half-heartedly. The Project explored the manner in which lighting, musical accompaniment and spatial arrangements affected audiences. The group put together *Re-Arrangements* (1979), a collage of images about social interaction, and *Tourists and Refugees* (1980), a study of homelessness. In this period, Chaikin also went back to acting – another manifestation of his qualms about leading an ensemble. He performed two monologues, *Tongues* (1978) and *Savage/Love* (1978) that he created in collaboration with Sam Shepard. Chaikin went through open-heart surgery in 1984 but continued to work well into the 1990s. In 1992 he directed an Obie-winning production of Samuel Beckett's *Texts for Nothing* and between 1994 and 1996 worked with Yankowitz on a new version of *Terminal*.

Ironically Chaikin's inconsistency with regard to the role of the director as leader led both to the institution of collaborative play-making, its richest product, and to the disbanding of the Open Theatre, its most fertile soil.

Notes

1 Sainer, A. (1975) *The Radical Theatre Notebook*, New York: Avon: 148–152.

2   Ibid.: 108.
3   Ibid.: 110.

Further reading

Blumenthal, E. (1984) *Joseph Chaikin*, Cambridge: Cambridge University Press.
Chaikin, J. (1972) *The Presence of the Actor*, New York: Atheneum.
Pasolli, R. (1970) *The Book of the Open Theatre*, New York: Bobbs-Merrill.

SHOMIT MITTER

EUGENIO BARBA (1936–)

No director since **Stanislavsky** has studied the art of acting more meticulously than Eugenio Barba. It is not surprising that Richard Schechner should have placed Barba and Savarese's *The Secret Art of the Performer* alongside Bharata's *Natyashastra* and Zeami's *Kadensho* as one of the most thorough and far-reaching investigations into what it is to be a performer. Not even **Grotowski**, Barba's mentor, compiled quite so comprehensive an account of the traits great performers all over the world have in common. Barba's systematic exploration of these features constitutes a formidable achievement – the likes of which would hardly have been conceivable in 1964 when the Italian from Gallipoli founded the Odin Teatret in Holstebro, a small town in northwest Denmark, with a group of would-be actors who had been rejected by the National Theatre School in Oslo.

At the time Barba's experience of the theatre was limited to having watched Grotowski's company at work for three years. Not surprisingly, Barba's early work consists almost entirely of introducing his fledgling company both to exercises such as somersaults, shoulder stands, head-stands and facial masks and to the exploration of the self through physical work, all of which were an intrinsic part of Grotowski's work during this period. As Iben Nagel Rasmussen observed:

> We were working very long hours training and rehearsing. It was during this intense work that I found my own voice, I found what was my own way out of exhaustion or through pushing past what blocked me. From here I had a beginning, a place to discover who I am as an actress.
>
> (Watson 1993: 49)

The important thing here was not that Rasmussen's voice had changed overnight into a rich and sonorous medium but that, in making this leap, Rasmussen had discovered something fundamental about herself. 'Training is a process of self-definition' wrote Barba (1986: 56), for whom theatre had become a way of testing one's responses at the limits of physical endurance.

It was appropriate, therefore, that Barba's actors should eventually begin to train independently. Ferdinando Taviani's description of a training session at the Odin is a study of harmony in diversity: what seems like anarchy is in fact an exercise in precision, the seeming bedlam a carefully orchestrated exploration of personality, tenacity and selfhood:

> Some actors begin with gymnastics, while others run or do acrobatic exercises ... [T]wo actors twist and turn on uni-cycles, like circus acrobats; Kathakali scenes appear as sudden flashes ...; a man in tails dances, as if an electric current is running through him; a swordsman duels with his shadow, the colors of Bali burst forth, followed immediately by the bright presence of the mute Kathrine from Mother Courage.
>
> (Watson 1993: 52)

In 1974 a number of sequences of these training routines were strung together in the form of a 'street theatre' production called *The Book of Dances*. The 'play' began with brightly costumed actors running helter-skelter through a small town in southern Italy, blowing whistles and beating drums to attract an audience. Once an audience had gathered, the actors reverted to presenting a number of their training routines such as mock combat and dances on stilts:

> Whirling around in virtuoso fashion on top of high stilts, three of them dialogued, changed the rhythm of the move-ment, took the villagers' breath away, ran into the yards and rapidly changed masks and facial expressions. In front of them went a drummer, one actress playing the harmonica, and two clowns ran among the children.
>
> (Ibid.: 112)

The Million (1979), which was presented in both 'street theatre' and 'studio' modes, was rather different from *The Book of Dances* in that it bore traces of a number of foreign forms of drama such as

Kathakali and Balinese dance. The influence of these forms of drama dates back to 1978 when various members of the company went to different parts of the world to study some of the local forms of theatre. The actors' intention was not so much to learn these arts but to use the systems of training they encountered to serve as catalysts to provoke them into deepening their own forms of presentation and expression. When the group returned to Holstebro they realised that, although the forms that they had studied varied hugely in evolution and appearance, the lessons they had gleaned had a great deal in common. The great masters of each of the traditions they had encountered used their bodies in very similar ways. For example, almost all tended to use posture and movement in such a way that the body seemed stretched between opposing forces. This, Barba observed, was precisely contrary to the manner in which people used their bodies in everyday life.

The parallels between the various traditions of performance the actors had studied were so striking that Barba decided to undertake a systematic study of these features. This was the beginning of ISTA, the International School of Theatre Anthropology, which Barba established in 1979. Barba's idea was to bring together performers from various parts of the world to address the question as to whether they used fundamentally similar techniques to generate presence on stage:

> Different actors, in different places and times, in spite of the stylistic forms specific to their traditions, have used certain principles which they have in common with actors from other traditions. To trace these 'recurrent principles' is the first task of theatre anthropology.
>
> (Barba 1986: 136)

Often, when we see two actors doing the same thing, Barba observed, one actor excites our attention and the other does not. Do those who captivate us have certain traits in common? Do they engage us for the same reasons?

Through the course of the 1980s Barba arranged a number of workshops and lecture demonstrations at which masters from various Oriental traditions such as Noh, Kyogen, Chhau, Bharatanatiyam and Odissi would meet to share their techniques and discuss the principles underlying their work. At the first session of ISTA, held in Bonn in 1980, for example, Barba conducted an open session in collaboration with the great Odissi dancer Sanjukhta Panigrahi:

Barba first asked Panigrahi to do a short dance with full musical and vocal accompaniment, following which he got her to repeat the dance without accompaniment. He then asked her to repeat the piece once again without musical backing, but this time requested that she stop and hold her body position at particular points in the dance in order for him to analyse the techniques underlying the odissi choreography. In doing this, Barba pointed out various elements embodied in the form, including the constant, yet precise, shifts and counterbalances in muscular tension; the changes in weight distribution; the continual alterations in the centre of gravity.

(Watson 1993: 152)

The elements of Panigrahi's dance to which Barba draws attention have less to do with the appearance of Odissi than with its mainsprings of energy. They also just happen to be those features that Odissi has in common with many other great performance traditions the world over. It follows that actors all over the world generate energy in much the same way – by changing posture and adjusting muscular tensions in certain fundamental ways. One such technique was dubbed the 'opposition principle':

According to the opposition principle, if one wants to go to the left, one begins by going to the right, then suddenly stops and turns left. If one wants to crouch down, one first rises up on tip-toe and then crouches down. ... I know now that this convention ... is a rule which can be found throughout the Orient.

(Barba and Savarese 1991: 176)

Although ISTA did not answer the question as to *why* spectators find the principle of opposition arresting, it did establish that the principle does recur almost universally and is widely recognised amongst performers as the 'secret' ingredient that brings vitality to their performances.

During the first ten years of the Odin, Barba produced only three major plays: *Ornitofilene* (1965), *Kaspariana* (1967) and *Ferai* (1969). Although each of these was based on an existing script, the text was used merely as a source of ideas around which the actors built improvisations, often working in isolation. Vocal work was also conducted separately from action and movement and re-combined only much later. This led to the amorphous nature of some of

Barba's productions whereby scenes follow one another in no easily discernible order and images are used to comment on the action. In *Ornitofilene*, for example, an executioner targets himself while his victim reads a letter from a condemned prisoner. A puppet attends a cross examination while a team of actors sing a song about institutional injustice. In *Kaspariana* a psalm is sung as news of a beheading is received. In *Ferai* a blanket represents both the swaddling clothes of a newborn baby and the shroud of a dead body, the two extreme points of human experience yoked together by the metaphorical capacity of a single object.

In the early 1970s Barba stopped working with existing scripts and began to put together performances based entirely on the actors' improvisations. Work on a new production would begin typically with a number of suggestions that would cohere around an idea that the group would retrospectively regard as a theme. The actor's improvisations would then present Barba with a range of visual options that he could combine into sequences at will. For *Brecht's Ashes 2* (1978), for example, the rape of Kattrin was a composite image which combined one actor's work with a bowl of water with another's attempt to get Kattrin to smoke when she didn't want to:

> Barba saw the two loose bits of material individually and then simultaneously. He then asked the actors instead of doing their 'scenes' on opposite ends of the room to put the bowl between Kattrin's legs. The juxtaposition of images worked, creating the equivalent of rape without rape.
>
> (Watson 1993: 88)

In the production the deliberate conflation of biographical details with the dramatic reality of **Brecht**'s plays was achieved entirely through the use of images composed in this way. Brecht decides to flee Berlin, for instance, after seeing the Cook from *Mother Courage* burn books in her frying pan. It is Arturo Ui who murders Walter Benjamin and then dances screaming through a set littered with coffee tables to an up-beat jazz rhythm hammered out on an organ.

As the actors came increasingly to rely on music rather than on words to communicate, they evolved a private language of sounds and rhythms, often played on musical instruments, to delineate character. A flute could become the trunk of an elephant, for instance, and an accordion a corpulent paunch. On occasion the instruments could be coaxed to speak to one another:

The 'voices' of the flute and the accordion, animated by two actors in the performance, commented on the action, dialoguing between themselves ... 'speaking' with detachment, commenting ironically on the 'passions' of the rich and noble people; then, on the contrary, they were obedient servants, working to create the setting of their masters' actions: the wind on the Siberian tundra, the noise of the horses' hooves....

(Barba 1986: 76–77)

The instruments were dropped for *Oxyrhincus Evangeliet* (1985) but the emphasis on using the voice as though it were an instrument remained as the dialogue was almost entirely comprised of resonant nonsense syllables synthesised out of approximations to Yiddish and Coptic. The purpose of these 'sound landscapes' was to ensure that the audience plunged into the emotional experience of the drama without trying fruitlessly to tease a rational structure out of its bizarre assemblage of images.

The irony of this attempt to involve the audience as fully as possible is that Barba's audiences are often repelled by the intellectual obscurity of his productions. A frequent criticism of Barba is that the almost complete absence of linear narrative in his work leads less to emotional absorption than to bafflement and confusion. The irony is compounded when one considers the amount of time and effort Barba has expended on discovering the means by which performers all over the world seek to draw their audiences into their performances.

Barba would of course argue that the reasons for this difference have less to do with the actor's technique than with the absence of a common ground of assumptions between performers and spectators in the West. While it will be impossible for Barba to institute homogeneous assumptions about performance styles in the West, his book, *The Secret Art of the Performer*, has gone a long way towards rationalising the art of the performer and providing actors and dancers in the West with their first coherent means of access to techniques that are practised the world over and go back centuries.

Further reading

Barba, E. (1985) *The Dilated Body*, trans. Richard Fowler, Rome: Zeami Libri.
—— (1986) *Beyond the Floating Islands*, trans. Judy Barba, Richard Fowler, Jerrold C. Rodesch and Saul Shapiro, New York: PAJ Publications.

—— (1995) *The Paper Canoe*, trans. Richard Fowler, London: Routledge.

Barba, E. and Savarese, N. (1991) *The Secret Art of the Performer: A Dictionary of Theatre Anthropology*, trans. Richard Fowler, London: Routledge.

Watson, I. (1993) *Towards a Third Theatre*, London: Routledge.

SHOMIT MITTER

YUKIO NINAGAWA (1936–)

Ninagawa has taken as his main repertoire the Greek tragedies and the plays of Shakespeare and Chekhov. His foremost concern in directing such classics is to find ways to bridge the spatio-temporal gap between present-day Japan and his audiences (usually Japanese) and the classical dramatic world.

This bridge frequently takes the form of a visual localisation or a meta-theatrical framework, or both, as happens in the *NINAGAWA Macbeth* (1980) set in the Samurai world of Japan's Azuchi-Momoyama period (1568–1600). The production opened with a scene in which the stage front was entirely occupied by a Buddhist home altar, many times its normal size. Two old women taken to be representative of ordinary people today came down the aisles of the auditorium. They mounted the stage and prayed in front of the huge altar. As they slowly opened its sliding-screen doors, *Macbeth* began, as if conjured up by the crones. The three weird sisters, played by *onnagata* (female impersonators), who were previously visible through the translucent doors dancing in the falling petals of cherry blossom, came forward to speak. The whole concept came to the director's mind when he found himself conversing with his dead father while he was praying at his family altar. This experience made him realise that the play could take the form of a story alluding to 'our' ancestors.

Another example is *The Tempest*, sub-titled 'A Rehearsal on a Noh Stage on Sado Island' (1987). For about thirty minutes before it started, actors and stagehands gathered on or near the stage, which held at its centre a dilapidated open-air Noh stage. Some actors warmed up individually, others chatted while putting on their costumes. Stagehands checked the sets and props, and drummers practised on the traditional Sado drums. By showing his actors going about their life in the theatre, the director called the audience's attention to the fact that the play was going to be acted by Japanese.

When it was time, the on-stage director, who was to play Prospero, called the cast and the technical crew around him and gave them instructions. The minute he gave the cue, two huge structures were pushed forward from each side of the upstage Noh stage, combining at the centre to form a looming ship. A sail dropped down, and sound effects of thunder and lightning created a violent tempest. Ninagawa thus made *The Tempest* a play-within-a-play, with Prospero's magic overlapping that of the theatre. Prospero's magic book was the player's promptbook. Towards the end of the performance, Prospero threw it away and broke his staff. The leaves of the book falling silently to the floor were totally blank.

Ninagawa made use of common factors between the play and Japanese history. Traditionally an island for exiles, Sado Island was the place where Zeami, the great Noh master of the Middle Ages, was exiled, and a few ancient open-air Noh stages still remain there. It seemed to Ninagawa that a Noh stage on Sado would be perfect for the 'revels' of the spirits of the island. This was a perfect example of his search for connections between the drama and the real life of both the past and the present.

Ninagawa's search for a visual localisation and/or meta-theatrical framework lies in the embarrassment he says that he feels when Japanese actors play the parts of European characters in Shakespeare or Greek tragedies. He thus tends to give the drama an Asian or Japanese visual context, thereby keeping actors and audiences deeply rooted in their racial memories as they watch a Western play. Even so, Ninagawa is faithful to the text. He simply designs it to fit the time available for performance. He once said: 'I do all that is written in the script, stage directions and all. But I allow myself to add what is not written' (personal communication, 18 December 1988).

Ninagawa's non-verbal additions are often extremely revealing and riveting. He opened *Richard III* (1999) with a scene in which Gloucester stood with his back to the audience while a white horse entered, running madly, from upstage right. The running horse soon fell dead, whereupon heavy, solid objects began to fall from the ceiling, thudding on to the stage: the bodies of a black horse and a boar, large bouquets of roses (red and white), cabbages, pots and pans, and so on. It was only then, while townspeople cleared the space, that Gloucester started his famous soliloquy. In this way, Ninagawa demonstrated that the 'glorious summer by this son of York' is actually the aftermath of a long, destructive war.

The young Lucius at the end of *Titus Andronicus* (2004) took a black baby from the arms of a Goth soldier. He carried the baby to the centre of the front of the stage and sat there for a while. He then started a repeated, high-pitched wail, his eyes raised up to heaven.

The audience could interpret this unforgettable scene as a sign that the chain of revenge had been stopped, or see the boy as the epitome of the misery of a battlefield full of orphans.

In *Pericles* (2003) a large group of Asian refugees entered from the auditorium to perform the play. The role of the Gower was played by a *biwa hoshi* (an itinerant, medieval Japanese lute player) and his wife, who were the heads of a dejected travelling company. Ninagawa said of this concept that the most unfortunate people have the right to dream of happiness. His *Pericles* was conceived as their dream, their hope, in response to the play's suggestion that its characters overcome their misfortunes and achieve happiness. As he often does, Ninagawa borrowed for this production from traditional Japanese performing arts – Kabuki, Noh and Bunraku puppet plays. These borrowings often strike non-Japanese audiences as oriental or exotic. However, they are not mere packaging for export, but are designed primarily for Japanese audiences.

Once he establishes his basic directorial concept, Ninagawa has his actors read the text through only once. On the second day, he throws them into rehearsal, with stage sets, as he has always done since his earliest days as a director. It is tacitly expected that the actors will have memorised their lines by then. Ninagawa tells them to read the text with their bodies, which is the opposite of what he experienced when he was an actor and spent half of the rehearsals reading the text, textual analysis being the sole purpose. He believes that the ability to analyse and verbalise is one thing, while the ability to represent and act is another. When they move, actors can 'read' in a way they cannot when seated around a rehearsal table. Ninagawa has them practice both word and action simultaneously throughout the rehearsals. That is to say, his approach is from the visible (the ocular) to the invisible; from the outer factors (movements, position, pose, stance, direction, facial expressions and costumes) to the inner workings of the characters. For example, during the rehearsal of Act 3 scene 1 of *Titus Andronicus*, Ninagawa found the actor playing Titus lacking in feeling when he sees Lavinia has been raped. He asked the costume designer to modify Lavinia's costume so that the actress' shoulders were completely bare and her breasts almost visible. When the Titus actor saw her like this, he spontaneously took off his coat to cover her nakedness without any instructions from the director.

According to Ninagawa, slow accumulation of emotions, thoughts and actions results in the theatrical embodiment of a play's characters. The personalities of the characters are not written in the text, but are born during rehearsals. He searches for the characters by participating with the actors in a process of trial and error and compares his duty as a director with that of a midwife who helps deliver a baby: the production is fathered by the text and given body by the 'mothering' actors.

In the same way that his direction seeks connections between the drama and real life, Ninagawa tells his actors to find connections between the dramatic situation, their roles and their selves. In his notes, he always gives examples of situations where he has felt anger, rage, restraint, pleasure or sorrow towards this or that person. He never puts himself in a safety zone, but exposes his 'self' freely to the actors and supporting staff during a rehearsal. Ninagawa is also a master of humorous similes and comparisons. He once compared Stephano, who tries to put on numerous 'glistering' garments, to a glutton who heaps his plate high at a buffet party. To the actor who played Caliban, he said: 'Be more jealous of Trinculo. Fawn on Stephano and stay close to him, like a street punk to his boss' (rehearsal, 6 May 2000).

However, Ninagawa knows that his inventiveness and imagination are most clearly shown through spectacle. When directing Prospero's long soliloquy in Act 5 scene 1 of *The Tempest* ('Ye elves of hills, brooks, standing lakes and groves'), Ninagawa had all the cast and stagehands appear from backstage to form a huge circle of listeners around the director-magician. At the first rehearsal of this scene for his 2000 revival of the 1987 production, he obviously identified himself with Prospero, and the stagehands with the 'elves, demi-puppets and weak masters':

> This is a scene in which a theatre person who is both a playwright and a director is saying that he has created a tempest, has created this kind of play, and is now giving thanks, for the last time, to the cast and the staff who have helped him in his work. Therefore, all of you have to listen to him carefully, deeply moved as you think that this may be his farewell, that this play may be his final work and his last piece of direction, that he may soon retire or even die. You stagehands will hate to appear on stage, but please understand my intention.
>
> (rehearsal, 10 May 2000)

Ninagawa's aspiration as a director is to grasp all aspects of the world and of human beings, which he admits is megalomaniac. With this as his goal he has directed, other than Shakespeare, *Oedipus Rex* (1976, 2002), *Medea* (1978), *Electra* (2003), John Barton's adaptation of ten Greek tragedies, known as *The Greeks* (2000), *The Seagull* (1999), *Three Sisters* (1984, 1992, 2000) and *The Cherry Orchard* (2003).

He is basically a visual artist in the theatre (he once aspired to becoming a painter) and his greatest achievement lies in how he has opened up great possibilities of interpreting the verbal in non-verbal dimensions, especially in his direction of Shakespeare. He creates different versions of plays, not least Shakespeare's, because he finds that, every time, he fails to seize the whole. Hence, for example, his five different versions of *Hamlet* (1978, 1988, 1995, 2001, 2003), three of *King Lear* (1975, 1991, 1999) and two of *Macbeth* (1980, 2001).

Further reading

Akihiko, Senda (1997) 'Scene III 1980–1987: The Period of Metatheatre' in *The Voyage of Contemporary Japanese Theatre*, trans. J. Thomas Rimer, Honolulu: University of Hawaii Press: 253–257.

—— (1998) 'The Rebirth of Shakespeare in Japan: From the 1960s to the 1990s', trans. Minami Ryuta, in Takashi Sasayama, Mulryne, J.R. and Shewring, Margaret (eds) *Shakespeare and the Japanese Stage*, Cambridge: Cambridge University Press: 21–26.

Ninagawa, Yukio (1994) Interview with Michael Billington, London, 14 March, trans. Yuriko Akishima, in Delgado, Maria M. and Heritage, Paul (eds) (1996) *In Contact With the Gods? Directors Talk Theatre*, Manchester and New York: Manchester University Press: 191–200.

—— (1995) Interview with Yasunari Takahashi, Tetsuo Anzai, Kazuko Matsuoka, Ted Motohashi and Ian Carruthers, 4 July, in Ryuta, Minami, Carruthers, Ian and Gillies, John (eds) (2001) *Performing Shakespeare in Japan*, Cambridge: Cambridge University Press: 208–219.

KAZUKO MATSUOKA

LEE BREUER (1937–)

Breuer has created a theatre which consciously absorbs the strategies and conventions of the mass media and popular entertainment. It is often dense, elliptical, lyrical rather than conventionally dramatic, and, in the case of his adaptations of established classics, controversial in its performance choices. His consistent ambition has been to connect American theatre to the vitality of its contemporary culture and to 'wait for poetry', composed out of the driving energy of the vernacular language, popular musical tradition, and refracted media images.[1] By cutting through the boundaries between genres and 'high' and 'low' forms that traditionally separate the arts, Breuer participated in the American experimental art reared in the social ferment of the 1960s and matured in the introspective 1970s. Through most of the 1970s, he worked with the theatre collective Mabou Mines, founded in 1970. This group aimed for a new experimental synthesis which would suffuse the ideal of artistic collectivity with the innovations of new painting, music and dance as well as the more traditional concerns of Stanislavskian 'truth', the tradition from which Breuer and most of the group had sprung.

Mabou Mines never viewed itself as the expression of a singular artistic vision. Even though Breuer dominated its beginning period with his series of Animations, written and directed by him, because of its collaborative ideal and the artistic strengths of the individuals comprising it, the group was never Breuer's theatre in the way that, say, the Ontological-Hysteric Theater *was* Richard **Foreman**. Since 1976, when JoAnne **Akalaitis** directed *Cascando*, the directorial baton has increasingly been passed around, with − in addition to Breuer and Akalaitis − Ruth Maleczech, Fred Neumann and Bill Raymond taking primary responsibility for shaping different Mabou Mines offerings. This sharing of directorial authority allowed Breuer to move outside Mabou Mines to direct a series of innovative productions of the classics for such institutions as the American Repertory Theater of Cambridge, Massachusetts (*Lulu*, 1980), the New York Shakespeare Festival (*The Tempest*, 1981) and the Brooklyn Academy of Music (*The Gospel at Colonus*, 1983; *The Warrior Ant*, 1988).

Two categories of work made the reputation of Mabou Mines in the early 1970s: ingenious stagings of plays and fiction by Samuel Beckett, and unconventional choral theatre pieces based on Breuer's poetic texts. They were originally performed in art galleries and museums, but soon moved beyond an art milieu. *Play* and *Come and Go*, and an adapted prose fragment, *The Lost Ones*, which Breuer directed in 1975, marked the group's major crossover into a theatre context. One of many startling images in *Come and Go* was created by how three actresses performed in the back of the house balcony while their reflected image was perceived on a slanted mirror before the audience. Most impressive of all was the stunning environmental realisation of *The Lost Ones*. Beckett envisioned purgatory as a

139

'flattened cylinder fifty meters round and eighteen high' into which are crammed two hundred 'lost bodies' each searching restlessly for its mate. David Warrilow was mesmerising as the narrator, his performance matched by the piece's brilliant set: a claustrophobic cubicle padded with grey foam rubber. The audience peered down at Warrilow's emaciated presence as he slowly unveiled a small sculptural representation of the cylinder he described, complete with a group of miniature toy bodies. With delicate precision, Warrilow used a pair of forceps to position these homunculi in the grooves of the cylindrical model. Each member of the audience was given a pair of binoculars with which to observe the proceedings in voyeuristic close-up. This molecular purgatory was evoked by ensemble member Philip Glass' tape-recorded music, which seemed 'to be played by electrons rather than instruments' (*Newsweek*, 25 October 1975).

Production innovations were also evident, although not as spectacularly, in the Animations. *The Red Horse Animation*, premiered at the Guggenheim Museum in 1970, was revised and expanded for the Whitney Museum in 1972. The piece unfolded on a bare floor backed by a wood-slatted wall, forming a ninety-degree angled performing space. Contact microphones underneath the floor allowed it to function as a percussive instrument. The actors interacted for the most part lying down on the floor rather than standing up, which was a radical violation of traditional performance. In *The B-Beaver Animation*, presented at both the Museum of Modern Art and the Theatre for the New City in 1974, a sculptural environment, which appeared to be no more than a makeshift construction of planks, ropes and floral-patterned drapes, was transformed in the course of the production into playing spaces suggestive of anarchic disorder. The Animations are intensely personal poems, each centred on an animal. Horse, beaver and dog serve as central images to illuminate the burdens of the contemporary consciousness assaulted by an overload of images and social roles. The horse evokes freedom and romance – journeys, burdens, speed, grace. The beaver creates defenses – a constructing mammal, 'a damning, dammed up and damned species'.[2] The dog (*The Shaggy Dog Animation*, 1978) is trapped in rituals of devotion and servitude – a figure, as Breuer's text notes, 'perceived only in the mirror of a master's eye' (Breuer 1979: 99).

Breuer, the poet, recognised that language, however fragmented and elliptical, was not enough. He learned from ensemble theatre that the group's collective consciousness must enhance the literary

text, and from art and film that visual imagery carries its own signification. He learned from music the power of pure,
non-programmatic sound. *The Red Horse Animation*, his first piece,
was partly based on Muybridge's photographic sequences of the
horse in motion. Thus, from the outset, Breuer's aesthetic was
indebted to film's vocabulary of shots, cuts, sequences, fades,
dissolves, voiceovers and overdubs. He also accepted theories of
literary deconstruction, particularly Roland Barthes' premise that
'the work of the commentary [read 'production' for Breuer], once it
is separated from any ideology of totality, consists precisely in
manhandling the text, interrupting it'.[3] Breuer manhandles his own
Animations texts for the same reasons that deconstructive critics
'misread' literary texts: to recuperate their many voices through the
intervention of performance. Breuer the director is not merely the
interpreter of Breuer the poet, but is his necessary accomplice.

A good example of this is *Hajj* (1983), Breuer's 'performance
poem' inspired by the deeply personal history of Ruth Maleczech, the
piece's sole live performer. The work has at its core the indelible
image of a parent's suicide. But despite premonitory outbursts, *Hajj*
does not confront this fact until the piece is half over. Before this
narrative turn, a woman, an actress, is at a make-up table, her back to
the audience. Her image is visible through a triptych of mirrored
reflections, which also reflect the audience. Images proliferate: mirror
images and images on mirrors, live video images of the actress from
different angles and depths of field, pre-recorded video images and
slides and film. Her monologue is often distorted by vocal overlay. An
expensive battery of equipment creates a collage of competing visual
and aural imagery. Video artist Craig Jones, and set and lighting
designer Julie Archer, collaborated fully in the work. Although *Hajj*
risked being overwhelmed by its elaborate technology, it never
succumbed because its multiple fragments and refractions meticulously created a moving, if not conventionally coherent, journey into
the self.

As long as Breuer's theatre focused on his own texts or those of
Beckett, it could be pigeonholed and dismissed by those unreceptive
to experimentation. When he moved outside Mabou Mines to
accept commissions for new productions of established classics, the
results were inevitably controversial because Breuer's aesthetic
remained committed to the values and strategies of his Mabou Mines
work: namely, if all texts are distorted by conflicting signals, performance re-interpretation is absolutely necessary to recuperate them.
For Breuer this meant that a new dialectic had to be forged between

the classic text, which was overlaid by the sedimentations of history, and contemporary performance styles. This was not always a felicitous conjunction. For example, his aggressively contemporary version of *The Tempest* (in Central Park, 1981) dressed Caliban in ragged jeans, open denim vest and dark spectacles; Ferdinand in white vinyl jumpsuit; a Mafia group of Antonio, Sebastian and Gonzalo (with Alonso as a godfather) in Palm Beach suits and big-brimmed fedoras, accompanied by pistol-packing guards. Trinculo and Stephano were modelled on Mae West and W.C. Fields. (The former was played by a woman, a gender transposition that Breuer was to carry to an extreme in his 1988 gender-reversed production of *Lear*.) Most outrageously, there were eleven Ariels, played by everyone from a Sumo wrestler to small children. The performers spoke in a variety of accents, ranging from punk cockney and Mafia guttural to Harlem street jive, all accompanied by Samba and Gamelan music. Even Breuer admits that he went too far, that he 'owes *The Tempest* another shot' (unpublished interview with author).

The piece confirmed Breuer's belief – a constant of his work – that 'high' and 'low' and 'seriousness' and 'entertainment' are not aesthetic antitheses and that popular forms project a vitality rarely duplicated by high art. Breuer's fascination with the power of popular art, particularly with its musical expression, has grown through the years. He wrote a doo wop poem about the Red Eye Special between Los Angeles and New York – produced with Mabou Mines as *Sister Suzie Cinema* (1980) with a real doo wop group called Fourteen Karat Soul. It also nostalgically evoked rhythm and blues and drive-in movie imagery, revealing 'a vulnerability to American imagery and its secret mythology'.[4]

Breuer's most successful recuperation of a classic text was his *Oedipus at Colonus*. Breuer and composer Bob Telson reconnected with the high, if recalcitrant, art of tragedy by placing its religious roots in the gospel tradition and using gospel performers such as the Five Blind Boys of Alabama. *The Gospel at Colonus* was in the form of a pentecostal church service, complete with preacher and congregants' hymns, prayers, sermons and benedictions. Oedipus was really blind, and divided between actor, Morgan Freeman, and singer, Clarence Fountain, as occurs in Asian theatre. *Gospel*, in Breuer's phrase, had 'white eyes and black ears'.[5] Despite how its meters were adapted to infectious gospel music, it was deeply faithful to Sophocles' tragedy.

In another collaboration with Telson, *The Warrior Ant* (1988), Breuer's animal-hero is a creature whose individuality is denied by its species. This mock-epic fable about the struggle against the anthill of conformity is staged multiculturally, Breuer using a variety of Western, Asian and African musical and theatrical forms. The warrior-ant was played by the Bunraku puppet of an eighteenth-century Samurai. As in *The Tempest*, the eclecticism proved counterproductive, the subtle artistry of the *Bunraku* masters overwhelmed by the three-ring circus ambience. None the less, it demonstrated Breuer's audacious willingness to embrace 'high' and 'low' and 'native' and 'exotic' artistic expressions. In his more recent *Peter and Wendy* (1996), there is only one performer who gives voice to an array of inventive puppets. Breuer is fearless in his search for recuperative strategies, for a theatre without risk cannot rediscover the mysteries American culture no longer understands.

Notes

1 Breuer, Lee (1980) 'Staging Poetry', *Village Voice*, 25 May: 85.
2 Munk, Erika (1977) 'Art of Damnation', *Village Voice*, 11 April: 81.
3 Barthes, Roland (1974) *S/Z*, New York: Hill & Wang: 15.
4 Breuer, Lee (1981) Interview in *Theatre*, Summer/Fall: 29.
5 Breuer, Lee (1983) 'Towards an American Classicism', *On the Next Wave*, November: 14.

Further reading

Breuer, Lee (1979) *Animations: A Trilogy for Mabou Mines*, New York: Performing Arts Journal Press.
—— (1983) *Hajj, Word Plays 3*, New York: Performing Arts Journal Press.
Marranca, Bonnie (1977) *The Theatre of Images*, New York: Drama Book Specialists.
Rabkin, Gerald (1983) 'Lee Breuer and His Double', *On the Next Wave*, November: 7–14.
Wetzsteon, Ross (1987) 'Wild Man of the American Theater', *Village Voice*, 19 May: 19–26.

GERALD RABKIN

RICHARD FOREMAN (1937–)

Born in New York City but raised in Scarsdale, Richard Foreman returned to the city in 1962 with a BA degree from Brown and an MFA degree from Yale, to pursue a conventional career in play-writing. He re-entered the city just as a new cross-disciplinary avant-garde movement was gathering momentum, partially in response to political imperatives. Foregoing genuine commercial prospects, the aspiring young playwright felt himself consumed by this experimental energy and ready to add his own contribution. Foreman's roots in the downtown arts community directed his artistic decisions: in starting his theatre, he did not search out a conventional playhouse but borrowed the ground floor loft of Jonas Mekas' Cinemateque on Wooster Street in the neighbourhood just then becoming known as SoHo. He did not seek out conventional actors: his performers were mostly avant-garde writers, filmmakers, painters or their friends. In this supportive context, Foreman's theatre made its debut with *Angelface* (1968). Although the play seemed to dramatise ordinary domestic situations, its dialogue, stripped of normal social interaction, made no conventional sense. Even the *cognoscenti* in the audience were bewildered. As Foreman conceded: 'For the first six years we knew that half our audience would walk out before the end of the play, often within the first twenty minutes' (Foreman 1992: 74).

It was not merely the absence of conventional narrative and characters that was disturbing. Audiences were used to this in the work of the Open Theater and other groups. But while the innovative work of **Chaikin**, Schechner and **Grotowski** affirmed strategies such as thematic unity, ensemble creation, performative presence and emotional commitment, Foreman actively rejected these. In their place, Foreman substituted their opposites: thematic fragmentation, auteurish creation, writerly presence, and Brechtian emotional estrangement carried to an extreme. He arrived early at an aesthetic to which he remained true: to purge art of emotional habit, through both the radical randomness of his drama and the jarring style of its staging.

Like **Brecht**, Foreman is the most intellectual of artists, enormously well read and discursively prolix. But just as Brecht was theatrically more practical and empirical than his theory of epic theatre would suggest, Foreman's theatre does not merely articulate his theoretical ideas. His theatre has sustained itself through the years because, at its best, it is *fun* – spirited, frenetic, dazzling, surprising, provocative, even as it is intellectually demanding. Foreman is not just an obsessive self-scrutiniser, a philosophical prober of recalcitrant reality. He is also a ring-master, melding text, performance, music, sound and objects into unique spectacles.

The dual nature of Foreman's work is reflected in the name he gave to his group: the Ontological-Hysteric Theater. The 'ontological' nature of Foreman's theatre resides in the fervent if unachievable quest for ultimate meaning. Hence the fierce concentration on the reality of each individual moment, which Foreman often replays in order to re-scrutinise. The 'hysteric' nature of the work lies in the manner in which it evokes physical vulnerability, terror and sexuality, an irrational counterbalance to the implacable rationality of Foreman's mental processes. The juxtaposition of ontology and hysteria reflects the relationship between Foreman the playwright and Foreman the director. Philosophy is – or should be – a rational quest, and Foreman's plays deny empathy because he does not want to pollute reason. On the other hand, theatre is nothing if not corporeal and, in the state of hysteria, the claims of the body swamp those of the mind. That is why Foreman chose the theatre as his main medium and not fiction, poetry or discursive prose. Theatre is here, now and palpable.

In the earliest plays, Foreman the director consciously served Foreman the playwright. 'The sets were extremely minimal … I built everything. But I added no decoration. I wanted … the look of my awkward carpentry' (ibid.: 71). By the time of *Hotel China* (1971–72), Foreman's interest began to shift away from his scrutiny of the psychological sub-texts that underlie the surface of conscious action. He increasingly felt that a minimally dressed space would not allow the text to ricochet fully between levels of meaning. Foreman the director/designer assumed a greater role in his self-collaboration. He saw the stage not as a platform on which to display action, but as 'a reverberation chamber which amplifies and projects the music of the action so it can reveal the full range of its overtones' (ibid.: 71). All the materials of theatre – scenery, props, lights, noises, bodies – were to be thrown together in polymorphous play.

Take, for example, the opening of *Hotel China*: there were two naked bulbs on floor stands and a man sitting behind each bulb. One had a sack over his head. A lamp was placed over the sack and a wrapped package was placed upon the other man's lap. Blackout. When the lights came up again, a rock had replaced the package. The un-hooded man said, 'Get this rock off'. The hooded one replied, 'I didn't notice it'. As the scene continued, there was another blackout accompanied by the sound of a rock being hit by a hammer. When the lights came back up, the men had gone and a gently swinging rock was suspended in the air, illuminated by a flashlight. The men returned. Signs were placed on the rear wall, one of which read: EACH ROCK IS CAPABLE OF VIBRATING INDEPENDENTLY. A screen descended. A film was shown. It consisted of shots of rocks being placed in different positions in different rooms. The film went to white. With the projector still running, a six-foot rock was rolled onto the stage. Birds chirped till the rock came to rest. A single bright floodlight illuminated the stage. The bird song faded. The crew placed small rocks around the big rock. There was the noise of a hammer striking a rock. This was repeated ten times. Then there was silence.

One visual element which made its first appearance in *Hotel China* and came, by subsequent repetition, to be synonymous with Foreman's theatrical style was the use of strings. In one scene Foreman attached strings to the sides of the stage in a widening funnel that came to a point on an actor's brow. The strings suggested lines of force emanating from the character's – and the author's – yearning mind. In the later plays, these ubiquitous strings, intensified by repetitive black dots, developed a life of their own. Feeling that theatrical space was insufficiently defined, Foreman wanted the strings, together with lights that were focused into the audience's eyes, to turn the stage into a participant-provocateur in the play, rather than have it remain a neutral site of performance.

The staging of Foreman's early plays was shaped by the space on lower Broadway that he had purchased as a home for his group. It was an eccentric loft only 14-feet wide. Converted into a theatre, it provided room for only seven rows of seats, which occupied less than a quarter of the space. The stage itself was a full 75-feet deep, the first 20 feet of which were at floor level. The next 30 feet ran at a steep rake, with the stage finally levelling off at about a 6-foot height for the remaining depth. Foreman used this eccentric depth to advantage: in performance, actors and objects would often roll down the 30–foot rake. Sliding walls would enter from the side of the stage to create a series of quickly changing areas that varied radically in depth. The stage floor, built from scratch, changed for each production. It could slope up and down like a series of hills, or a wall could move in and isolate a shallow area. Throughout each show, the performance space would alternately close and open up, shifting back and forth vertiginously, the perfect site for a theatre of dis-equilibrium.

As Foreman's reputation spread beyond the downtown arts community, new theatrical opportunities presented themselves. Institutional theatres came calling with increasing frequency, particularly as his status grew in Europe. In 1976 he received an offer to stage a revival of Brecht's *Threepenny Opera* at the Vivian Beaumont Theater in the Lincoln Center. Foreman had never staged the work of any playwright other than himself, but his affinity with Brecht was deep. In his production he worked to recover the savagery that Marc Blitzstein's popular Off-Broadway success had sacrificed. *Threepenny Opera* was the first of eight Foreman productions under Joseph Papp's auspices over the next dozen years, three of which (*Penguin Touquet* (1981), *Egyptology* (1983) and *What Did He See?* (1988)) were written by Foreman in the Ontological-Hysteric tradition.

Foreman closed his theatre on lower Broadway in 1979. The Wooster Group offered the O-H Theater its home space, the Performing Garage. From 1985 to 1990 Foreman presented four plays at the Garage: two with the Wooster Group ensemble − *Miss Universal Happiness* (1985) and *Symphony of Rats* (1988) − and two without − *The Cure* (1986) and *Lava* (1989). Foreman acknowledges that the visceral acting style of the Wooster Group − so different from the ironic deadpan he usually coaxed from his performers − clearly moved their collaborations in hyper-kinetic directions:

> [The] actors from the Wooster Group ... didn't hesitate to expand on my suggestions to get louder and faster.... They threw themselves into it with a vengeance that moved the performance faster and faster, and I indulged myself by asking for more violent physical activity than I ever had in the past.
>
> (Ibid.: 97)

In 1991 Foreman took over the historic upstairs theatre at St Mark's Church on Second Avenue in New York's East Village. This space, home to Foreman's most recent work, has shaped his directorial vision, just as his earlier work was shaped by his Broadway space. While the latter was deep and narrow, hence accenting distancing, the St Mark's space is wide and shallow, expanding like a large Corneillian box yearning to be filled with objects. After the scenic simplicity of the inaugural play in the new space, *The Mind King* (1992), the St Mark's plays have increased their visual component. *Samuel's Major Problems* (1993) was set in a littered room in which a party had taken place: balloons, streamers, loose paper and confetti were scattered about and pictures of skulls on the wall replicated some real skulls that were mixed in with other strange objects on the shelves. In *My Head Was a Sledgehammer* (1994), the set was a room with blackboards, tall bookcases and tiny flags hung around. It could have been a lecture room, a studio or a gymnasium − or all of them at once. *I've Got the Shakes* (1995) repeated the image of doomed festivities: balloons and streamers again festooned the space and white flowers cascaded near the ceiling. Characters and narratives remained typically elusive, but themes were perhaps more accessible than before. With age, Foreman had turned towards themes of death and self-assessment.

Richard Foreman will persevere. Like Beckett's Unnamable, he can't go on but he will go on. As he confessed in *Permanent Brain Damage* (1996), 'an angry man, disillusioned and weary of life, nevertheless sustains the blind faith that something amazing and beautiful will emerge from the chaos surrounding him'. In his most accessible book, *Unbalancing Acts* (1992), Foreman notes that 'essentially, an artist does one thing throughout his career' (ibid.: 85). Indeed, Foreman has continually recycled visual images (variegated strings, collagist detail, lines of force, etc.), titles (*My Head Was a Sledgehammer, I've Got the Shakes*), intellectual concerns and directorial strategies (presentational non-acting acting, constant interruption, Brechtian distancing through blinding lights, buzzers and musical fragmentation). His vision remains steadfast and adversarial: Foreman maintains that when conservative critics attack contemporary art because they fear that it will undermine Western culture, they have a valid fear. Not now, but 'in the long run'. Until then, Foreman will keep going – thirty years and counting – by continuing to create serious art in a culture he perceives hostile to serious art.

Further reading

Foreman, R. (1976) *Richard Foreman: Plays and Manifestos*, ed. Kate Davy, New York: New York University Press.

—— (1985) *Reverberation Machines: The Later Plays and Essays*, Barrytown, NY: Station Hill Press.

—— (1992) *Unbalancing Acts: Foundations for a Theatre*, New York: Pantheon Books.

Rabkin, Gerald (ed.) (1999) *Richard Foreman*, Baltimore: Johns Hopkins University Press.

GERALD RABKIN

PETER STEIN (1937–)

The German director Peter Stein's place in history is analogous to that of an adolescent's within a family – at once rebellious and accommodating, fighting off mentors and being shaped by them. Stein's 1969 *Tasso* was quite clearly the attempt of a young German director working in what was inevitably **Brecht**'s shadow to test the legacy of the master against the growing authority of his own artistic sensibility. Stein's rearrangement of scenes in *Tasso* owes a great deal to Brecht: episodes are grouped together without an overt sense of sequence. As Michael Patterson observes, 'By undermining the absoluteness of the play's dramatic structure, Stein challenged the absoluteness of the social structure it reflected' (Patterson 1981: 21): there could of course be no clearer definition of the 'epic' in Brechtian theatre. Patterson also notes that the actor 'Bruno Ganz did not identify with Tasso but "quoted" him' (ibid.: 26) – a reference to an acting technique used by Brecht to introduce a distinction between the actor and the role. Patterson notes the 'blasphemous shock-effect' (ibid.: 24) achieved by Edith Clever's deliberately inappropriate line delivery, a standard Brechtian way of subjecting social norms to scrutiny by reviewing them in an unusual aspect.

In 1970 Stein decided to apply the principle of alienation not only to the texts he produced, but to the manner in which theatres in Germany were run. In a radical move, he introduced the Schaubühne, the theatre he had just taken over, to the principles of democracy and egalitarianism that had been a characteristic feature of some of the plays he had directed. This flew in the face of the tradition of autocratic control which directors in Germany were accustomed to exercising, but drew on Stein's conviction that actors were more likely to give better performances if they had a say in what the company as a whole was trying to achieve. Stein chose Brecht's *The Mother* (1970) to be his first production at the Schaubühne. The choice of play was symbolic: just as the characters in the drama lose their bourgeois instincts and gradually embrace community-oriented thinking, so also the rehearsal process, Stein hoped, would abandon traditional authoritarianism and embrace a more democratic mode of functioning. Stein placed himself in a triumvirate of directors who were a part of a larger collective comprising the whole company. All actors attended all rehearsals so as to contribute to the daily meetings held to discuss the direction the production should take. Even the technicians were copied in on the thinking of the directors and their views scrupulously considered. In an effort to widen the circle of participants in Stein's fledgling democracy, post-performance discussions were instituted so as to encourage the audience to contribute to the process of creating performances. As Stein remarked in an interview with Bernard Dort, 'what we intend to explore … is a form of theatre where the audience are ultimately the ones who create the theatre…. [W]hat is shown will directly concern the audience and involve them in debate, indeed make them question their own way of debating'.[1]

It rapidly became apparent, however, that Stein's actors and technicians treated the greater responsibility of running the theatre as burdensome rather than fulfilling. The longer hours were tiring and, with a large number of conflicting views to accommodate, the process of discussion became frustrating. Practical considerations eventually led to the directors having to do the bulk of the decision-making. Even this did not prove sufficiently cohesive, with the very different contributions made by each of the directors inevitably pulling the performance in different directions. The decision to give major actors walk-on parts so as to give lesser actors an opportunity to receive star billing turned out to be a grossly wasteful dissipation of resources. The decision to give technicians and directors equal voting rights on matters seriously affecting the company's policy also proved misguided: after considerable wrangling over the fate of an engineer who had been dismissed, a more stable equilibrium was reached whereby members of the team with temporary contracts did not have the right to veto committee decisions.

Stein came away from his experiment with democracy both bruised and impatient. His frustration erupted into an over-zealous preoccupation with its ideological opposite – the theatre of bourgeois nostalgia. Stein was quite clear about his reasons for abandoning his short-lived career as a spokesman for the proletariat: the company would have to accept, he argued, that both its members and its audience was essentially middle class, and that, by playing to a revolutionary brief, they were being both condescending and hypocritical:

> The theatre cannot be a means of realising the ideology of the working classes. This realisation can only be achieved in practical political struggle. The means are those of the word, of writing, of pictures etc. and not the interaction which takes place between two or three people in an enclosed space in front of a maximum of 1300 people.[2]

When Stein vehemently declared, 'I refuse to put bad plays which deal with the so-called problems of the working classes in our programme just to prove how leftish we are' (in *Der Abend*, 21 July 1977), his tone was that of a man for whom the rejection of the socialist model was in effect the rejection of a family ethic. This was the adolescent again, protesting in excess of the facts because of the bonds that had formed between his sensibility and a particular way of thinking.

Socialist revolutions, Stein repeatedly argued, were best played out on the stage of life, not the theatre. Not only were revolutions ill suited to theatrical treatment, but the theatre was itself compromised by limiting itself exclusively to revolutionary material. His next production, Ibsen's *Peer Gynt* (1971), Stein announced with the zeal of the convert, would aim instead 'to develop an understanding of our own bourgeois origins'.[3] In fact, there is a greater similarity between the techniques used in *The Mother* and *Peer Gynt* than Stein's ideological indignation would have us believe. The single thread running through each of the changes Stein made to Ibsen's text was a concern with exposing the social structures underlying the dramatic action:

> Thus the Strange Passenger, instead of asking Peer about his experience of 'dread,' now posed questions like ... 'Have you ever tried to find out the facts about social conditions in Norway?'
>
> (Patterson 1981: 70)

In the troll scene Peer's lines were adapted to read not 'I'm whatever you want – a Turk, a sinner, a troll' but 'I'm whatever you want – a liar, a capitalist, a troll' (ibid.: 84). The actors were included in the discussion about alterations to the text and Stein accepted majority decisions about casting. The Schaubühne's commitment to ensemble acting was accommodated by dividing the role of Peer into a number of parts that were played by six actors. The actors' instructions were explicitly Brechtian: they had to 'act the role *and* criticize it'.[4]

A number of commentators have linked the greater element of realism that entered into Stein's staging in the 1970s and 1980s with his supposedly growing interest in 'bourgeois theatre'. In fact Stein's use of reality is interesting precisely because it *destroys* illusion on stage. The rain in *Piggy Bank* (1973), for example, was so real that it destroyed the game of 'let's pretend' that naturalistic actors traditionally rely upon to sustain stage illusion. The technique dates back to one of Stein's earliest productions, Edward Bond's *Saved* (1967), in which Stein put a real boat on stage but deliberately failed to paint in the trees and the water that the boating scene required. The act of insinuating an incongruously real object into the fictitious context of a piece of theatre had the effect of challenging the audience's sense of the real – which was Stein's precise intention.

One of the most memorable aspects of Stein's best-known production, Gorky's *Summerfolk* (1974), was the use of real trees which, when the production moved to London, had to be carefully selected and felled in Epping Forest before being planted and watered in specially prepared soil on stage. The trees belonged to the same category of intentionally intrusive reality that had repeatedly been used by Stein through the course of his career to break the carefully cultivated naturalism of the actors. Just as in Brecht the naturalism of a scene had to be built up before it could be broken, so also in Stein the involvement of the audience was an essential precondition to the destruction of the spell that made for effective 'alienation'. Repeatedly in *Summerfolk* the painstakingly created spontaneity of the characters would be broken with a freeze – and laid over with a commentary on the action. Stein would encourage his actors 'to seek for detail for no other reason than that it was lifelike' (ibid.: 113–114); but he would also have his actors periodically stand still and address the audience directly, thereby destroying any 'illusion' their lifelike acting may have created.

Stein began work on *Summerfolk* by giving a lecture on Gorky. His co-director Sturm followed with a lecture on nineteenth-century Russian literature. Work on *As You Like It* (1977) began in the same vein – with a series of seminars on Shakespeare and Elizabethan culture. A reading list was compiled comprising works on a host of subjects including philosophy and science. Actors selected fields of research and were required to report their findings at weekly conferences. There were even readings from Jung 'to illustrate utopian love in the symbol of the hermaphrodite' (ibid.: 134) – a subject as academically remote from the hurly-burly of practical work in the theatre as it is possible to imagine. The actors did work on acquiring physical skills such as Morris dancing, but these were approached as one would approach artefacts in a museum – and indeed were presented as such in a work-in-progress performance entitled *Shakespeare's Memory* (1976). In an age when the exploration of the space outside language was very much the vogue, Stein rigidly held on to the value of studying the world of a play intellectually before beginning physically to inhabit it. Stein's rejection of body-oriented work was analogous to his rejection of socialist theatre: in both cases an outmoded method of working was preferred to a more recent and fashionable alternative. What was revolutionary about Stein was that he was reactionary.

As You Like It was performed in a film studio. Stein liked the flexibility the space gave him: it permitted him to move the audience around and have sequences of action playing concurrently in different locations. While some court scenes were played as set pieces upon a stage, others involved the actors moving amongst the spectators who had to accommodate the action as though it were taking place on a street. The audience then followed the actors through a door in a wall which led, by way of a narrow passage, into 'Arden' – a vast arena bathed in bird song and autumnal light, littered with trees and pools, foliage, butter churns and spinning looms. The action took place all over this vast space simultaneously. As the eye wandered over the action, certain moments were caught and others lost. Indeed, it was the tension between what was gleaned and what was missed that constituted a vital element of the interest of the production.

Perhaps the most memorable – and controversial – aspect of Stein's more recent productions is an extension of this preoccupation with scale. Stein moved the Schaubühne into a new building, which was designed to meet his growing need for a large, flexible space, at a cost of £25 million. Stein left the Schaubühne in 1985 with his appetite for space undiminished: his 1992 *Julius Caesar* used 200 extras on a 45–metre stage. The *Faust* he put on in 2000 was performed over twenty hours and cost DM24m – a price that was, for some, very much at odds with the image of a director who had begun his career doing Peter Weiss' *Vietnam Discourse* (1968) as a series of agit-prop performances which ended with a nightly collection to fund weapons for the Vietcong. For some, Stein had 'sold out'. For others, Stein had finally shaken off the burden of his cultural past and come of age as a director with an independent vision.

Notes

1   Stein, Peter (1972) Interview with Bernard Dort, *Travail Theatral*: 24.
2   Stein in a meeting with actors and staff, 30 November 1975 (Schaubühne Protocol No. 502).
3   Stein quoted in a Schaubühne Protocol of 5 April 1970.
4   Canaris, Volker (1971) on Stein's *Peer Gynt* in *Theatre heute* 13: 32.

Further reading

Lackner, P. (1977) 'Peter Stein', *Drama Review*, T74 June.
Patterson, M. (1981) *Peter Stein*, Cambridge: Cambridge University Press.

SHOMIT MITTER

JOANNE AKALAITIS (1939–)

JoAnne Akalaitis is one of America's most innovative and controversial stage directors whose work ranges from original theatre pieces to unconventional interpretations of classic plays. Noted for her imagistic and sculptural approach to staging, Akalaitis' multi-layered, collage-like works combine text, acting and design to create highly evocative theatrical environments. Her approach to creating theatre is a profoundly physical one. In her work, the dramatic event is palpably present in the bodies of the actors and in the scenic architecture of space, image, light, sound and music. While Akalaitis considers these concrete, physical aspects of theatre to be compositional elements, they do more than contribute structure and form to her work. They convey emotion also. Theatrical space is psychological space; physical geography is emotional geography. What matters most of all, according to this iconoclastic director, is 'the inside and the outside coming together.'[1]

For twenty years, Akalaitis was a member of Mabou Mines, the New York-based collaborative theatre group she co-founded in 1970 with Lee **Breuer**, Ruth Maleczech, David Warrilow and Philip Glass. Mabou Mines has distinguished itself by a complex visual sensibility, intellectual rigour, democratic principles and a tradition of collaborating with artists from various disciplines. The company has remained dedicated to the creative process rather than the commercial product, developing its theatre pieces over lengthy rehearsal periods and keeping them in the repertory for several years. From her early days with Mabou Mines, Akalaitis has recognised the importance of working collaboratively. She considers actors to be intelligent individuals who think creatively and independently rather than merely execute the vision of the director, and endeavors to create a democratic rehearsal environment in which all participants have freedom to invent and explore. She also believes it is crucial for actors to develop a sense of ensemble over the course of a rehearsal period, and expects each actor cast in her productions to participate in daily physical warm-up sessions. Whether the actors explore images, movements and gestures in one of the exercises, or while working on a scene, Akalaitis continually reminds them that they are 'in it together'.

For Akalaitis, the primal element of theatre is bodies moving in space on stage. She seeks out actors who inhabit their own bodies in an easy and expressive manner, who 'possess the habit of being emotional but who also like to work physically'. And in her rehearsals, a large part of the actor's work involves developing a physical connection to the text, to fellow actors and to the scenographic space itself. Akalaitis believes that all great plays require the actor to be 'pre-narrative', to be able to exist in a kind of primeval, subconscious state that is open to the worlds of the play. To this end, Akalaitis has developed a series of physical exercises which are central to her directing process. The exercises, performed by the entire cast of actors throughout the rehearsal period, are not about creating improvisational situations or scenes. Their focus is to establish this pre-narrative, open and alert state in a manner that avoids defining the *actual* physicality of the actors' characters too early on in the rehearsal process. Once established, this foundation of primitive physicality underlies the more detailed scenework that Akalaitis and her actors engage in as they continue their exploration of the play.

In recent years, Akalaitis has devoted an increasing amount of time to 'tablework' during the early days of rehearsals. Even so, she gets her actors on their feet by the first or second day, engaging in a complex series of physical exercises which lasts anywhere from twenty minutes to several hours, and supports the work on the text itself. Discussing the rehearsal process for her production of Pinter's *The Birthday Party* at the American Repertory Theatre (2004), Akalaitis explains that her movement exercises 'help develop a company' and 'help the actors learn to talk to each other with their bodies'. She adds that she 'would never do a show without these exercises. It's very hard for me to go into rehearsal and just start working – I need the actors to do something first. The actors lead me to exploration, I don't lead them' (Saivetz 2000: 188). As the actors perform these exercises, Akalaitis either watches attentively, goes through the exercises herself in her imagination, or allows her mind to wander freely. At times she asks the actors to improvise on their own while she jots down ideas and images. She emphasises that the exercises are for the actors' rather than her own benefit, and refers to them as 'pure actor-research'.

While each exercise has its own purpose and set of instructions, most of them require the actors to move about the rehearsal space to music that Akalaitis associates – thematically, emotionally or structurally – with the particular text, or project, she is directing.[2] She continually coaches from the sidelines, urging the actors to be aware of the physical sensation of the space around them, particularly the space between them. She reminds the actors to be aware of and to 'use' the music, even if what they happen to be doing physically occurs in opposition to it (for example, moving in slow motion to music with a frenetic beat). The actors are asked not to choreograph their actions to the music, but to be conscious of the music's emotional qualities and 'to let the music in'. In this way, the music facilitates the actors' investigation of images arising from their personal histories, the text, the director's suggestions, or from design elements in the physical space. Over time, the exercises strengthen the actors' connection to each other and to the space around them, which eventually will contain scenery, props, lighting and music. They become accustomed to working as an ensemble, and to creating both a personal and shared vocabulary of images, movement and gestures that can be invoked throughout the rehearsal process.

Akalaitis compares the actor's sense of energy to that of a team athlete whose reflexes are automatic and consistently oriented towards the physical task of moving. The actor, like the athlete, uses peripheral vision to sense another player's approach, to sense the energy coming from the spectators, to sense how to shape the rhythm and dynamics of the moment. Akalaitis has said that she dislikes 'people standing [onstage] in front of scenery, talking to each other'.

Whether they are performing a physical exercises or a scripted scene from the play, Akalaitis' actors are urged to 'be in it and see themselves in it'. They are encouraged to give themselves over equally to the *fictive* circumstances of the exercise or scene, and to the *actual* 'where' and 'who' that actor is – specifically, a body moving in theatrical space, investigating a dramaturgical/emotional/architectural structure with clarity and sincerity. According to Akalaitis, the actors must be open to everything around them without becoming 'lost in the emotion'; they must, at every moment, be aware of their exact location in the physical and emotional geography of the work. The type of on-stage presence that Akalaitis asks her actors to investigate calls upon them to be responsive to, and responsible for, something greater than their own individual roles. The actor in an Akalaitis production not only *is* the image but also *casts* it, knowing exactly what he or she is contributing to the totality of the on-stage composition. In doing so, the actors eventually come to view themselves not merely as components, but also as shapers of the entire on-stage 'picture.'

Akalaitis offers the following insight into the imagistic base of her directorial approach: 'I get most of my ideas from pictures. In fact, all images in the theatre are visual, even language – it's impossible to read without making pictures in your mind. The crucial thing for me is always to remain true to your images.'[3] She has developed her physical exercises to help actors explore, within a shared space, the connections between their physicality and these very pictures in their minds, and to encourage them to be true to their own personal images.

At New York University's Second Annual Design Symposium, which focused on the relationship between design and the performer, Akalaitis spoke about her willingness to use stage design to challenge actors, as well as her interest in working with actors who 'can see it all – who can both see the space and see themselves in that space'.[4] She believes that a physically demanding set poses no problem for actors and is in fact desirable because it contributes an 'interesting tension' to the performance.[5] Akalaitis explains that actors work in a very private, hermetic, deeply subjective manner, which they eventually must translate into a way of working that is public, objective and physicalised:

> The actor has to put himself or herself into space, and that's a very hard thing to do. Actors say, 'Oh, the set is so hard to work on.' They all say that. They should say that. They need to say that. And then they need to get on to the next step, which is to understand that the set supports them and embraces them. And they have to figure out how to domi-nate. I often say that the actors have to possess the space. And they usually do.

It is ironic that Akalaitis, while often referred to as a designer's rather than an actor's director, in fact endows her actors with an unusual degree of imagistic responsibility. Particularly during the early stages of rehearsal, Akalaitis encourages her actors to think directorially, inventing images that may find their way into the fully-staged production. She, in a sense, empowers them to become, in Roland Barthes' phrase, 'masters of meaning'.[6] If the actors are willing to commit to Akalaitis' exercises and have faith in her direc-torial approach, they open themselves to the possibility of experiencing an unusual degree of spontaneity, individuality and passion on stage. As a result, the stage becomes a maelstrom in which image, emotion and the body whirl together.

Akalaitis has remarked that, for her, 'chaos, not conflict, is the essence of drama' – the illogical, the disruptive and the reckless. She habitually unearths the strange and perverse in history, politics and culture. While Akalaitis frequently stages works written by and about people from cultures other than the United States, her imagination is caught by those aspects of the collective American psyche that are twisted, demented, ugly and frightening, and that, with our peculiar tendency toward naive optimism, we sentimentalise or repress. Her productions have dealt with such disturbing subjects as the sexism and patriarchy surrounding the development of atomic energy (*Dead End Kids: A History of Nuclear Power*, stage 1980, film 1986); the intertwining of political failure and sexual tragedy in fascist Italy (*'Tis Pity She's a Whore*, 1990); the current of hypocrisy and fraud that runs through the Mormon religion (*The Mormon Project Workshop*, 1990); and the grotesque system of capital punishment carried out through a horrific yet strangely glorious execution machine (*In the Penal Colony*, 2000–01). Commenting on the 'joyous and dangerous reunion of violence and humor' in the plays of Euripides, Shakespeare, Beckett and Pinter, Akalaitis suggests that these plays allow us to live the part of our life that we are forbidden to experience: 'I think this interest in violence is healthy. Violence has to do with chaos and darkness, and chaos and darkness are part of religion, drama, literature, theatre, and music. We want to dip into that from time to time'.[7]

Drawn to subjects and texts that address aspects of chaos in the individual and society, Akalaitis also embraces the chaos of the unknown as an inevitable aspect of the creative process. Her physical exercises serve as formal structures to shape and contain this chaos, allowing the actors to investigate personal, textual and scenic images in an emotionally 'safe' environment. They become active participants in the image-making aspect of theatre, an area traditionally considered the province of the director and designer. As the membrane between acting and design becomes more permeable, the actors perform with, and within, the design instead of merely in front of it. The integration of acting and design is thus at the core of Akalaitis' directing process.

Since the early 1970s Akalaitis has been considered a provocative director of at times astounding, at times flawed, experimental work. Because she values the visual, spatial and compositional aspects of theatre, her work tends to provoke grumbling among certain critics and spectators who conclude that she therefore devalues the inner processes of the actor. In fact, Akalaitis respects the actor's emotional life and considers her actors to be intelligent and active collaborators in the overall fabric of her productions. She is a director who subverts aesthetic boundaries, shrugging off attempts by even the most appreciative critics and scholars to describe her work, style and taste. Her imagination is as intrigued by social structures and systems of power relationships as by her own dreams. She grapples with complex social, philosophical and aesthetic questions without settling for easy answers and expects no less of her colleagues, critics and audiences.

Notes

1   Unless otherwise noted, all quotes attributed to Akalaitis are drawn from the author's rehearsal notes for *'Tis Pity She's a Whore*, directed by Akalaitis, Goodman Theatre, Chicago, 1990, and *The Mormon Project Workshop*, directed by Akalaitis, Atlantic Center for the Arts, New Smyrna Beach, Florida, 1990, as well as from personal interviews and informal conversations.
2   Examples of Akalaitis' rehearsal music include Jimmy Cliff's 'By the Waters of Babylon' and David Byrne's 'Burning Down the House' for *The Mormon Project Workshop* and songs by Marvin Gaye for *The Trojan Women*.
3   Wetzsteon, R. (1981) 'Mabou Mines', *New York Magazine*, 23 February: 30.
4   Smith, R. (1992) 'Actors, Designers Face Off: Can They Be Partners?', *American Theatre*, April: 49.
5   Ibid.
6   (1977) 'Diderot, Brecht, Eisenstein' in *Image-Music-Text*, ed. and trans. S. Heath, New York: Hill-Farar: 74.
7   McKittrick, R. (2003) 'Party Politics', interview with JoAnne Akalaitis, American Repertory Theatre website, Cambridge, MA. Available at: <www.amrep.org/articles/2_3b/party.html>

Further reading

Bartow, A. (1988) 'JoAnne Akalaitis' in Bartow, Arthur (ed.) *The Director's Voice: Twenty-One Interviews*, New York: Theatre Communications Group: 1–19.

Cattaneo, A. and Diamond, D. (1996) 'We Are the Ones', interview with JoAnne Akalaitis, *The Journal for Stage Directors & Choreographers* 10 (1): 9–17.

Daniels, R. (1996) *Women Stage Directors Speak: Exploring the Influence of Gender on Their Work*, Jefferson, NC: McFarland.

Saivetz, D. (2000) *An Event in Space: JoAnne Akalaitis in Rehearsal*, Lyme, NH: Smith & Kraus.

DEBORAH SAIVETZ

ARIANE MNOUCHKINE (1939–)

Theatre, for Mnouchkine, is a matter of three interrelated priorities under which all other objectives are subsumed: collective construction of productions rather than the single vision of a director; theatricality rather than realistic representation; political engagement rather than aestheticism. Her ideas and practice have evolved within these parameters during the forty years that she has worked exclusively with the Théâtre du Soleil in Paris.

The company, which she co-founded in 1964, was a non-hierarchical organisation of equal salaries and shared responsibilities, expressing the broadly Left politics of its members. Not specifically aligned to any party, it participated in the student and workers' revolt of May '68, touring *La Cuisine* (Arnold Wesker's *Kitchen*) to factories on strike. Mnouchkine thus shared with **Vilar** the principles of inclusivity and accessibility defined by his notion of 'popular theatre', and with **Brecht** the idea that theatre was instrumental in bringing about social change.

Nevertheless, she has consistently rejected such descriptions of her work as 'didactic' or 'militant' – allegedly 'Brechtian' characteristics, as seen in the French context of the 1960s and 1970s. The terms had stuck since the seminal *1789* (1970) and *1793* (1972), both in promenade form. The Soleil had staged these extraordinary frescoes of the French Revolution as something of an analogy with the egalitarian movements of May '68. Yet Mnouchkine did not think of these productions as aiming to instruct or persuade audiences, but as an attempt to understand, *with* audiences, a past and present history of which they all had some knowledge. Everyone in France had covered the same school curriculum, and everyone had gone through May '68.

By calling upon the idea that theatre is a conduit for *learning* from history rather than transforming it, as Brecht had envisaged, Mnouchkine shifted the balance away from what might be termed direct politics to a more fluid concept for which ideology is far less important than people's living involvement with events that concern them. It also throws into relief Mnouchkine's holistic view of the relationship between theatre, society and history, which, for her, is not a matter of national, but of world history:

> Does life consist of staying locked in by four walls or of knowing others, of travelling, in all the senses that we can give to this term? When we make theatre, we create, we construct a world view on the stage, around the stage and through the way audiences receive us. In actual fact, I don't like speaking about all that as if it were detached from the rest. This is history. Our lives are situated at every moment in a historical period: we either decide from early child-hood that we are a girl or a boy who is going to participate in history; or we decide that history is made without us, and put our head in a black hole and do not move.
>
> (*Le Monde*, 26 February 1998)[1]

Mnouchkine here is discussing *Et soudain, des nuits d'éveil* (*And Suddenly, Nights of Awakening*, 1997), which treats the genocide and exile of the Tibetan people. She continues:

> When one speaks of these cultures that are disappearing, from Tibet, from Cambodia, they are pieces of us, of humanity, that are disappearing. My one treasure is the world. I am neither disinterested nor altruistic in wishing to have it as little devastated as possible.
>
> (Ibid.)

This could be described as a humanist and humanitarian politics whose importance is especially palpable in Mnouchkine's themes since 1985, when she staged the ten-hour *L'Histoire terrible mais inachevée de Norodom Sihanouk, roi de Cambodge* (*The Terrible but Unfinished Story of Norodom Sihanouk, King of Cambodia*). Summarised, they draw a devastating image: the mass destruction of peoples, regicide, matricide, war, struggle against political and moral oppression and social injustice, religious fanaticism, abusive authority, intolerance, exile, asylum-seeking and homelessness. All these, for Mnouchkine, are global occurrences that destroy 'humanity'. No other director working at the end of the twentieth century has put such urgent and all-embracing subject matter at the very heart of his/her theatre.

Where composition is concerned, the Soleil first drew interna-tional attention for its practice of *création collective*, which succeeded in mounting large-scale art-theatre productions. *Création collective* refers to the collective writing on stage, not on paper, from which the early productions were developed – *Les Clowns* (1969), *1789, 1793* and *L'Age d'or* (*The Golden Age*, 1975). All members of the company researched their material. Scripts were written from improvised situations, stories, scenes and characters. Mnouchkine believes this is necessary because 'actors are authors more with their sensibilities and their bodies than they would be with a blank sheet of paper' (Williams 1999: 55). Scripting physically included experimenting with costumes and make-up from the very start so that the performers could visualise their work. This seeing approach has become a permanent feature of the Soleil.

When *1789* was made, Mnouchkine observed that she was uncertain about her exact role in the company, although she believed she was 'there to encourage, to energise' (Babelet and Babelet 1979: 48). By the time of *L'Age d'or*, however, she was quite sure that collective work did not imply 'the suppression of the specific place of each individual', but relied on everyone occupying their place in a certain 'democratic centralism' so as to ensure 'maximum creativity in each function' fulfilled by them (Mnouchkine in Williams 1999: 57). Her special function was to centralise activity. Mnouchkine, then, defines her role of director in functional terms, which are not the same as hierarchical ones, and has retained her role accordingly to this day.

Création collective after *L'Age d'or* refers to collaboration with delineated artistic tasks. The actors continued to improvise, but no longer invented the script. Mnouchkine wrote *Méphisto* (1979) herself and directed Shakespeare's *Richard II* (1981), *Twelfth Night* (*La Nuit de rois*, 1982) and *Henry IV* (1984). She continued her exploration of 'great' texts with *Les Atrides* (1990–92), a tetralogy in which *Iphigenia in Aulis* by Euripides precedes Aeschylus' *Oresteia* to help audiences understand the events of the latter. Mnouchkine's return to pre-existing texts was motivated by two major difficulties that she had encountered previously: she could not develop the art of the actor, her concern from the very beginning of her career, unless she grasped the principles of acting in Asia; nor could she stage contemporary events adequately unless the whole company learned how Shakespeare and the Greeks had handled their cataclysmic history.

Her need to come to grips with the horrors of our own history led Mnouchkine to feminist author Hélène Cixous, who, she believed, was properly placed as a *writer* to provide the kind of texts she required. Cixous' work sustained the Soleil's humanitarian themes: *Norodom*, on the massacres perpetrated by the Khmer Rouge; *L'Indiade, ou L'Inde de leurs rêves* (*The Indiad, or the India of their Dreams*, 1987), on India's struggle for independence; *La Ville parjure* (*The Perjured City*, 1994), on homelessness and the HIV-contaminated blood scandal in France in the early 1990s; *Les Tambours sur la digue* (*The Flood Drummers*, 1999), on how self-interest and greed destroy communities and whole societies. For *Et soudain*, Cixous arranged the company's hundreds of hours of improvised scenes into four hours. After fifteen years of close collaboration, she must be considered as integral to the Soleil's development.

Création collective also incorporates other activities for which the Soleil is renowned. The actors help to make costumes, sets and props and clean and cook by roster. They prepare meals for audiences as well, whom they serve at a counter in costume and make-up during intervals. This is consistent with Mnouchkine's idea of the theatre as a total event: the place in which a production is performed should be a visual and sensual extension of it. For *Et soudain*, hundreds of small images of Buddha filled the playing area of the Cartoucherie, the disused cartridge factory and warehouse where, with *1789*, the Soleil had made its home. Tibetan food was served, and a gigantic map of the country and its location in Asia covered the entire back wall of the vast central hangar of the Cartoucherie, where people meet, eat and talk. The convivial atmosphere and sense of occasion are fundamental to Mnouchkine's notion of theatricality, understood, here, as a charge bringing the environment and the actors and spectators together.

Space, for Mnouchkine, is not something that is filled, but is structured for the needs of each production. In *1789* it holds multiple platforms to enhance action (often echoed from platform to platform), narrative and movement and to create the excitement of history in the making. Space in the Shakespeare productions has a *hanamichi*-like lay out, allowing actors to gather momentum for superb entrances and exits in leaps and bounds. In *The Flood Drummers*, it is contained, as in a puppet show, which is fitting for a production whose actors play marionettes playing characters (the first and last of its type for the Soleil). The space beneath the tiered seating for the audience is the actors' dressing rooms. In *La Ville parjure*, a runway slopes upwards from it towards the stage. The Furies (Cixous' cross-reference to the Furies of *Les Atrides*) sweep along it to great effect to reach earth from Hades.

Immediacy of impact is one of the defining features of Mnouchkine's theatricality, as is the sense of otherness the actors create through their persona of Actor. Spectators watch them dress and apply elaborate make-up – Mnouchkine's innovation, for European theatre, from Asian tradition. That spectators may witness this crossover from reality to fantasy is essential because Mnouchkine's productions are elliptical figurations of historical events, never literal representations of them. Realism is anathema to Mnouchkine, especially when it involves psychological probing into 'character'. *Et soudain*, for example, deals with the political situation of Tibet through numerous metaphors of displacement and destitution. Its main metaphor is an itinerant troupe of Tibetan performers who stand for the people of Tibet as a whole. A subsidiary metaphor is a homeless tramp who is not realistic, but a mixture of Charlie Chaplin and *commedia dell'arte*'s Arlecchino.

Mnouchkine's premise is that the theatre must use metaphorical transposition, from which the actor's *état* ('state') is inseparable, to speak effectively about the world. *Etat* is very much Mnouchkine's word and defines something intrinsic to her goals:

> In our work, what we call the 'state' is the primary passion which preoccupies the actor. When he is 'angry', he must draw the *anger*, he must *act*. Shakespeare's characters often contemplate their interior landscape. The passion they feel must be translated by the actor. There is a chemistry. It's not just a question of feeling; it's a question of showing. Of course one can't show what one doesn't know or what one can't imagine, but there should be a chemistry, a transformation. An actor is a person who finds a metaphor for an emotion.
>
> (Williams 1999: 96)

An *état* must be extreme, since to temper it would be to succumb to psychological theatre. This idea guides Mnouchkine's persistent direction to actors not to indulge in states, but to move rapidly across them 'in ruptured discontinuity' (ibid.: 8). Actors must always be physically and mentally concentrated – 'there' or 'present', as she puts it – in their successive states so as to project them fully. Apart from drawing on improvisation to achieve these ends, she uses various *commedia* techniques, including acrobatics and masks, and adapts Jacques Lecoq's principles of corporeal expression. In *Le Tartuffe* (1995), for instance, a sideways gait is a metaphor for lust, which combines with other physicalised metaphors (for domination, oppression and so on) to show the production's critique of religious fundamentalism. Metaphoricity gives Mnouchkine tremendous scope for tackling the problems of the world – in disguise, one might say, since metaphor is an indirect mode of address.

Although European physical theatre helped to shape her work, Asian theatre became Mnouchkine's main reference because it provides the technical, emotional, sensual and imaginative resources she needs for an optimal 'theatricality': words, music and dance, together with sumptuous textures and colours in costumes, headgear and make-up. 'Western theatre', she maintains, has created magnificent texts – Shakespeare, Molière and Aeschylus, whom she has staged – but 'Oriental theatre is the art of the actor ... the Orient knows what an actor is'.[2] Her Shakespeare productions explore the dynamics of Kabuki and Noh through the way the actors run with bent knees, hold a pose with knees apart, stylise arm movements, and so on, some recalling Kurosawa's Samurai films. *Les Atrides* draws primarily on Kathakali's articulation of the eyes, hands, fingers and feet, and its use of ornate headgear. *Et soudain* has dances from Tibet, the company having been taught them by the Tibetan performer Dolma Choden. *The Flood Drummers* is an extraordinary attempt at grasping the 'secrets' of Bunraku. Many of Mnouchkine's productions use masks in the manner of Balinese Topeng, on occasion merged with *commedia* mask work. Faces are whitened, as in Kabuki as well as in *commedia* and clowning, while eyes and brows are generally heavily marked out in black. White on faces is also a form of masking. Music is played virtually without a break in all her productions, and can be seen as another reference to performance practices in Asia. Written and performed by Jean-Jacques Lemêtre, who makes most of his instruments, it is full of unusual sounds, but really sounds only like itself.

Mnouchkine's attraction to Asian theatre is by no means unique, but her relationship with it is exceptionally intense for four reasons. She thoroughly explores a broad spectrum of Asian performance forms; concentrates on one form in a production before she focuses on another form; merges these forms with non-Asian texts, contents and contexts; and systematically transforms them in performance for both theatrical and social purposes. Her productions are not Asian. They are a Mnouchkine-variety of European theatre, a culturally and formally hybridised theatre whose aim is to generate emotion, joy and pleasure, and inspire audiences to assess what they see. She believes that her theatre could be described as a 'citizen's theatre' precisely because, over and above any political imperative, spectators are fully capable of exercising their civic responsibility.[3] This, to her mind, is what constitutes a genuine socio-political perspective, which is grounded, of necessity, in individual and collective ethics.

Mnouchkine's seven-hour long *Le Dernier caravansérail* (*Odyssées*) in 2003 no longer appropriates Oriental forms. Here she returns to the principles of *création collective* established by *1789* and to a less metaphorical, more direct and emotionally charged engagement with a 'citizen's theatre'. The production concerns the global situation of refugees. Mnouchkine and several actors collected hundreds of hours of interviews with refugees in the detention centres of Sangatte in France and Villawood in Australia. The company as a whole devised motifs running through these accounts. The result is a montage of powerful incidents in juxtaposed times, places and spaces. It is performed in French, Farsi (for the Iranian and Afghan characters), German, Russian, English and several other languages, the whole indicating linguistically the widely international composition of the some forty actors constituting the company since the 1980s. Displacement, destitution, violence and terror: the Soleil brings home, with verve, the state of humanity today.

Notes

1 My translation.
2 Shevtsova, Maria (1995) 'Sur *La Ville parjure* – Un Théâtre qui parle aux citoyens: entretien avec Ariane Mnouchkine', *Alternatives Théâtrales* 48: 72. Translated by me as 'A Theatre that Speaks to Citizens: Interview with Ariane Mnouchkine', *Western European Stages* 7 (3): 5–12.
3 Ibid.: 72. Mnouchkine affirms that 'when audiences are treated like citizens, they are already being asked to be citizens'.

Further reading

Babelet, Marie-Louise and Babelet, Denis (1979) *Le Théâtre du Soleil ou la quête du bonheur*, Paris: CNRS Editions, Diapolivre.

Kiernander, Adrian (1993) *Ariane Mnouchkine and the Théâtre du Soleil*, Cambridge: Cambridge University Press.

Quillet, Françoise (1999) *L'Orient au Théâtre du Soleil*, Paris: L'Harmattan.

Williams, David (compiled and ed.) (1999) *Collaborative Theatre: The Théâtre du Soleil Sourcebook*, London: Routledge.

MARIA SHEVTSOVA

TADASHI SUZUKI (1939–)

Since 1972, when *On the Dramatic Passions II* was first seen at the Théâtre des Nations Festival in Paris, Suzuki's productions have been acclaimed worldwide for the extraordinary intensity of their acting and their provocative revisioning of classic texts. Tagged '*le Grotowski japonais*' by the French-speaking press, his work was seen as a Kabukiesque realisation of **Artaud**'s 'Theatre of Cruelty'. Underpinning these accolades was a training system based on a new synthesis of traditional and modern techniques and a rigorously original application of surrealism to the 'making visible' of human fantasies. This used a postmodern collage of classical plays, the familiarity of which helped foreground the originality of their semantic reorganisation.

Suzuki claims that 'the actor composes ... on the basis of ... sense of contact with the ground' (Rimer 1986: 8) and that this 'determines even the strength and nuance of the actor's voice' (ibid.: 6). As he told James Brandon in 1976:

> Suppression [*tame*] is fundamental to traditional Japanese theatre.... There is nothing natural about a *mie* (squint-eyed pose) or the leaping *roppô* exit in Kabuki.... So there is this almost unbearable tension in the actor ... using unnatural movements and voice to express natural emotions.... The Kabuki actor engulfs the spectator in his overwhelmingly dynamic stage image. *The secret of this kind of acting is instantaneous release of suppressed action, then [further] suppression ... [release] and so on....* I suppose you call it tension, but it is not muscular tension, it is psychological tension.
>
> (Brandon 1978: 29–42; my italics)

But Suzuki is not atavistic. In showing his awareness that powerful foot-stamping was 'originally used to magically ward off evil', as Origuchi Shinobu claims, Suzuki is equally aware that, in the contemporary world, its usage is simply to 'eradicate the ordinary, everyday sense of the body' in order to build a powerfully expressive stage presence (Rimer 1986: 11). For him, 'the [actor's] self must answer to the desires that other people place upon them.... The actor's role can be compared to the role of a "shaman" in this respect'.[1] He knows that the strongest contemporary 'possession' is likely to be consumerist and signals it by arming Chekhov's three sisters with Department Store shopping bags when they pine for Moscow, and by placing large cylindrical red-and-white Marlboro ash-cans on the stage of his *Bacchae*. As Heiner Müller puts it pithily in *Hamletmachine*, 'Heil Coca Cola'.

Suzuki's postmodern training and acting style work best in performance spaces that combine elements old and new. Isozaki Arata's renovated farmhouse, the Mountain Hall (*Sanbô*) Theatre, with its high-tech anodised aluminium dance floor, is reminiscent of, but significantly *different* from, a Noh space. The latter has its one point of stage entry and exit along the *hashigakari* (raised walkway); however Suzuki's Mountain Hall ingeniously and economically 'consists of two walkways which themselves serve as the playing space. In between the forward and rear walkways, a flexible partition-like structure (*shôji*) is installed' (ibid.: 23). Any of these shutters, whether paper, wood or reflecting/opaque glass can become an exit or entry point. His playing space aims to optimise continuous flows of movement (elsewhere, he has referred to the director as 'a traffic conductor'):[2]

> It is my view ... that a modern man, who has no place to call his own and whose gods have departed, lives best on the kind of stage I have constructed. All of us, at all times, everywhere now seem to live a life of composed passages.
>
> (Ibid.: 24)

For example, in a production of *Electra* at the Delphi Stadium in 1995, Suzuki used zebra-crossing walkways that intersected 'at the navel of the world'. These suggested both a modern traffic intersection and an abode of the dead, for the black and white strips of cloth he used were Japanese funeral awnings. Such flexible playing spaces, in which architectural structures and set designs frame and accentuate actor rhythms and proxemics, are well suited to Suzuki's postmodern style of performance and collage of texts.

The aforementioned principle of suppression (*tame*) underwrites Suzuki's training system. To create a strong sense of presence on stage, the actor needs to build an artificial sense of resistance in the *hara* (the psycho-physical centre between the hips). This is the home of the breath, the platform on which we place our torso, our centre of gravity. Suzuki has likened the basic pre-acting position of body-readiness (*kamae*) to a Boeing 747 on the runway just before take-off: engines are revving at high speed, but the brakes are on. Nowhere on stage is this tension completely relaxed. In the words of Kanze Hideo: 'Energy ... is the consequence of tension between opposing forces.'[3] In Japanese performance tradition, this state is called *hippari-ai*.[4]

One of the mental images given to help the trainee find the necessary resistance-energy in the *hara* is that of the actor as a puppet: one string pulls upwards from the crown of the head, another drags downward from the pelvis, a third draws forward from the belly button and a fourth restrains from the small of the back. All of these imagined lines of force help to build resistance in the centre. With practice the actor can get into this charged state instantly just by going into *kamae* (the 'ready' position), but the trainee needs further disciplines to help build deeper awareness of this sensibility.

Amongst other exercises, Suzuki has also devised a series of artificial walks, each of which challenges the centre of balance in expressively distinctive ways.[5] How this feeds into performance expressivity can be suggested by an example from *The Chronicle of Macbeth* (1992) in which the Farewell Cult 'witches' entered to 'Slow Walks', holding a copy of *Macbeth* as their catechism; in training, the specific way each actor found to walk with the book became the first stage of a physical exploration of individual case histories of collective obsession and despair.

As the above suggests, Suzuki training is a structured system that aims to build energy, stamina, stability and concentration in a modular, choral manner. It moves from the simple to the complex, and from the mechanical to the creative. Creativity is an individual matter and is revealed by the quality of the individual actor's imaginative engagement with the different sensibilities generated in each exercise and their technical ability to relate combinations of these 'patterns' to the expressive needs of the performance moment. Suzuki provides space for his actors' own creativity. For instance, in *The Chronicle of Macbeth*, the three actors involved in Lady Macbeth's sleepwalking scene choreographed their own presentation at home (within the guidelines set) before Suzuki set about refining and shaping it in rehearsals.

The actor's ability to fascinate is created by the amount and quality of energy radiated by the body in all directions. This energy is built through a coherent system of restraint (*tame*). As in Noh, the actor builds presence by creating the will to move, but deliberately holds back on doing so until the inner tension becomes unbearably high. Once in motion, the goal is to become conscious of the body's entire structure as a kind of moving sculpture. The influence of Kabuki principles, in which action flows from one climactic freeze-pose (*mie*) to the next, is clear here – but so are its affinities with non-Japanese theatre forms. **Meyerhold**, in particular, refers to the stage as 'a pedestal for sculpture'.[6]

While Suzuki has admitted that his training could serve other styles of performance, he asserts that, for him, it both emerges out of his postmodern awareness of the fissures in our world and serves his dramaturgical underlining of those 'gaps' (Ryuta, Carruthers and Gillies 2001: 199):

> I think I'm close to Beckett.... This means I believe there is no absolute standard which can objectify the self or establish identity.... But what I'm saying is that people who live in the real world also have fantasies and illusions. And I'm saying that these have no end and cannot be solved.
>
> (Ibid.: 201–202)

Suzuki's long term concentration on this problematic channels his work between narrow banks in an extraordinarily deep, rich and strange way. As he has observed: 'Usually an insane person is my main character' (ibid.: 196). By collaging and replaying theatre classics – such as *The Trojan Women*, *King Lear* and *The Cherry Orchard* – through the distorting consciousness of a senile, mad or alienated man or woman, he underwrites a strategy for uncovering and 'making visible' the invisible world of the human subconscious by which we are all 'possessed'.[7] Suzuki is perhaps unique amongst contemporary directors in choosing to base his theatrical life work on an exploration of this ubiquitous, but hitherto largely unexplored territory.

The critic Senda Akihiko observes:

> It's rather easy to be radical and carried away by ideas [in the theatre], and Suzuki knows very well that this is often achieved when the lower body is forgotten. Against the 'floating' quality of ideas, Suzuki and his company set 'miserableness' as a sign of the lower body. This feeling is a constant thread running throughout the drama he produces.... This 'miserableness' in the form of theatrical expression opens a fissure at many different levels of human existence. On Suzuki's stage, the upper and lower halves of the body – the conceptual and physical, the conscious and unconscious, dream and reality, script and body language – always have a big gap between them, though they are also entwined and in a state of tension and struggle.
>
> (Saitoh 1982: 151–152)

In Suzuki's words:

> If I gave a script to my actors, they would give it a psycho-logical reading.... They would kill it. That was why I [first] tried in *Dramatic Passions I* [1969] to separate the lines from their concrete physical self-consciousness on stage. I was trying to cancel out the lines' [original] significance and create a semantic field in which there was no correct approach' to lean on.... I don't do a reading of the script.... The best action is to create a whirlpool of new material creation out of the old.
>
> (Ibid.: 152–153)

Acting technique, dramaturgical collage of play materials and eclectic *mise-en-scène* are all combined to emphasise our 'ungrounded' post-modern cultural condition. For example, in *Dramatic Passions II*, the set is constructed to symbolise the subconscious of an old woman locked up by her daughter who amuses herself by acting out scenes from her favourite Kabuki and Shinpa plays. As the lights go up, numerous *shôji* (paper doors) are revealed, hung from the ceiling in a seemingly haphazard pattern that suggests a surrealist collage – perhaps even a Cubist fragmentation of the humanist organisation of experience through 'character and setting'. As the stage directions indicate, they 'look as if they're flying away into the sky' like the old woman's thoughts, unmoored from their everyday contexts.

Like the Noh fan, Suzuki's props can take on different significa-tions through inter-subjectivity. In *Dramatic Passions II*, the old woman triumphantly presents a toilet roll to Sakura as 'our family treasure, the Miyakodori scroll'. In *Three Sisters*, the ways Olga, Masha and Irena hold open umbrellas overhead, even when eating a meal, suggest their differing obsessions, while Juliet's umbrella in *Waiting for Romeo* takes on a life of its own, indicating the strength of her desire by tugging her about like a puppet whenever 'Romeo' passes. In *The Chronicle of Macbeth*, when the old man who imagines himself to be Macbeth demands 'Give me mine armour!', Seyton-the-cook's response is to take the napkin that had covered his meals-on-wheels dinner and tie it round the neck of this nursing home 'Macbeth' like a bib.

Suzuki's costumes and music also serve to indicate 'gaps'. In *Ivanov*, Suzuki takes his cue from Chekhov's reference to the local gentry as 'Zulus' to physicalise our sense of Ivanov's alienation.[8] He dresses them in weird lampshade hats and military decorations, plastic horn-rim glasses and false noses, and places them in baskets (as 'basket cases') and wheelchairs (as the spiritually challenged). Suzuki says:

> For me plays present what goes on inside of us. For example, when an ambitious person trying to reform society is worn down or made a scapegoat by other people, he begins to lose confidence and feels a growing sense of isolation from his surroundings; he loses interest in others and starts to see them as aliens. As a result he either becomes autistic or easily emotional and escapes into a hobby or solitude. I wanted to describe the process by which one falls into 'madness' through rupture with the external world, whether through excessive self-reflection, daydreaming or being oppressed.[9]

To increase this sense in *Ivanov*, Roger Reynolds' specially commissioned music suggests such things as lonely whale calls and the creaks and groans of a submarine that, to avoid attack, has dived too deep. In *Trojan Women*, on the other hand, a blast of pop music (*enka*) returns us from the dream of a dispossessed old bag-lady to the harsh realities of her wasteland world.

As Charles Jencks reminds us, postmodernism is 'conceived as a wide language which cuts across high and low taste cultures with a double-coding that still holds the integrity of each voice'.[10] Through intercultural productions that sustain the integrity of differently coded voices, Suzuki has spent thirty years exploring the gap between traditional and modern, and mainstream and marginal cultures. Perhaps the clearest example of this is his *Bacchae*, in which mixed casts of Japanese and American actors speak powerfully to each other – and to their audiences at home and abroad – through signs and in tongues (Carruthers and Yasunari 2004: chapter 7).

Notes

1 Deborah Leiser-Moore's Toga training notes: 6.
2 Interview following *Dionysus* in the NHK TV series *Suzuki Tadashi no sekai* (The World of Suzuki Tadashi), July 1993.
3 Barba, Eugenio and Savarese, Nicola (1991) *A Dictionary of Theatre Anthropology: The Secret Art of the Performer*, London: Methuen: 12.
4 Ibid.
5 For descriptions of these walks and how they may be creatively applied to performance, see Carruthers and Yasunari (2004).

6 Braun, Edward (1969) *Meyerhold on Theatre*, London: Methuen: 89, 91.
7 Suzuki, Tadashi (1973) *Naikaku no wa: Suzuki Tadashi engeki ronshū (The Sum of the Interior Angles: Suzuki Tadashi's Collected Theatre Writings)*, Tokyo: Jiritsushôbô: 54, 317–318.
8 Fen, Elisaveta (trans.) (1954) *Chekhov Plays*, Harmondsworth: Penguin: 64.
9 Interview following *Ivanov* in the NHK TV series *Suzuki Tadashi no sekai*, trans. Kazuko Eguchi and Ian Carruthers.
10 Papadakis, Andreas (ed.) (1990) *Post-Modernism on Trial*, London: Academy Group: 25.

Further reading

Brandon, James (1978) 'Training at the Waseda Little Theatre: The Suzuki Method', *The Drama Review* 22: 4.
Carruthers, Ian and Yasunari, Takahashi (2004) *The Theatre of Suzuki Tadashi*, Cambridge: Cambridge University Press.
Rimer, J. Thomas (1986) *The Way of Acting: the Theatre Writings of Tadashi Suzuki*, New York: Theatre Communications Group.
Ryuta, Minami, Carruthers, Ian and Gillies, John (eds) (2001) *Performing Shakespeare in Japan*, Cambridge: Cambridge University Press.
Saitoh, Setsurô (ed.) (1982) *Suzuki Tadashi no sekai*, Tokyo: Shinpyôsha.

IAN CARRUTHERS

PINA BAUSCH (1940–)

Famously saying that she was 'not so much interested in how people move as in what moves them', Pina Bausch has developed a theatre of dance energised by the visceral emotions which also provide its enduring themes.[1] Anxiety, insecurity, pain, humiliation, abjection and fear predominate, unmitigated by the abundant quirky humour and irony and, on occasion, satire of her work. However, the need for love is shown to power above all else the vying tensions she perceives to be integral to human relationships, the latter essentially defined by gender and sexual antagonisms. Never before has dance so openly embraced the everyday realities which have historically been the concern of the theatre, or so radically generated hybrid and crossover idioms.

Bausch founded the Tanztheater Wuppertal in 1973. She trained under Kurt Jooss until 1959 at the Folkswang Hoschule in Essen where she acquired the principles of classical ballet as well as those of *Ausdruckstanz*, the theatrical 'expression dance' of the 1910s and 1920s revived in Germany after the Second World War. Previous exponents included Mary Wigman, Rudolf Laban and Jooss himself. She studied at the Juilliard School of Music in New York and performed with the New American Ballet directed by Antony Tudor. She returned to Germany in 1962 to explore the idea that was to underly her entire choreographic production, namely, that movement is not primarily a matter of technique, virtuosity, or shape and image, but is a process through which human beings discover each other and themselves.

Like all great innovators, Bausch uses her pedigree to transcend it. She subverts the canons of classical ballet, no more cruelly than in *Bandeon* (1980) when a dancer dances *en pointe* while the blood oozes from the raw steaks she had ostentatiously stuffed inside her shoes. Bausch tirelessly extends the expressive possibilities of the human body as she questions the very notion of dance for the stage. Thus she incorporates numerous forms of social dancing in her pieces – ballroom/party/line dancing in *Kontakthof*, for example (1978; to 1930s movie music), or the non-Western styles which she adapts to her explorations, as occurs in a step-and-sway chain dance sequence in *Masurca Fogo* (1998; to Cape Verde popular music and song).

The dancing body liberated of constraints also has limitless potential for violence. This is especially clear in *Café Müller* (1978) where, in a role reserved for herself, Bausch repeatedly hits her body against a wall before her character falls into a comotose state. Another dancer repeatedly hurls herself onto the floor or slaps her body onto a table. The harsh noise of this physical abuse becomes part of the work's rhythmic patterns, showing, as does Dido's lament from Purcell's *Dido and Aeneas* which accompanies Bausch's confrontation with the wall, how skillfully she underscores events with sound, musical or otherwise, instead of interpreting or illustrating them in any narratorial or psychological kind of way.

By the same token, she exploits theatrical devices. A Brechtian-style *Verfremdungseffekt* fractures physically demanding as well as poignant moments. Direct address to the audience in cabaret chatter, random lines or fragments of the performers' personal stories, which they usually speak impersonally, counterpoint the movement phrases. Her aesthetic has been described as 'not dance in the conventional sense, since her dancers seldom dance. It isn't orthodox theatre in that dialogue does not sustain her drama' (Cody 1998: 119). Montage structures, generally on a monumental scale and of long duration (most of her later works are evening-length), throw into relief the dance variations, re-iterations, distortions and elisions, and sharp compositional and emotional reversals that surprise, delight and discomfort audiences. All of these effects are designed to stimulate perception on multiple planes where questions about dance-theatre are also questions about social life, and where nothing can be held to be unequivocally true.

Indeed, Bausch cultivates equivocation to an unprecedented degree. The suave men in beautifully cut suits who feature in so many of her pieces cause spectators to reflect upon the elegance of lithe and relaxed bodies in motion. Yet they also inspire doubt. Do they comment on social decorum, on social oppression, or on the particular type of oppression of women generated by overconfident, self-possessed men? Are the women in various states of dress or undress, according to a given scene, sex objects, victims, predators or sanely empowered agents of their own actions? What does clothing signify beyond the daily grind of social appearances? Are the stiletto heels of her women dancers – a Bausch trademark – signs of desire, seduction, weapons of destruction (in a misogynistic scenario) or merely of self-inflicted torture (in a sado-masochistic script)? And the exhibitionistic quality of the dance invites variegated responses in that it is liberating, sensual, aggressive, comically self-mocking and seriously self-indulgent all at once.

Spectators, like the performers, are kept alert by the shifting perspectives opened out by each piece, and by the body of her work as a whole, and given the freedom to see according to their own predilections. In this way, and more than any other choreographer preceding her or who has been inspired by her, Bausch engages spectators directly in the choreographic process. The fact that her dancers speak to the audience from the edge of the stage – more recently in her 1997 *Der Fensterputzer* (*The Window Cleaner*) – stresses the importance of such engagement. This is given a new twist in the 2000 revised version of *Kontakthof* performed by people over the age of sixty-five who have relinquished the status of spectator for that of dancer-actor. Here might well lie the strongest case for understanding Bausch's most recent work, including *Wiesenland* (2000) and *Água* (2001), as epitomising current concerns about the agency of individuals and how they are increasingly disempowered by controlling global forces.

Bausch's crossover principle underpins such early dance-opera as *Iphigenie auf Tauris* (1975) and *Blaubart* (1977) where Bartók's music is reorganised for the sake of the work's claustrophobic atmosphere. The women's long hair, apart from bearding their faces in a dark joke on the opera's themes of autocracy and murder, is used as a dance element. Bausch had already explored its whiplash movements in *Le Sacre du printemps* (1975) and was to return to it thereafter, even obsessively. She was to rework *Le Sacre* for the Ballet de l'Opéra National de Paris in 1997, mindful of this company's extraordinary balletic training. She uses short film clips or else projects on-going series of images onto transparent screens, as occurs in *Masurca Fogo* where, in a witty *trompe l'œil*, dancers sleep in gigantic blossoms that wave and close like anemones beneath the sea. Her experience of acting in Fellini's *And the Ship Sails On* (1983) led her to her film-dance *The Lament of the Empress* (1987–90).

No one has so thoroughly transformed the surface of performance space with natural elements, thereby affecting the execution of movement. Turf covers the floor of *Le Sacre*, dead leaves that of *Blaubart*, carnations for *Nelken* (1982), mud for *Viktor* (1986). Dancers perform in water up to their shins in *Arien* (1979), in the rubble of a concrete wall that crumbles on stage in *Palermo, Palermo* (1990), up and down uneven slopes and on salt in *Tanzabend 2* (1991), on a mound of red tulip petals in *Der Fensterputzer* and among the forest of redwoods on the stage of *Nur Du* (*Only You*, 1996). These environments expose the dancers to physical danger as they evoke political associations (the Berlin wall and the decay of urban living in *Palermo, Palermo*) or ecological ones. They may contain nostalgic references to a 'lost' countryside and perhaps wry thoughts on the cult of nature expressed in *Ausdruckstanz* as practised by Laban.

Animals, too, recall the organic world. There are hens and dogs. Alsatian dogs reined in by guards in *Nelken* suggest Nazi camps. A black poodle appears in *Two Cigarettes in the Dark* (1985), a sheep in *Viktor*. A fake hippopotamus creates laughter in *Arien*. Objects create obstacles, as do the numerous chairs of *Café Müller*, and function like ready-mades in the manner of Marcel Duchamps or Andy Warhol. Cigarettes, toys, washing bowls and other domestic items recall humdrum everyday life. Red balloons dress a woman in *Masurca Fogo* in a gag about women as market goods.

Articles of clothing, notably the frocks occasionally worn by men, suggest you make do with what you find. There is nothing pantomimic about these images of cross-dressing, although they may well be a wink at dance transvestism from ballet to cabaret and club drag. Nor are they hip, although Bausch was a trend-setter in using them in serious-art contemporary dance without any qualms or any inhibition. Rather, they query the idea of fixed gender identities, often with some *angst*. Bausch contours her dance as well from what could be termed *mouvements trouvés* such as walking, washing, carrying babies, caressing, kissing, smoking and all sorts of less obvious routine movements. The less likely their provenance, the more startling they appear to the spectator's eye.

Devising is key to Bausch's practice. She asks her dancers a wide range of questions on which they improvise, and asks them to push back their psychological limits while they go 'from the inside out', as she puts it, as if she were quoting **Stanislavsky**.[2] Bausch uses their personal experiences, especially their anxieties, as the very subject matter of performance. Cues reorient their direction as she edits and re-edits their inventions. Instead of being crafted upon, they craft themselves into what eventually become performance pieces. Such participation in choreography gives dancers a sense of ownership. Bausch's approach as a whole is shared not so much by choreographers (William Forsythe being a major exception) as by experimental theatre directors, and resembles most of all the working methods of Lev **Dodin**. She has not yet been superseded, even by the most border-breaking choreographers of today, in her sublime celebration of the mental and physical powers of dancers who are consummate performers in the strongest sense of this term.

Notes

1   Quoted in Manning, S. Allene and Benson, M. (1986) 'Interrupted Continuities: Modern Dance in Germany', *The Drama Review* 30 (2): 43.
2   Quoted in Hoghe, R. (1987) *Pina Bausch: Histoires de théâtre dansé*, Paris: L'Arche: 42.

Further reading

Cody, G. (1998) 'Woman, Man, Dog, Tree: Two Decades of Intimate and Monumental Bodies in Pina Bausch's Tanztheater', *The Drama Review* 42 (2): 115–129.

Manning, S. Allene (1986) 'An American Perspective on Tanztheater', *The Drama Review* 30 (2): 57–79.

Müller, H. and Servos, N. (1984) 'Expressionism? "Ausdruckstanz" and the New Dance Theatre in Germany', *Dance Theatre Journal* 2 (1): 11–15.

Servos, N. (1984) *Pina Bausch Wuppertal Tanztheater or The Art of Training a Goldfish*, trans. P. Stadié, Cologne: Ballett-Bühnen-Verlag.

MARIA SHEVTSOVA

REX CRAMPHORN (1941–91)

In 1985, Rex Cramphorn staged *Hamlet* and *Measure for Measure* in repertory at the Playbox Theatre in Melbourne.

> The plays were presented on a bare stage, around which the actors and one musician sat or knelt on small Japanese stools and were visible to the audience throughout. The stage was lit with a broad wash of white light, and the only lighting change was a low light state for the night scenes. The actors and musician supplied music and sound effects using small percussion instruments and tuned wine glasses … the minimal setting, props and lighting meant that the actors' and audiences' concentration was entirely on words and position….[1]

The stage itself was painted with an interlocking red, green, silver and black pattern characteristic of Cramphorn's over-coding of spatial relations. Many of his projects featured such designs marked out on the bare platform stage, schematising and activating spatial semiotics, and foregrounding the proxemic relations between characters. Across this bare space, transected by vectors and tangents, the characters would move with geometric precision. As Mark Minchinton, an actor who worked extensively with Cramphorn, notes, this rigorous stripping back of theatrical apparatus made huge demands upon actors and audience alike, a reflection of Cramphorn's desire to make theatre *hard* – an exacting experience. Minchinton recalls that '[t]ypically, he had little interest in what audiences made of the productions, remarking that he thought audiences should have to sit an exam before attending'.[2]

The 1985 *Hamlet* and *Measure* were the culmination of The Actors' Development Stream at the Playbox, one of Cramphorn's ill-fated attempts to establish an ensemble company of actors committed to a sustained, intensive examination of the actor–director relationship. A desire to work with such a company drove Cramphorn throughout his career. Towards the end of his life, he was still pursuing that goal, seeking funding for an ensemble company which would work towards the

> establishment of a performance style which arises directly from a close study of classic texts (i.e. a style in conscious reaction to or developed in full awareness of current naturalism) with an aesthetic which is appropriate to an heir of

English-speaking tradition with a multicultural future in a
Southeast Asian location … a classic company, capable of
drawing from the best available academic and professional
resources and developing a valid Australian contribution to
world theatre.[3]

The company was never set up. Cramphorn, having spent close to
two decades struggling against a tide of theatrical conservatism,
instead enrolled as a student at the Australian Film, Television and
Radio School, pursuing his love of cinema instead.

Cramphorn's was a career characterised by sustained attempts to
establish a vital, new theatre within what he saw as an oppressively
conservative, anti-intellectual and institutionally unsupportive
milieu. In 1968, Cramphorn took stock of the state of play in local
theatre, writing of the 'free-for-all commercial struggle with no
security of any kind, no opportunity for learning':[4]

No one here is experimenting with acting … [a] nation as
politically and socially apathetic as we are is unlikely to
have anything serious to say in a theatre. Until theatre has
something serious to say, or a distinctive statement to make
– that is, until it demands to be taken seriously – it will
remain a withering mistletoe on our gum-tree culture.[5]

As Cramphorn observed, 'in Australia, the "newest" theatre comes
from overseas … it begins and ends with the *Time* review. Like sex-
educated children we know it all without experience'.[6] The only
counter-model of theatre available in Australia at the time was that
of the Melbourne Theatre Company, where George Ogilvie – a
student of Lecoq, and an acting tutor under Peter **Brook** at the
Royal Shakespeare Company in the early 1960s – was able to maintain an ensemble of 'twenty or so actors' engaged in daily classes and
working in an environment in which 'actors can develop and directors experiment'.[7]

Rather than yielding to the temptation simply to stop wasting his
time writing about such a desolate theatrical culture, Cramphorn
instead composed a manifesto for a new Australian theatre:

I take theatre's unique asset to be the actor's physical presence, and I take its major misdirection to be the foisting of
psychological realism, what Artaud calls 'storytelling
psychology' on him.[8]

Alternatives to the sclerotic insularity of emergent Australian naturalism – the 'gum-tree culture' – would require 'an elastic training scheme as a basis for arduous research and experiment, resulting in an original stylistic communication of an unforeseeable nature, but relevant to its Australian environment in the way that, say, Grotoski's [sic] is to Poland'.[9] Cramphorn's was to be an indigenous Australian theatre, but one based upon the revolutionary training, practices and ensemble ideas of **Grotowski** and **Copeau**, the writings of **Artaud** and a repertoire built on a balance of devised work and European classical texts – in particular, those of Shakespeare and the French neo-classicists (which he translated for himself).

Towards the end of 1969, Cramphorn and a group of recently graduated actors got hold of a photocopy of the just-published English translation of Grotowski's seminal text, *Towards A Poor Theatre*. Spurred by their collective distaste for the professional and commercial theatre, the group worked systematically through Grotowski's exercises. In 1970 this core group joined with three other graduates to form a company for a season of productions at the Jane Street Theatre. Generous funding from the Australian Council for the Arts allowed the company of seven actors and three directors to work as an ensemble with commissioned writers on new texts. Rehearsals started in March 1970 with eight weeks of full-time classes in yoga, movement, mime, singing, voice work and 'Brechtian' acting. The classes continued for a further four weeks as the company moved into improvisations with preliminary script ideas. Each of the season's three productions was then rehearsed full time for two weeks. Cramphorn directed the season's second work, a meditation on themes of exploration titled *10,000 Miles Away*. The company worked with the Grotowskian model, developing from a range of tumbling and falling exercises a physical language of flight, flow and continuous movement, generating in turn a percussive performance rhythm. This was augmented by a series of texts contributed by Willy Young, reflecting his own particular interests: space travel, the film *2001: A Space Odyssey* and endurance cycling.[10]

10,000 Miles Away began with the cast, dressed in white judo suits, meditating on a square white mat as the audience entered, taking seats on two sides of the performance space. A narrative developed out of apparently meaningless chanting: four of the performers – the core 'Grotowski group' – were space travellers in search of distant radio signals, the 'Siren Song' that drew them away from 'Home Base'. Their journey was rendered as a clockwise running around the central mats. The actors ran

> till their feet blistered and bled.... Their running vibrates the building, giving a constant percussive accompaniment to speech in which the words are often just sounds ... the performers test the limits of human endurance. They go beyond speed, beyond death, and in [a section titled] 'Supersex' in countless bouts of lovemaking, beyond pleasure. The limitations of their flesh are left behind.[11]

One reviewer suggested that 'Grotowski from 10,000 miles away' might have been a more appropriate title (*The Australian*, 8 July 1970) – certainly the work contrasted markedly with the talk-heavy, naturalistic Australian-ness dominating local stages.

More importantly, the whole experience suggested a sustainable model for innovative, actor-based work. Cramphorn and the core members of the company applied to the Australian Council for the Arts under the name 'Performance Syndicate', the first of Cramphorn's four attempts to create ensemble companies which would provide financial and artistic stability for actors, writers and directors. Performance Syndicate is best remembered for *The Tempest* (1972), set on a flat stage, surrounded by the audience, with the cast sitting around the edges providing musical accompaniment. 'Asian in music, in look ... the performance astonished utterly', wrote one reviewer:

> Each gesture of finger, of foot, of body, was mannered.... Drums reverberated; flutes played; bells and finger cymbals clanged and tinkled; a dulcimer, guitar and harmonium lent plagency. The tempest broke, symbolized by thunder on the drums, and by lightning – banners of white cloth zig-zagging through the air.... The island [was] marked out by a [chalked] magician's circle.[12]

In the course of preparing and touring *The Tempest*, the ensemble discovered 'a new unifying interest in the development of musical skills ... learning to play a new instrument and improvising together were seen as a parallel to the actor's skill'.[13]

At the same time, however, the ensemble-as-commune ideal was fraying: the lack of a secure rehearsal and performance venue, the pressures of touring, the lack of sustained funding, and drug use were taking their toll. A decision to accept a residency at St Martin's Theatre in Melbourne for six months in 1973 proved disastrous: the Syndicate found itself at loggerheads with a management fearful of losing its conservative subscribers, pressuring the company to deliver commercially viable productions and unwilling to provide the promised financial resources to sustain class work. By 1975 the experiment was over. By the late 1970s Cramphorn was moving increasingly towards academic circles, within which, he noted, 'I seem to be a raffish experiment' although 'in practical circles I get branded as an academic'.[14] Another attempt to establish an ensemble company – the Paris Theatre, with Jim **Sharman** – failed, and Cramphorn went to work as a freelance director for major subsidised companies.

In 1980 Cramphorn received a major grant to work with a group of actors for six months on Shakespeare. 'A Shakespeare Company' was Cramphorn's experiment with what he called an 'anti-interpretational focus' and an 'unimposed directorial style'. Salaried for twenty-four weeks, nine actors were able to withdraw from the busy routine of normal demands made on them and to participate in an administrative and artistic 'democracy'. In many ways the project was a critique of the director as auteur. A few years later, Cramphorn quoted Copeau to explain his approach:

> Nothing is more frightening than a director who has ideas. The director's role is not to have ideas but to understand and communicate those of the author; not to force them or reduce them to nothing but to translate them faithfully into the language of theatre…. What is for others just a string of words, black on white … for the director is straight away a world of forms, sounds, colour and movement. They aren't invented, they are discovered.[15]

A Shakespeare Company experimented with open rehearsals, cross- and contrary-to-type-casting, a rigorously academic approach to the texts – *Two Gentlemen of Verona* and *Measure for Measure* – and various forms of documentation of the process.

As Resident Director at the Playbox Company in Melbourne, where, once again, he confronted the limits of experimentation within a major company milieu, Cramphorn developed the Actors' Development Stream: a core company of actors working on classic texts and structured around nine statements of principle, ranging from an assertion of 'each individual's right to be here' through 'a belief in theatre as a spiritual, political, social microcosm', to the desire to 'build a new aesthetic from our differences'.[16] These ideals were accompanied by practical exercises which formed the basis of the ensemble's daily practice, and elaborate schematisations of rehearsal processes: a four-week block focused on script analysis – Cramphorn called this the 'Question' phase – followed by a six-week rehearsal 'Answer' phase. At the core of Cramphorn's schema is this formulation of the work of theatre:

Philosophical Frame: A belief in the relevance of the work to the audience ... to *be* the meaning not to demonstrate it.

Practical Aims: To allow the audience to make its own connections; to engage an audience; to endow the audience with the power of discernment, with wit and knowledge; to stimulate the circular nature of the communication.

Practical Exercises: Each actor has 'a line' – a spine scenario, a meaning; Each 'line' converges in a unified presentation (with an overall meaning on which all agree).... Every action is necessary; We are aware of the audience/stage relationship and we develop the performance in relation to the specific demands of the theatre space being used.[17]

Once again, commercial pressures overwhelmed even modest ambition: the Playbox Actors' Development Stream was wound up by 1985. Cramphorn returned to Sydney to attend film school, having failed to secure funding for his own company, which was to have been called Performance Syndicate 2. In the course of seeking that funding, Cramphorn again articulated his thinking about rehearsal:

I do not see rehearsal as a process in which the meaning, intellectually perceived from reading a difficult or obscure text, is imposed on the material to clarify it (still less do I now see it as a process which attempts to re-animate the text without any attempt to clarify it), but rather as one in which an unformed but actual entity is coaxed into physical materialisation using the minds and bodies available with whatever compromises of the original text are needed to make the present manifestation accurately communicable.[18]

Such an approach, of course, is not without risks. As Minchinton observes, Cramphorn's cultivation of autonomy on the part of actors did not appeal to everyone:

when working with actors unable or unwilling to step out
of the routines of mainstream work he could be cruel in
refusing to acknowledge or to work with their confusion.[19]

Minchinton notes Cramphorn's 'inability or unwillingness to negotiate' when tension arose between his own understanding of a play
and the results of his commitment to allowing actors to 'find and
express their own agendas and needs' in response to that play.
'Cramphorn', he observed, 'did not like conflict, and seemed unable
to deal with it explicitly – as a colleague put it, he often "just disappeared" '.[20]

Most actors loved working with Cramphorn, and would take any
opportunity to work with him, right up to the weeks preceding his
death when he was working, again, on *The Tempest*. His determination to give actors time, space and creative responsibility, to create
conditions within which actors might develop their own craft and
take on roles that otherwise, for reasons of sex, age, race, physical
characteristics and so on, they might never play, has had effects still
being felt today in Australian theatre. At a time when the dream of
an ensemble company is more remote than ever, Cramphorn's
legacy has, in no small way sowed the seeds of possibility for what
theatre in Australia might, one day, become.

Notes

1 Minchinton, Mark (2001) 'Rex Cramphorn and "Measure for
  Measure", 1973–88' in Golder, John and Madelaine, Richard (eds) *O
  Brave New World: Two Centuries of Shakepeare on the Australian Stage*,
  Sydney: Currency Press: 206.
2 Ibid.
3 Cramphorn, R., 'Professional Stocktaking', attachment to an application
  to the Theatre Board of the Australia Council, in 'Papers of Rex Roy
  Cramphorn', Box 20, file S. Much of the material used in this chapter
  has been taken directly from Cramphorn's personal papers, archived at
  the Department of Performance Studies at the University of Sydney.
  Cramphorn published his reviews in *The Bulletin* and *Sunday Australian*
  as Rex Cramphorne, dropping the 'e' (a parent's affectation) in the mid-
  1970s.
4 Cramphorne, R. (1968) 'Ideals and Actualities', *The Bulletin*, 9
  November: 24.
5 Cramphorne, R. (1970) 'A Withering Mistletoe on our Gum-Tree
  Culture', *The Bulletin*, 3 January: 29.
6 Cramphorne (1969) 'Theatre in Sydney', *The Bulletin*, 4 January: 39.
7 Cramphorne (1968).
8 Cramphorne (1970).
9 Ibid.

10 Spinks, Kim (1985) '10,000 Miles Away', *Aspect Art and Literature Nos 32–33: Theatre in Australia*: 12–23.
11 Ibid.: 12, 18.
12 Frizell, Helen (1973) 'A Tempest is Brewing – On and Off Stage', *Sydney Morning Herald*, 6 August: 6.
13 Cramphorn, R. (1974) Application to the Australian Council for the Arts.
14 Cramphorn, R. (1976) Address to the Inaugural Conference of the Australian Theatre Studies Centre (University of New South Wales), August.
15 Cramphorn, R. (1985) Application to the Australia Council, quoting Kim Spinks' translation of Copeau, Jacques (1974) 'Une rénovation dramatique est-elle possible?' in *Registres I: Appels*, Paris: Editions Gallimard: 268–269.
16 Playbox Actors Development Stream document, 1984.
17 Ibid.
18 Cramphorn (1985).
19 Minchinton, Mark (1998) 'The Right and Only Direction: Rex Cramphorn, Shakespeare, and the Actors' Development Stream', *Australasian Drama Studies* 33: 132.
20 Ibid.: 143.

Further reading

Cramphorn, R. (1987) '*L'Illusion Comique* to *Theatrical Illusion*: Textual Changes for Performance' in McAuley, G. (ed.) *From Page to Stage: L'Illusion Comique*, Sydney: University of Sydney Theatre Studies Services Unit: 59–71.

McAuley, G. (1999) *Space in Performance: Making Meaning in the Theatre*, Ann Arbor: University of Michigan Press.

Spinks, K. (1987) 'Notes from the Casebook' in McAuley, G. (ed.) *From Page to Stage: L'Illusion Comique*, Sydney: University of Sydney Theatre Studies Services Unit: 11–32.

IAN MAXWELL

ROBERT WILSON (1941–)

Not many directors have done as much as Robert Wilson to displace language from the centre of the theatre act. In Wilson's work, the script is often absent and the performance is structured around the movement of bodies in a space. Wilson's dramas are like mobile sculptures: compositions in sound and colour, silence and light that have no 'meaning' apart from their concrete presence:

185

> Go [to my performances] like you would to a museum, like
> you would look at a painting. Appreciate the color of the
> apple, the line of the dress, the glow of the light.... You
> don't have to think about the story, because there isn't any.
> You don't have to listen to words, because the words don't
> mean anything. You just enjoy the scenery, the architectural
> arrangements in time and space, the music, the feelings they
> all evoke. Listen to the pictures.
>
> (Wilson, quoted in Robert Brustein's introduction to
> Shyer 1990: xv)

No story, no characters, no dialogue: just motion, tone, angles, lines
and tints. 'A light moves or a prop moves and it's timing, it's a
construction in time and space.'[1]

Wilson's attraction to form at the cost of narrative goes back to
his background in painting. What Wilson's early experience of the
fine arts gives his theatre is the capacity to explore space rather than
language as the medium in which a work is created:

> When I make a play, I start with a form, even before I know
> the subject matter. I start with a visual structure, and in the
> form I know the content. The form tells me what to do.
>
> (Holmberg 1996: 84)

When Wilson is asked to explain a point he often responds
simply by making a drawing. When he described *the CIVIL warS*
(1983) as 'a play about triangles' (ibid.: 100), he was not being
evasive. It is simply the case that he thinks visually rather than
semantically. The substance of *Einstein on the Beach* (1976) simply
had less to do with the relativity of perception in an unstable
universe than with the manner in which vertical columns break up a
horizontal plane when bodies move slowly in straight lines parallel
to the proscenium.

For the painter in Wilson, the most salient feature of a production is its use of light:

> Light is the most important part of theatre.... From the
> beginning I was concerned with light, how it reveals
> objects, how objects change when light changes, how light
> creates space, how space changes when light changes.... I
> paint, I build, I compose with light. Light is a magic wand.
>
> (ibid.: 121)

In a Robert Wilson production, light is 'the most important actor on stage' (ibid.: 128). The redefinition of space as a consequence of altered lighting is a vital fraction of the value of the drama. Walls of light upstage create silhouettes; the interplay of yellow and blue light creates varying degrees of three-dimensionality; sidelights emphasise the lateral movement of bodies. Different parts of a body are lit with different lights so as to sculpt the actor's figure as it moves across space. For *When We Dead Awaken* (1991), Wilson used sixty hours of technical rehearsal. Wilson's 1987 production *Quartet* had 400 lighting cues spread over ninety minutes. He spent two whole days lighting the prologue and is rumoured to have spent three hours lighting one hand gesture.

The two aspects of Wilson's work as a theatre director that should not by rights derive from his background as a painter are movement and time. Yet Wilson does contrive to use movement in a manner that is distinctly painterly. Movement, in Wilson's work, is important not because it narrates something outside itself but because it alters the visual field. The actor is a body and a voice, an interruption in space. The actor's body moves not so as to express emotion or tell a story but to modulate the forces operating in that space, to create a hiatus or regulate a contrast. Movement replaces plot in Wilson's theatre: the action of a drama may consist of a group of actors filling a space and then emptying it. In rehearsals the actors are not told what a scene means or what they are required to express. Instead, they are told where to walk and what precise positions to assume:

> I had to walk across the room in a straight line on a count of 10, sit down on a count of 21, put my hand to my forehead on a count of 13.... It's all about precision of movement. He demands meticulous attention to detail, down to the angle of the fingers and the eyes.
>
> (Thomas Derrah, quoted in Holmberg 1996: 137)

As Seth Goldstein recalls, 'All I thought about was timing. Bob didn't talk about family dynamics or subtext' (ibid.). Strict time-keeping not only guarantees the integrity of the visual structure but also ensures that the actors are physically constrained from indulging their habitual forays into the world of character and motivation.

For any actor the reduction of the body to the status of a stage property would be fraught with difficulty. In the case of Wilson's actors, they have to face an additional problem: much of the action in Wilson's performances takes a very long time to unfold. In *The*

Life and Times of Sigmund Freud (1969) a tortoise took over an hour to make its way across the stage. In *the CIVIL warS* a soldier spent the entire duration of the performance traversing the stage. For Wilson this is 'NOT in slow motion, it's in natural time. Most theatre deals with speeded-up time, but I use the kind of natural time in which it takes the sun to set, a cloud to change, a day to dawn' (Shyer 1990: xvi). Wilson's actors take quite the opposite view: Sheryl Sutton, who first worked with Wilson on *Deafman Glance*, recalls the problem of working with a radically altered perception of time:

> It's very difficult. In general I think anyone can come close to approximating five minutes of real time. You have a kind of sense about it. But when you have to do something extremely slowly within that five minutes you lose all perception of clock time. The way I approached the scene was to break down the action into inner cells of contrasting speeds so that I could pace myself through it.
>
> (Ibid.: 6)

When one considers that *Deafman Glance* lasted eight hours in performance, one gets some idea of the difficulty of the actor's task in Wilson's theatre.

Deafman Glance began with a silent tableau: a woman dressed in black stood on stage with her back to the audience. A boy sat on a stool near her reading a comic book. A little girl lay asleep on the floor. Nothing moved. Eventually, the woman, moving extremely slowly, poured a glass of milk for the little boy. The boy drank the milk slowly, was put to bed and was then stabbed in slow motion by the woman. The woman wiped the knife and then stabbed the girl. An older boy screamed. The wall behind the actors was removed to reveal a pink figure moving backwards. Nine ladies in white gowns listened to Beethoven. A frog sat at a table sipping a drink. A bee and a rabbit danced to pop music. A group of monkeys picked up red apples. An umbrella caught fire. Stars fell from the sky – and the spectators began to wonder if they had ever seen anything like this.

In 1976 Wilson produced his best-known work, *Einstein on the Beach*, an opera created in collaboration with the composer Philip Glass and the choreographers Lucinda Childs and Andrew de Groat. The opera was built around three sets of incongruous images that appeared every third scene over nine scenes: a train and a building, a courtroom and a bed, and a field with a spaceship. Each scene had a musical theme associated with it. The music was repetitive, as was the dancing. In the first scene a young boy watched a train move onto the stage in extreme slow motion, surrounded by a number of performers who repeatedly executed the same dance steps for over half an hour. In the courtroom the judges scribbled in their books. A woman holding a pipe walked to and fro making frenzied movements with her arm. A second woman jumped periodically for no apparent reason. A boy in a sailor suit flew through the air. Two glass coffins moved in straight lines around the stage.

What *Deafman Glance* and *Einstein on the Beach* have in common with the bulk of Wilson's work is his need to destabilise language by breaking up sequences of words and creating contradictions between levels of speech and action. In *Einstein on the Beach* a woman crawled across a bed and delivered a speech that was repeated 35 times. A number of voices were heard, some singing 'o', some repeating '1966', some asking, 'What is it?' Occasionally a voice screamed 'No!' The music was interspersed with phrases that were spoken over and over so that they lost all semblance of meaning:

> But a court where it could happen. So when David Cassidy
> tells you all of you to go on get going get going. So this
> one in like on WABC New York ... JAY REYNOLDS ....
>
> (Passage from *Einstein on the Beach*,
> quoted in Holmberg 1996: 54)

For Wilson, language has a disturbing tendency to tip over into sense. Hence the manner in which Wilson deforms language in his dramas batters it till every vestige of connotation evaporates and we are left with sounds, noises and patterns. This can be both profound and childish, subtle and churlish. When, for instance, fragments of sentences are suspended in midair as beginnings fail to find ends and questions remain unanswered, one gets a vividly evocative picture of loneliness and isolation worthy of Beckett. When, on the other hand, Wilson writes 'This is not a pipe' under a picture of a pipe, or has two actors make mutually exclusive statements, we get not a profound comment on the limits of language but a gimmick. In *Hamletmachine* (1986), a number of different performers claim to be Ophelia, one of whom then goes on to assert that she is Electra as well. We do not as a result ponder the ultimate mystery of being; we merely become conscious of a ploy. When, in *Einstein on the Beach*, a radio timetable tells us first that Donovan is on from 6.00 to 10.00

189

and then that Donovan is on from 4.30 to 6.00, we do not question the ability of language accurately to describe the world but note that we are in the presence of work that delights in mystifying the spectator.

Having said that, one has to concede that Wilson's uncompromising stance on the issue of pure being has produced a form of theatre that is as rare as it is sublime. Wilson's fields of contrasting images, his collages of sensory impressions drawing on a startlingly diverse fund of experience, are unforgettable. They altered the course of twentieth-century theatre so profoundly that productions less cryptic, less singularly enigmatic, seem like relics of a previous age.

Notes

1   Wilson in Delgado, Maria M. and Heritage, Paul (eds) (1996) *In Contact With the Gods? Directors Talk Theatre*, Manchester and New York: Manchester University Press: 306.

Further reading

Brecht, S. (1978) *The Theatre of Visions: Robert Wilson*, New York: Methuen Drama.

Holmberg, A. (1996) *The Theatre of Robert Wilson*, Cambridge: Cambridge University Press.

Quadri, F., Bertoni, F. and Stearns, R. (1997) *Robert Wilson*, New York: Rizzoli.

Shyer, L. (1990) *Robert Wilson and his Collaborators*, New York: Theatre Communications Group.

SHOMIT MITTER

ANATOLY VASILYEV (1942–)

Born in Rostov-on-Don, Vasilyev trained as a director under Andrei Popov and Maria Knebel, who had been a pupil of Mikhail Chekhov and **Stanislavsky**. After his graduation, he was invited to work at the Moscow Art Theatre, where he made his debut with Oswald Zahradnik's *Solo for a Striking Clock* (1973). The production involved the 'old generation' of the Art Theatre's actors. He gradually departed from the psychological realism that had dominated Soviet theatre for much of the twentieth century, which assumed that actors emotionally experienced the role they played (*perezhivanie*); filled it with the knowledge of the 'given circum-stances' and their own affective memory; and found a character's motivation in a precipitating event.

Over the past thirty years Vasilyev has shed these basic principles and moved toward a theatre based on improvisation, using texts and developing improvisation within what he calls their 'rigid struc-tures'. The personality of the actor is effaced behind the role. The actor does not create a psychologically and physically real character by drawing on his/her affective memory of the past, but works towards a predefined objective, taking time on the path leading towards it to engage in playful, ludic explorations of the situations that arise. Vasilyev's search for a new theatre developed in three distinct phases: exploration of new dramatic and theatrical forms (1977–87); experiment with improvisation (1987–95); and definition of a 'verbal' theatre (1996 to present).

His 1978 production of Gorky's *Vassa Zheleznova* established the basic concept of space for Vasilyev's theatre. He and the architect and designer, Igor Popov, created a set the walls and furniture of which narrowed the stage. The space opened only at the top, where a cage holding Prokhor's beloved pigeons was suspended. Prokhor's death from a heart attack was caused by the feathers of his own birds being thrown at him. He was suffocated by what he loved most, both literally and figuratively. In 1979, Vasilyev directed Viktor Slavkin's *A Young Man's Grown-Up Daughter*, a play about the meeting of old university friends who are now in their forties, but were jazz fans and teddy boys (*stilyagi*) in their youth. Vasilyev contrasted the present and the past: the 1970s were set in the narrow space of a flat that unfolds along a diagonal wall, diminishing the stage; the 1950s were expressed through the jazz music that opened the enclosed space acoustically.

While these two productions created a furore in the Moscow theatre scene of the late 'stagnation' period under Brezhnev, they were steps towards a new way of directing that found its full expres-sion in *Cerceau* (1985). Slavkin's play consists of lived experience and collated literary material. It centres around the mid-life crisis of a group of forty-year-olds whose world is dominated by past hopes and present despair. The characters go through a series of happy recollections of the past, attaining a glimpse of the chance for a brighter, happier future at the end. The collage of texts includes Thomas Cook's train timetable, the brochure 'How to Play Cerceau', remarks made by the Swedish cultural attaché Lars Kleberg (on whom the figure of Lars was modelled) and pieces from

Gogol's *Selected Passages from Correspondence with Friends*, Chekhov's plays and Pushkin's correspondence. One of the characters, Petushok, invites several of his colleagues, neighbours and chance acquaintances for a weekend to a *dacha*. All of them had led their own lives without revealing their true feelings for each other. After a series of excursions into the past, triggered off by letters found in the attic, their tragic isolation from each other becomes apparent. Nevertheless, they continue as before. Vasilyev's production elevated Slavkin's fragmentary text to a sophisticated four-hour performance. It recreated the past through costumes and props such as the sticks and hoops used when playing cerceau and the trunk full of letters, which the characters had discovered in the *dacha* and which also contained possessions of its previous owners.

Cerceau demonstrated Vasilyev's work on ludic structures very well. Within the fragmentation of the dramatic text, the absence of any apparent dramatic development and the inertia of the characters, Vasilyev developed a method that enabled the actors to engage in a series of sketches, short games and scenes which, taken together, formed an aesthetic unity. He located certain 'knots' in the 'rigid structures' of the text, defining them as mini-objectives between which the actors were free to improvise and 'play'.

When Vasilyev founded his own theatre, the School of Dramatic Art, in 1987, censorship and bans on improvisation no longer existed. His production of Pirandello's *Six Characters in Search of an Author* (1987) was a new achievement in his method of improvisation within the parameters of fixed ('rigid') textual structures. Scenes were repeated with variations in text and performance, the latter by using different actors. A variety of styles and moods entered the production, making it impossible to pinpoint reality.

In 1990 and 1991 Vasilyev explored dialogic structures in Dostoevsky's novels, *The Possessed* and *The Idiot*, demonstrating that the word precedes action and causes a response or emotion in the character. He worked with Plato's philosophical treatises (1991), searching for ways of expressing the idea contained in a text or speech, the formation of ideas in a character's mind, and the relationship of the speaker to the idea contained in Plato's text. In order for the word to ring true rather than be a well-rehearsed and meaningless sound, he required actors to be free from any prior knowledge or emotion and to allow their roles to develop on the basis of words spoken and words heard. The all-powerful word triggers action.

With *Amphitryon* (1995) and *The Stone Guest* (1998), Vasilyev began to deprive the text of its narrative function and to reduce it to a pure sign and sound system in order to reveal new meanings. This practice established him as the founder of a new theatre which may be called 'verbal', 'conceptual', 'metaphysical' or 'ritual' theatre. Vasilyev's approach essentially inverts Stanislavsky's 'system'. Instead of creating the illusion of an (interior) space on stage, he explores the parameters of the architectural space constructed within the theatrical space, never fully blurring the borders between the two. Instead of the emotional experience of the situation and the psychological exploration of the action, Vasilyev concentrates on the meaning of the word, dismissing the pre-history of the character provided in the given circumstances. He orients his characters towards the future, using the principal event of a play as its driving force. Instead of providing an emotional trigger for action, the philosophical content compels a character to act (Vassiliev 1999).

The classical Pushkin text, *Mozart and Salieri*, is pronounced on stage in a manner that insults the Russian ear in that Pushkin's verse resonates in a chopped and truncated manner. Phrases and words are deprived of their usual intonation and stress patterns. In everyday speech, words are connected to each other through a linear intonation (with a drop at the end of the phrase) to form a narrative. In order to destroy the narrative intonation, Vasilyev has each word pronounced with a dropping intonation, which lays bare the metaphysical quality of the word, its 'pure' meaning. According to Vasilyev, most texts are submerged in layers of interpretation, and the intonation tells the story, covering up the real meaning of the words. Intonation thus becomes the carrier of information, whereas words, for many postmodernist writers, have become the means for betrayal and power, even weapons that have the potential to destroy. Vasilyev's technique of recitation is highly unusual, but it assists in uncovering the original or 'pure' meaning of the word. The actors are not driven by the past, but are drawn towards the same, principal event which will happen – the murder of Mozart – and take Mozart and Salieri to be blank pages on which any story can be written. The actor stands beside the character, while the play takes place in the gap between the actor and the character.[1]

The actors gain freedom within the structures of a given text and are able to approach it in a playful manner, which gives them ironic distance from it. The unemotional acting, combined with the symbolism of the props, creates a ritual performance that is prescribed in every single detail. A ritual or mystery play is based on a fixed form that opens up toward the absolute truth (God); the stages of the path are predetermined. The 'stops on the road' (knots) allow for interludes, games in-between characters who diverge for a short moment in their paths before they reconvene.

The organisation of the theatrical space reflects the binaries of order and chaos, vertical and horizontal planes of action, and narrative and metaphysical discourse. There is a high temple staircase on stage left, and an empty space which is gradually filled with the chairs, easels and other clutter on the right. Adjacent to the staircase is a space encircled by transparent plastic (a glass house), which contains the chairs and table for the scene of Mozart's and Salieri's dinner. Their dialogue in the glass house and in the empty space pertains to metaphysical issues, and reverberates like a series of hard sounds, largely consonant-based words, that are thrown like arrows into the empty space. Vasilyev juxtaposes this way of reciting the text with the narrative discourse and playfulness of conversation held in the space that fills with furniture.

For Vasilyev, *Mozart and Salieri* is not a psychological drama that explores the reason and motives for Salieri's crime, but is a metaphysical discourse on the nature of harmony. Mozart is in harmony with the world. He moves with ease between high and low, order and chaos, and is able to create harmony out of the surrounding chaos. Salieri cannot do that. He is reduced to immobility and unable to compose after Mozart's death. His genius depended on Mozart and, by destroying him, Salieri upset the harmonious balance of their co-existence.

Vasilyev's reading of dramatic texts as treatises provides a key for interpreting and staging the dramas of ideas. Moreover, his method of turning texts into non-narrative has proven to be a useful tool for the production of contemporary plays which are distinguished from traditional ones by their fragmented structure and their lack of a linear plot-line or narrative.

Notes

1   See for these points, Grotowski, J. (1975) 'Actor's Training (1966)' in *Towards a Poor Theatre*, London: Methuen: 175–204. Grotowski differentiates between head voice, mouth voice, occipital voice, chest voice and belly voice, and these concepts were adopted by Vasilyev, who worked with Grotowski at Pontedera during the 1990s.

Further reading

Beumers, Birgit (2002) 'Spinning the Text: the Play with Infinity in Contemporary Russian Theatre', *Modern Language Review* 97 (1): 135–148.

Brauckhoff, Maria (1999) *Das Theater Anatolij Vasil'evs*, Bochum: Projekt Verlag, dissertation.

Vasil'ev, Anatolij (2003) *Dem Einzigen Leser*, Berlin: Alexander Verlag.

Vassiliev, Anatoli (1997) *Maître de stage: a propos de* Bal masque *de Mikhaïl Lermontov*, Carnières-Morlanwelz: Lansman Editeur.

—— (1999) *Sept ou Huit Leçons de Théâtre*, Paris: P.O.L.

Wyneken-Galibin, Ruth (1993) *Anatolij Wassiljew*, Frankfurt: Fischer Verlag.

BIRGIT BEUMERS

PATRICE CHÉREAU (1944–)

Chéreau's is the brilliant career of an *enfant prodige* frequently seen to be an *enfant terrible*. It covers theatre, opera and film, each of which he masters with equal aplomb. His pathway through the theatre began in 1966, when he was only twenty-two years old and already the managing and artistic director of the Théâtre de Sartrouville, a municipal theatre in the Parisian suburbs. He stopped working in the theatre in 1990, apparently definitively, but returned with a visceral *Phèdre* at the Odéon-Théâtre de l'Europe in 2003. He directed the *Contes d'Hoffman* (1974) and *Lulu* (1979) at the Paris Opera and Wagner's *Ring* with Pierre Boulez at Bayreuth (1976–80) whose counterpoint to the established 'Bayreuth' productions earned him international notoriety – Wagner set in the industrial world rather than in the glory of myth and legend. Having abandoned the opera, he returned to it with Berg's *Woyzeck* at the Châtelet Theatre in Paris in 1996. He directed opera the way he staged his theatre productions, requiring singers to identify the dramatic purpose and significance of their roles and to perform them as actors who sing.

As a director of film, Chéreau was equally decisive, despite the restless pattern of his professional life. He made several experimental films before *La Reine Margot* (1994), his first box-office success, controversial for its political and sexual violence. Then, after the off-beat, subtly gay *Ceux qui m'aiment prendront le train* (*Those Who Love Me Will Take The Train*, 1998), he made *Intimacy* in English (2001) with Mark Rylance in the principal male role. (Chereau's casting appears provocative since Rylance, who is the director of the Globe Theatre in London, is renowned for his female roles at the Globe). About family values, conjugal infidelity and overwhelming hetero-sexual desire, *Intimacy* was threatened with censorship in Britain because it showed Rylance's erect penis during the sexual act. Yet the issue for Chéreau here, as elsewhere in his film and stage work, was not controversy for publicity or didactic purposes, but about being truthful to what he sees regarding human beings. As he observed in 1977: 'I talk about things that I want to see or about the life of people whose secret I wish to penetrate. I gave up wanting to teach people lessons long ago' (Aslan 1986: 18).[1] *Son Frère* (2003) is Chéreau's last film to date.

At Sartrouville, Chéreau took a **Brecht**ian perspective on **Vilar**'s principles for a 'people's theatre', radicalising them through explicitly political collaborations with trade unions and schools. If he lost interest in teaching 'lessons', he never stopped thinking from the left of the political spectrum, as his mentors, **Strehler** and Planchon, had not. He learned at the Piccolo Teatro (1969–72) about poetic composition, the necessity of harmony between the elements of a production and the importance of design for the theatre in all its forms. Roger Planchon, with whom Chéreau began to co-direct the Théâtre National Populaire de Villeurbanne (Lyon) in 1972, nurtured Chéreau's 'feel' for dramaturgical research, particularly for sociological and historical contexts. This was consistently to sustain Chéreau's works, irrespective of their genre. Planchon also encouraged the taste Chéreau shared with German Expressionist cinema for architectural monumentalism, startling images, shadows and silhouettes.

These features distinguished Chéreau's 1973 staging of *La Dispute* by Marivaux in Villeurbanne which, having attracted considerable attention, was revised in Paris in 1975. No less distinctive was Chéreau's thick smoke, enormous mirrors, which reflected both characters and spectators, and a runway to the stage with a tower on it, which extended playing space outwards and upwards away from the centre. Apart from its visual strangeness, the production revealed a Marivaux whose dialogue was cruel, thus nothing like the frivolous banter (*marivaudage*) for which he was known. Marivaux's fable tells of a Prince who isolates a brother and a sister at birth so as to bring them together in early adolescence as an experiment on human behaviour. Chéreau re-evaluated it, showing that the Prince was not a benign seeker of knowledge, but an emblem of perversity legitimated by power; and crystallised his interpretation in an image of the Prince spying, half-hidden from view in the tower, on the adolescents' rites of passage. Chéreau also framed the fable with a prologue constructed out of other texts by Marivaux. The moral debate in the prologue underpinned his re-organisation of Marivaux's twenty scenes into seven nights, each one leading the young characters to despair, madness and death. His textual 'tampering', rare at the time in France, was part of the shock of the unexpected which was to become typically 'Chéreau'.

La Dispute was the source of other trademarks: Chéreau's idea that a director's point of view is necessarily different from the author's (or allegedly the author's); his conviction that the directorial viewpoint must be visible in the sequences and entire structure of a given production (ibid.: 37); his encouragement of the actors' research into their own acting potentiality and possibilities; his emphasis on the actors' externalised, articulate play; his use of natural elements – real trees, water, earth – in ostentatiously artificial environments, which reiterate his affinity with Germanic culture, this time via Pina **Bausch**. In *Peer Gynt* (1981) the protagonist peels an onion in a constructivist set of planks. Earth fills the whole space of *Combat de nègre et de chiens* (*Combat with Black Dogs*, 1983), where a huge flyover, cars, a caravan, a shack, a tree and prowling dogs seem all the more out of place for being real. A horse ridden by Hamlet's father gallops across the floor boards with a ringing sound (1988). The boards, in colour, are arranged to look like a picture of a Renaissance palace surrounded by darkness.

Chéreau's stage world is essentially nocturnal, the seven-hour *Peer Gynt* being an extreme example, comparable only to his *Ring*: low shafts of light, creeping mists and, on occasion, a full moon on the horizon reinforce its pervasive obscurity. Planks, pulleys, swings, platforms and walls shift and creak (design by Richard Peduzzi) to suggest dark mountains, crevices and valleys, and caves inhabited by trolls. The design facilitates Chéreau's urge to push beyond the limits of the stage, which is largely why he left it to embrace the spatial freedom of the cinema. Action occurs on the planks, and so on, which lift, tilt and fall in diagonals, verticals and horizontals, scattering the space in all directions. Space reaches into the audience, even to the top rows where the actors run, speaking their lines. Chéreau manipulates focal points by using the cinematographic techniques of travelling shots, zooms and close-ups. These techniques are evident in all his theatre productions, without exception, and substantiate a claim he repeated frequently in the late 1990s that the universes of the cinema and the theatre were not incompatible.

Chéreau constantly reviews his use of space. In *Combat de nègre et de chiens* he merges the stage and auditorium, transforming the whole theatre into a cavernous hangar. In *Hamlet*, an apron protruding well into the audience is Hamlet's space. His father's ghost invades it, thereby indicating physically the production's guiding thread: his father, a symbol of the time 'out of joint' and who is on a horse like a horse of the Apocalypse, places an impossible burden on Hamlet's shoulders, that of setting to set the times right. Critics in Moscow, in the middle of *perestroika*, quickly grasped this point when *Hamlet* was shown there in 1989, one year after its premiere at the Avignon Festival (De Nussac 1990: 238). The apron is also the space for Hamlet's 'To be or not to be', which he speaks softly with his back to the audience, dark space in front of him. His position denotes his vulnerability, and the space, the insurmountable difficulties that lie ahead. Play in *Les Paravents* (Genet's *The Screens*, 1983) oscillates between stage and audience spaces. Chéreau has Genet's colonised Algerians hold the stage, indicating by this how they move to the centre of history when they make their own history through independence and revolution. He places the colonisers in the 'margins', to the side of the audience. Once again, Chéreau demonstrates that his play with space is not purely a formal affair, but is in dialogue with the substance of his productions and their – in this case, political – perspectives.

Peer Gynt is something of a matrix for Chéreau's cinematographic use of sound. Its three-dimensional soundscape of seven hours, as long as the production itself, disperses all sorts of natural sounds – birds, thunder, rain – among abstract ones. Many replace decor in that they accompany actors as they move through the auditorium, suggesting changes of place from village to mountain path or chasm, or to the sea which carries Peer across the world and back, in search of himself. All of them build a hallucinatory atmosphere for Chéreau's critical view of Peer's existential crisis, which he takes to represent the crisis of modern individualism. And he links the latter to the entrepreneurial drive of capitalism.

A similar cluster of ideas pervades *The Ring*. Peduzzi designs Valhalla, the seat of the gods, as a cross between a manor house and a huge factory. Wotan wears a frockcoat of the kind worn by prosperous men and, indeed, by Wagner himself. The other gods are in salon-type clothing. The Rhinemaidens in *The Rhinegold* are Belle Epoque prostitutes. The Nibelungs are dressed as miners. Space, in the four operas, is in multiple dimensions to suggest journeys, distances, heights and depths, and miraculous feats. Voluminous smoke, illusions of fire, water, forests and burning gold, and disappearing stairs and walls mark what is, for Chéreau, Wagner's infinitely cruel universe. Chéreau's task was to observe Wagner's stage directions by following his own taste for 'theatrical magic' and the 'rules of theatrical play', and his conviction that 'the strings and the pulleys' of production should be exposed to view (Chéreau

1994: 42–43). He urged the singers to avoid automatic responses to the words, arguing that 'the text says a hundred things, but you do not play it if you play only what is written' (ibid.: 76). Playing what was not written meant going 'behind' each libretto. He unearthed, in *Siegfried*, a host of anti-Semitic prejudices which he was not afraid to display in Bayreuth, a place with a Nazi past. He found 'disoriented humanity' in *The Twilight of the Gods* (ibid.: 53). For its sheer interpretative and theatrical audacity, Chéreau's *Ring* is a major event in the history of opera production.

Chéreau's baptism by fire in the 1970s prepared him for his co-directorship with Catherine Tasca of the Théâtre des Amandiers in Nanterre, in western Paris (1982–90). He transformed the Amandiers from a peripheral venue into a centre with a broad cultural remit unmatched by any theatre in France. He gave priority to artistic rather than practical demands; established a school for actors; brought together his old-time collaborators, among them the actors Maria Casarès and Gérard Desarthe, his scenographer Peduzzi, costume designer Jacques Schmidt and sound designer André Serré; gathered up new actors, many of them stars of the cinema (Michel Piccoli, Bulle Ogier), not just because they had exceptional skills, but because 'a whole humanity passes through them' (Aslan 1986: 68). He did not aim to build an ensemble company, but an artistic team. In addition, he invited national and international directors (**Wilson**, **Ronconi**, **Stein**, **Sellars**, Luc Bondy) and international troupes; developed new techniques and technologies; had rehearsal and cinema studios on the premises; and organised concerts and talks.

Not least among his achievements was his engagement with young authors, most notably Bernard-Marie Koltès, whom he virtually put on the map. Apart from *Combat*, he staged *Quai ouest* (*Key West*, 1986), *Dans la solitude des champs de coton* (*In the Solitude of the Cotton Fields*, 1987), in which he performed, and *Retour au désert* (*Return to the Desert*, 1988). In Chéreau's big style, they all give due weight to Koltès' notion that power and control are expressions of fear, suspicion, competition and loathing. All his Amandiers productions, among them Marivaux's *La Fausse suivante* (1985), Chekhov's *Platonov* (1987) and, of course, *Hamlet*, pick up these concerns, but none deal with them as brutally as his productions of Koltès. None show as plainly as his Koltès productions that violence is not a matter of thematics, but is a fact of life.

At Amandiers Chéreau attempted to bring his actors' faces into closer view, as occurs in film, and pushed his actors' physicality so that they could bodily tear their characters' passions open. He rediscovered these qualities in *Phèdre*, performed in a long and narrow space by his old-time actors who spoke Racine's august verse as if they were speaking everyday language and who gave the spectators, right under their nose, an astounding emotional experience of the kind no production emulating the classical rules of prosody and affective delivery could have given them.

Notes

1   All translations are my own.

Further reading

Aslan, Odette (ed.) (1986) *Chéreau, Les Voies de la Création Théâtrale* XIV, Paris: CNRS Editions.

Chéreau, Patrice (1994) *Lorsque cinq ans seront passés: sur le* Ring *de Richard Wagner*, Toulouse: Editions Ombres.

De Nussac, Sylvie (compiled) (1990) *Nanterre Amandiers, Les Années Chéreau 1982–1990*, Paris: Editions Imprimerie Nationale.

Mervant-Roux, Marie-Madeleine (1998) 'Le *Hamlet* de P. Chéreau à Moscou. Etude d'une tournée' in *L'Assise du Théâtre: pour une étude du spectateur*, Paris: CNRS Editions: 195–217.

Shevtsova, Maria (1993) '*Peer Gynt* in France Directed by Patrice Chéreau' in *Theatre and Cultural Interaction*, Sydney: Sydney Studies: 55–80.

MARIA SHEVTSOVA

LEV DODIN (1944–)

Dodin's achievements are virtually unthinkable without the Maly Drama Theatre of St Petersburg, which he has directed since 1983. No other company in the world today is as tightly-knit or as exclusively focused on working intensively, continually and permanently together as is this ensemble. It has built its 'common language' on a school-company continuum, Dodin having trained three generations of actors at the Leningrad State Theatre Institute (now the St Petersburg Academy of Theatre Arts) where he began to teach in 1967. The Maly incorporates everybody from technicians and stage hands to the voice, music and dance teachers who help to prepare Dodin's students and who coach them still as professionals. The enduring commitment to its collaborative principles of their company of 64 actors and a total of 220 people also defines its unique ensemble dynamics.

For Dodin, the training of actors cannot be reduced to 'technique', 'exercise' or 'method'. It consists of a 'training of the heart and of the nervous system', that is, of feeling, sensation and sensory receptivity (unpublished interview with author, Paris, 8 April 1994). His perspective is broadly Stanislavskian in so far as he believes that technique awakens emotions, but he is critical of the **Stanislavsky** 'system', seeing it as little more than mechanisms that prevent actors from tuning into their innermost 'aliveness'.[1] The actors' task is to reach this 'aliveness', which activates their growth and sparks off a chain reaction from actor to actor to spectator – a process Dodin describes as 'infection' to indicate its organic quality. Above all, training develops the spiritual, intellectual and cultural evolution of the human being who inhabits the actor. The theatre made by him/her thereby becomes a place of similar possibilities for spectators.

The students who graduated in 1990 with *Gaudeamus* demonstrate Dodin's development-centred approach to training. They learned to play brass and wind instruments especially for the production and toured *Gaudeamus* to great international acclaim during the early 1990s, accompanied by their music teachers who monitored their progress. So effective was this ongoing learning that, by the time Dodin staged Chekhov's *A Play With No Name* in 1997 (usually known as *Platonov*), they were able to perform entire pieces at an extraordinarily high standard quite at odds with their late start. Their achievement as actors (by now they were fully integrated in the company) was intertwined, in their view, with their personal growth (conversation with Sergey Kurishev, Weimar, 7 July 1997).

Reading may serve as another example. Dodin and the actors construct scripts out of novels, which they read to each other over a number of years while they perform productions already in the repertoire. Reading aloud sharpens the actors' capacity for listening to and hearing each other on stage; encourages an immediate response to a specific situation, and thus improvisation around that response; and helps actors to make discoveries together, which, apart from reinforcing their ensemble identity, inspires them to extend their personal imaginative and intellectual resources through further reading. Reading Dostoevsky's *The Devils* together led the actors to everything Dostoevsky is believed to have read while writing his book. This accumulated culture resonated in the scenes they devised and guided their critical perception of them. *Chevengur* (1998), from the novel by Andrey Platonov, followed a similar pattern. The actors invented multiple scenes which they performed to Dodin who, as usually happens, observed, probed, prodded and talked generally around their work rather than commented directly on it. The actors then internalised his contribution, processing it through their 'nervous system' before coming up with alternatives. Gradually, Dodin directed a piece out of successive devisings, sometimes going backwards to earlier versions, at other times anticipating new ones, which the actors played around with and refined.

These procedures are slow, but have the advantage of drawing into their collaborative efforts all the experiences undergone by their participants during the passage of time. *Their* maturation is integral to the maturation of the work. For this reason, Dodin's principal task as a director is best described as catalytic: he prompts actors to 'dig' through the layers of their existence – memories and subconscious experiences included – in order to find in themselves whatever they are playing and stimulate their existential and creative potential.

Acting, Dodin believes, is driven by 'inner energy', which he defines as 'the feeling and thought that move, disturb and excite us, and do not give us peace; energy does not mean being louder or more nervous, but asking sharper, more astute questions' which engender actions (unpublished interview with author, St Petersburg, 30 September 1998). The actor involved in this process is not primed to be a mere interpreter or, worse still, to execute the director's will, but becomes what Dodin calls an 'active co-author' of a production along its entire research path or 'journey of birth' (unpublished interview with author, Weimar, 9 July 1997). The cognates of 'birth', notably 'giving birth anew', are integral to Dodin's vocabulary and are consistent with his view that a production is a 'living organism' and the theatre a place of spiritual regeneration and renewal – *re*birth, in some sense of the word – for all who engage with it.

Since co-authoring is crucial to the company's objectives, actors are expected to attend all devising sessions and rehearsals, irrespective of whether they will be required to play on a particular day or not. This means that everybody shares the discoveries made in a particular scene and understands their domino effect on subsequent reworkings. Unbroken participation is also essential because casting is not pre-set: different combinations of performers and roles are tried out for a production over a number of years until the right cast emerges from the process.

The Maly's rehearsals are also distinguished by the fact that teachers, assistants, designers, stage and props managers and technicians and administrators attend them to co-author work. They anticipate where they may be needed, help an individual or a group to overcome a difficulty, and adjust choices that have been made, or propose new ones. For example, everybody selected music for *A Play With No Name*, which took twelve hours to play. The teachers searched for scores, transcribed pieces from recordings and transposed music to different keys or vocal registers. They helped to narrow down the sheer quantity of music for the three and a half hours of the production's 'final' version. The music that remains is played almost non-stop, and covers a wide range of genres and periods – jazz, blues, classical pieces, Russian romances, opera arias, waltzes, charlestons, tangos – all of it reflecting the input of the different people involved in the work's development.

Rehearsals, for Dodin, are performances in their own right, which is why actors perform fully in them, as if already in front of an audience. Rehearsals are also a zone of unconditional freedom where actors and director open themselves to each other through improvisations and what Stanislavsky called *études*. Dodin extends the scope of *études* through demanding physical work, notably ballet and acrobatics, on the assumption that physical articulation unites body and mind, emotion and thought, intention and action, conscious and unconscious desire and motivation, and artistic imaging and framing. And he fuses Stanislavsky with **Meyerhold** by following two main Meyerholdian principles: play the internal outwardly with a strong sense of fantasy and theatrical projection; play it with a self-awareness that generates humour, irony and reflexivity regarding the material or how it is performed.

The 'theatre of prose' is one of Dodin's main innovations and has nothing in common with the Russian tradition of adapting playscripts from novels. Dodin's actors perform a novel in its entirety, writing what eventually becomes a script through the physical process itself. *The Devils*, for example, took more than three years and generated countless hours of play. This mass was whittled down to about twenty hours, then eventually reduced to eight and divided into three parts. What became the production went through several phases, the book's themes, motifs and issues being highlighted in various combinations. Dodin culled, cut and assembled, much like a literary editor, except that he did it with living people. Several potential productions fell by the wayside during this intense research, many of them worthy of public viewing (conversation with Nikolay Lavrov, St Petersburg, 29 September 1998).

The Maly's repertoire is largely composed of 'theatre of prose'. Its signature piece, *Brothers and Sisters* (1985), is from Fyodor Abramov's trilogy about the hardships of peasant life in northern Russia at the end of the Second World War. Dodin had already directed *The House* by Abramov in 1980 at the Maly. Apart from the titles noted previously – *The Devils*, *Chevengur* and *Gaudeamus* (from Sergey Kaledin's 1988 novel, *The Construction Battalion*) – there are *Lord of the Flies* (1985, from William Golding's novel) and *Claustrophobia* (1994), devised by the class of *Gaudeamus* as a collage of fragments from contemporary fiction, woven through operatic and balletic idioms. The actors defy physical-spatial limits. They crawl up the walls and sway perilously away from them, or crash their way through them. They walk on ledges and dance on barres. Men dance *en pointe*. Dialogue is sung. Brass instruments are played satirically as barbed asides on socio-political realities. In one funny scene, they are used as medical instruments by 'doctors' attempting to revive Lenin's corpse.

Plays are given less priority, although in the 1960s and 1970s Dodin staged various 'dissident' Soviet playwrights as well as Tennessee Williams and Hauptman; and, in 1987, *Stars in the Morning Sky* by Sergey Galin. Set in 1980 during the Moscow Olympics, *Stars* deals with prostitution, drunkenness, violence and rape. Its extroverted performance style is interspersed with moments of elegiac beauty, including the first nude love scene in the history of the Russian theatre. It was showcased with *Brothers and Sisters* when the Maly first travelled to Western Europe in 1988, soon to become the Russian company most toured abroad since the Moscow Art Theatre. Dodin directed Kleist's *The Broken Jug* and O'Neill's *Desire Under the Elms* in 1992, and Chekhov, his only Russian classical dramatist, for the first time with *The Cherry Orchard* in 1994, followed by *A Play*, *The Seagull* (2001) and *Uncle Vanya* (2003).

Dodin's Chekhov productions concentrate on uncertainty, precarity, egocentrism, cruelty and misguided love. *The Cherry Orchard* is the most sombre of them, its concerns encapsulated in Eduard Kochergin's design: a group of black triptychs intimating screens, corridors, doors, windows and altars which unseen hands tear apart leaving bare frames, like the frames of a ruined house, at the end of the performance. Branches of blossom are attached to the back of these transparent windows, bringing together the outside and the inside, the orchard and the house, and the physical and mental state of the characters. The construction falls apart about them, no more poignantly than when they weave a dance in and out of the corridors of their house-mind. Dodin avoids pathos, as in all his Chekhov productions, and seeks generalising power from the specific instances embodied by his actors. The theatre, in his view, fulfils its most important purpose when it shows people their common humanity.

The symbiosis between direction and scenography in *The Cherry Orchard* is a Maly principle. Kochergin's design for *Brothers and Sisters*, which is a multi-purpose platform of logs, allows Dodin to change time, place, scene, situation and action in an instant. The logs are a hut, a bath house, a wheat field, a lorry that collects grain for the state leaving the villagers hungry, a wall on which they watch propaganda films and an attic for making love. In *The Devils*, a system of planks and pulleys suggests the nooks and crannies of the city slums in which the characters torment and pursue each other, in some cases to madness and death. In *A Play With No Name*, designed by Alexey Poray-Koshits who also designed *Gaudeamus*, *Claustrophobia*, *Chevengur* and *The Seagull*, water is the dominant element. The actors swim in it, play instruments in it as they swim, kiss and dance in it, and float candles upon it. Platonov, the protagonist, is caught in a net in it, like a fish. Besides indicating a country estate, the water is a metaphor for life, despair and death, and for the production's central idea that, as in Chekhov's period, people today are adrift in a precarious world.

Scenes are always connected seamlessly, although for different purposes. Seamless composition in *Brothers* is symphonic, and its rhythms, phrasing and cadences change according to section, movement or motif. In *The Devils*, it channels attention to the actors' concentration and intensity. In *A Play*, Dodin runs scenes simultaneously. Several scenes are spoken at once. Singing in one scene does not drown out the speech of a concurrent scene, any more than does the non-stop music. Simultaneity not only creates multiple visual and spatial dimensions, but also textures sound. Dodin's innovations in *A Play* confirm his belief that the theatre is virtually without limits, providing its actors are developed beyond their presumed limits. He trains his actors to be versatile and virtuosic, and inculcates in them the virtues of mental agility, flexibility, boldness and risk-taking, and the feeling that they are able to do anything.

Dodin's achievements as a director include his staging of seven operas: *Elektra* by Richard Strauss at Salzburg (1966); *Lady Macbeth of*

Mtensk by Shostakovich in Florence (1998); *The Queen of Spades* by Tchaikovsky in Amsterdam (1998); *Mazepa* by Tchaikovsky in Milan (1999); *The Demon* by Anton Rubinstein in Paris (2003); *Otello* by Verdi in Florence (2003); and *Salomé* by Richard Strauss in Paris (2003). Like Stanislavsky and Meyerhold before him, he seeks in this most comprehensive and synthetic of arts its veritable theatricality. This means treating opera as if it were spoken theatre, and singers as if they were actors. It means, as well, allowing the music and the dramatic action to do their respective work and not merely to illustrate each other. On these points, Dodin joins **Brook** and **Strehler** who, in any case, advanced what Stanislavsky and Meyerhold had begun.

Notes

1   A term at the heart of Dodin's vocabulary, which like 'common language' above cannot be assigned to a single date. All translations are mine.

Further reading

Autant-Mathieu, Marie-Christine (1994) 'Le Théâtre russe après l'URSS', *Théâtre/Public* 116: 21–39; section on Dodin and the Maly: 31–35.

Dmitrevskaya, Marina (1986) ' "Ishchem my sel', ishchem my bol' etoi zemli" ' (' "We seek salt, we seek the pain of this land" '), *Teatr* 4: 89–102.

Shevtsova, Maria (2004) *Dodin and the Maly Drama Theatre: Process to Performance*, London and New York: Routledge.

MARIA SHEVTSOVA

ELIZABETH LECOMPTE (1944–)

LeCompte has been the artistic director of the Wooster Group since 1975. Based in their theatre space, the Performing Garage, New York, the Wooster Group have become notorious for their radical deconstruction of canonical theatre texts, their extensive use of technology on the stage and their subversive approach to identity in performance. LeCompte has been at the centre of this work, directing fourteen theatre and dance productions, four films and three radio plays in the twenty-eight years of the company's life, gaining a reputation for her witty and fiercely critical engagement with the theatrical canon. Elinor Fuchs has argued that LeCompte's work 'announce[s] performance itself as the field of raw material'.[1] It is certainly true that LeCompte's work is characterised by her interest in the political effects of theatrical representation. It demonstrates an uneasy awareness of the ways in which the performance of identity on stage can shape spectators' attitudes towards hierarchies of race, gender and sexuality. Performance is both the aesthetic material with which LeCompte works, and the political target which she interrogates and critiques.

It would be a mistake to single LeCompte out as a director without taking into account the collective and collaborative nature of the Wooster Group's work. LeCompte's directing is rooted inextricably within the creative impulses of the company as a whole, and an analysis of her work must take account of the processes through which the Wooster Group as a company develop and perform their work on the stage. The company's productions take over two years to develop into fully realised performance pieces, and not only performers, but technicians, designers, dramaturgs, translators and administrators are involved in the creative process from the very beginning. Mistakes, accidental discoveries and jokes developed in rehearsals are often incorporated into the work, and the company reshapes and reformulates their performance material over many years. LeCompte works more like a film editor than a traditional auteur theatre director in rehearsal in that she edits and shapes the material developed rather than imposing a vision constructed in advance of rehearsals. Reference here to the Wooster Group rather than solely to LeCompte acknowledges the collaborative nature of this company's structures and approach.

The Wooster Group have become famous for their deconstructive approach to identity. They interrogate essentialised attitudes to gender, race and the body by undermining and fragmenting the actor's presence on the stage, and by constructing consciously inauthentic bodies in performance. Televisions, plasma screens and microphones on metal stands proliferate, allowing the performers to demonstrate the work of acting through the objects of technology, and using technology to produce a mediated and distorted vision of the human body. The company are also famous for their controversial appropriation of performance styles and 'bodies': Japanese theatre techniques, blackface minstrelsy, vaudeville and burlesque, contemporary dance, and popular film. The Group emphasise and exaggerate the artificiality of these appropriated racial, historical and gendered 'bodies', and foreground their own inability to offer new identities in place of the old, repressive ones. They contest stereotypes through the subversive and hyperbolic conformity to them in performance.

While the company approaches theatricality as a central characteristic of identity, there is also a sense of regret in their work that bodies are inevitably mediated through representation. This is shown in the kind of 'bodies' the company chooses to explore in performance. The Wooster Group have implicated the theatre in the formation of unequal hierarchies of identity by linking the traditions of blackface minstrelsy with the racism of American society, by interrogating the reductive representation of femininity in canonical play-texts, and by examining the ways in which technology can construct and medicalise the human body in post-AIDS culture. The company's complex approach to the representation of identity has been articulated in a number of different ways: exploration of blackface minstrelsy in works such as *Route 1&9* (1981), *LSD (...Just the High Points...)* (1984), *The Emperor Jones* (1993) and *The Hairy Ape* (1995); engagement with Japanese staging techniques and costume in productions such as *Brace Up!* (1991) and *Fish Story* (1994); and use of technology as a means of mediating and meditating on gender in productions such as *House/Lights* (1999) and *To You The Birdie* (2002).

An example of how blackface and Orientalism combined to construct a subversive vision of racial identity in performance can be seen in *The Emperor Jones*. Eugene O'Neill's expressionist play centres on an escaped African-American chain-gang convict, Brutus Jones, who becomes the tyrannical emperor of a Caribbean Island. While O'Neill's play was praised in 1920 for casting a black actor in the title role, by the 1990s theatre critics had rejected the play for its racist stereotyping of black identity. The Wooster Group's production complicated the racial representations in the play by casting Kate Valk in the title role in blackface, while Willem Dafoe played the white Cockney trader, Smithers, in white make-up resembling a Kabuki mask. Both actors were dressed in simulations of Japanese Samurai clothing, distancing the production from a naturalist or realist portrait of racial identity.

LeCompte's production showed that racial identity is produced through performance. Valk's blackface first appeared to simply represent the play's central black character. However, next to Dafoe's whiteface, the use of blackface functioned not as a literal rendering of blackness, but as a theatrical mask. The production denaturalised race by placing two evidently artificial performances of colour side by side on the stage, undermining the implication that Valk's blackface was a mimetic rendering of 'real' blackness. Race became a social and theatrical performance, and the fact that the rest of the performers' bodies were left unpainted maintained this effect, reminding the audience that the actors' coloured faces were a theatrical rather than a biological construct. By dislocating colour from race, and showing racial identity to be constructed from a series of gestural and vocal signs rather than being innate to the coloured body, the Wooster Group showed the racial body to have been (partly) produced through theatre practice. Blackface minstrelsy was not critiqued as an 'inaccurate' reflection of race, but was shown to be a deeply and tragically formative performance practice which has shaped the contours of white and black identity in American society. LeCompte's production interrogated the ways in which race is formed on the stage and in the audience, unearthing the ways in which O'Neill's text – and potentially her own performance work – could mediate how spectators related to racial identity.

The production echoed Eric Lott's observation of the formative effects of blackface minstrelsy:

> It was hard to see the real thing without being reminded, even unfavourably of the copy, the 'cover version' that effectively did its work of cultural coverage. Nor, just as surely, could the copy be seen without reminding one of the real thing.[2]

The Wooster Group's theatrical interrogation of blackface and whiteface did the important work of destabilising racial binaries by making not only blackness, but also whiteness, strange on stage. However, the company has been criticised for its appropriation of a racist theatre form, and some critics have rejected their work as formalist experimentation which has little to do with race as lived experience. The Group's work teeters on the brink between subverting and affirming the stereotypes they investigate, and they have attracted controversy for not rejecting minstrelsy outright in their work. The company's investigation of racial stereotypes belies their uneasiness with the formative effects of performance, while also running the risk of affirming the racial inequalities they interrogate.

The complex and problematic ways in which LeCompte and The Wooster Group investigate identity is also apparent in *To You The Birdie*, a performance of Racine's *Phèdre*. Racine's text was layered with and interrupted by technological 'masks', disjointed voice-overs, bodies 'made strange' and contemporary dance to provide a meditation on the contemporary fascination with image, body and celebrity in Western culture. Racine's neo-classical tragedy of illegitimate love was transformed into a contemporary tragedy of the media age. LeCompte also interrogated Racine's text for its deeply problematic vision of female sexuality, and foregrounded the objectification of the female body in Racine's play. Technology, central to the Wooster Group's aesthetic practice, became a trap in this production, mediating and confining female subjectivity in performance.

Both Valk as Phèdre and Frances McDormand as Oenone wore distressed seventeenth-century style corsets, but their elbows were tied to their corsets, giving them limited movement in their upper body. Valk's corset had two metal hoops on its back which her servants used to move her while on stage, place her in various positions and sit her into a bath chair, whereupon they attended to her with enemas and colostomy bags, helping her to defecate and urinate. The spectacle of the female body rendered helpless by the constricting effects of misogyny was further maintained by the fact that actor Scott Shepherd spoke all of Phèdre's lines, leaving Valk a silent and physically helpless figure, mouthing words spoken by a male voice. The use of video continued the production's link between entrapment and spectacle by visually splicing performers' bodies in half on the screens, forcing the actors to mimic film of their own body parts. Valk's body became a spectacle to herself as she mimed to video footage of her feet, which corresponded with Phèdre's body as a spectacle of tragedy and femininity, incapable of any greater physical action than being looked upon.

The production's mediation of physical identity extended also to the male performers, with Ari Flakios as Hippolytus freezing into various Greek statue-like poses and Dafoe as Theseus establishing his masculinity through his body-builder movements and the grotesque distortions of his torso and ribcage. While femininity was the focus of this production, masculinity was also shown to be trapped, immobilised by the effects of mediation. Although the Group critiqued Racine's construction of gender roles, they did not offer an alternative to these roles. Nevertheless, the hyperbolic nature of the Group's performances meant that the production offered the possibility of doing gender 'wrong' and denaturalising its seeming hegemonic inevitability. Gender stereotyping was resisted through its wholesale endorsement in *To You The Birdie*, a strategy which, like the company's use of blackface minstrelsy, runs the risk of maintaining the values it seeks to undermine.

The Wooster Group show the mediated nature of identity to be a tragic inevitability. While they examine the theatre's role in the formation of identity, the identities they explore are frequently negative ones. Representation is implicated in producing the grotesque masks of minstrelsy, the repressive and confining images of gender, the medicalised bodies of the post-AIDS era and the distorted bodies of the celebrity age. One critic has described the company's famous use of multi-media effects on the stage as 'reluctantly technocentric',[3] and the company could also be said to be 'reluctantly theatre-centric'. While the Group show identity to be inevitably constructed and mediated through representation, the dystopian effects of their work come from the sense that they mourn and decry this fact. The Wooster Group show theatricality to be the *only* available mode of identity in a mediated and post-industrial universe. Nonetheless, there is an ever-present sense of loss in their theatrical world, a sense of despair at the irresistible effects of representation. The Wooster Group show theatricality to be an inescapable tragedy.

Notes

1   (1996) *The Death Of Character: Perspectives On Theater After Modernism*, Bloomington and Indianapolis: Indiana University Press: 174.
2   (1993) *Love And Theft, Blackface Minstrelsy And The American Working Class*, Oxford: Oxford University Press: 115.
3   Kalb, Jonathan (1998) 'Theater', *New York Press*, 25–31 March: 6.

Further reading

Aronson, Arnold (2000) *American Avant-Garde Theatre: a History*, London: Routledge.

Auslander, Phillip (1992) *Presence and Resistance, Postmodernism and Cultural Politics in Contemporary American Performance*, Michigan: Michigan University Press.

Butler, Judith (1990) *Gender Trouble: Feminism and the Subversion of Identity*, New York and London: Routledge.

—— (1993) *Bodies That Matter: on the Discursive Limits of 'Sex'*, New York and London: Routledge.

Savran, David (1988) *Breaking The Rules, The Wooster Group*, New York: Theatre Communications Group.

AOIFE MONKS

JIM SHARMAN (1945–)

In the mid-1970s, not yet thirty years old, a successful director on the London stage, the prime mover behind a new genre of popular musicals, and with a major film success in the can, Jim Sharman made what, to some, may have appeared to be a strange decision: to return to Australia.

In so doing, Sharman was not so much turning his back on international stardom as making a commitment to creating an outward-looking, rather than introspective, antipodean theatrical culture. His aim was to synthesise and foster an indigenous theatre combining influences from continental Europe and Asia, the formal gravity of classical tragedy and the carnivalesque vigour of the Elizabethan stage. Such is the significance of his work that it is not an overstatement to credit Sharman with being the driving force behind a generation of Australian theatre workers – actors, directors, writers, designers – and, with the Lighthouse Company in Adelaide, providing a (since unattained) model for theatre-making in Australia.

To write about Jim Sharman is necessarily to write about his relationship with the dramas of Patrick White and the design work of Brian Thomson – Sharman himself pinpoints his 1979 revival of White's epic play *A Cheery Soul* for the newly formed Sydney Theatre Company as a defining moment both in his own career and for Australian theatre in general. The 'cheery soul' of the play's title, Miss Docker, was based on a neighbour of White's – a do-gooder, spreading disaster through a fictional Australian suburb. A Melbourne production in the early 1960s, striving for a naturalistic realisation based on the playwright's elaborate stage directions, had floundered, struggling to come to terms with both the play's theme – a tragic meditation on the destructive power of good taken to militant proportions – and with White's poetic treatment of a darkly expressionistic psychological terrain.

The venue for Sharman's production, the Drama Theatre of the Sydney Opera House, offered a broad, shallow-aproned stage in a panavision proscenium opening, facing a steeply raked auditorium of high-backed seats. Intended originally as a cinema, the space was converted to accommodate main-stage theatre, and, limited by narrow wings and awkward sightlines, had a reputation as a difficult space in which to work. Sharman and Thomson chose to ignore White's staging suggestions, confronting the audience instead with a dropped fire curtain, upon which was painted the cast list like a huge vaudeville poster. When it rose, the actors were dotted about a brilliantly lit stage, bare except for a piano. There was a soft chord as all the inhabitants of Sarsaparilla except Miss Docker turned to face the audience. They stood stock still for the second chord, and on a third Robyn Nevin's Miss Docker turned, her face locked in a silent scream.[1]

A half-curtain crossed the expanse of the proscenium, drawn by Nevin to change scenes.

> The side of the stage was lined with benches used by actors when not directly involved in the action ... a Brechtian emphasis on theatricality of performance allowed non-naturalistic elements of the play to become a natural part of life on stage, as well as heightening the audience's awareness of language and characterisation. The actors often played directly to the auditorium, discussing action and events in a technique which produced the notion of an imagined reality. The world of the play was as real and as imagined, as ordinary and as fantastic, as only life in the theatre can be.[2]

And so Sharman brought **Brecht** to main-stage Australian theatre – not a didactic, austere Brecht, but a richly theatrical Brecht; Brecht via the carnival, the fantastical and the poetic. In turning his gaze outwards, towards the continental European theatre of Genet, Lorca, Wedekind and Strindberg, Sharman was seeking a break with what he perceived as an Anglocentric insularity dominating the antipodean stage, all the better to determine an Australian voice, to create an indigenous theatre, in David Marr's words, of 'myth and magic with a dash of vaudeville'.[3]

Sharman and White met in 1966. White had found himself 'led blindfolded one night' to a 'rather crummy'[4] theatre to watch the 'topical revue *Terror Australis*, which a respected critic had panned'.[5] The show was, in White's words, an 'abrasive, shit-slinging' political cabaret into which the audience was herded through sheep railings 'while the cast stood on stage baaing their way through the national anthem'.[6] The director was Jim Sharman, newly graduated from the National Institute of Dramatic Art (NIDA) in Sydney. Excited by the experience, White wrote a rebuttal to the nay-saying critic's pan, and, some months later, was collared outside a record shop by 'a scruffy young man in T-shirt, jeans, and sneakers'.[7] It was Sharman, wanting to thank White for defending his work in the press. They exchanged awkward small talk, and White did not expect that the two of them – the well-established, middle-aged literary figure and the 'wonderkid of Australian theatre, idol of the young'[8] – would cross paths again. As Katherine Brisbane notes, however, Sharman was 'a man as pre-occupied as White with the task of communicating in physical terms the landscape of the imagination'.[9]

Sharman's star was already on the rise. In 1967 he directed *Don Giovanni*, staged on a huge chequerboard, for the Elizabethan Trust Opera Company, alienating conservative audiences while attracting the young. The entrepreneur Harry M. Miller liked what he saw, and invited Sharman to direct the local production of *Hair*. Among the legacies of that work was Sharman's subsequent commitment to 'multi-cultural' casting (a theme that also drew him to Genet's writings). He counts among his contributions to Australian theatre his willingness to allow non-Anglo-Saxon actors to play a range of roles, from Mary Magdalene to Ariel. *Hair* was a tremendous success; following productions in Melbourne, Tokyo and Boston, in 1972 Miller and Sharman again collaborated on the Australian premiere of *Jesus Christ Superstar*. Brian Thomson designed, marking the beginning of what commentator Martin Thomas has called 'the strongest director–designer partnership in Australian theatre'.[10] Thomson's design was extraordinary: a multi-levelled perspex and chrome constructivist fantasy built into the grand proscenium of the Capitol Theatre in downtown Sydney, the catwalks connected by a clear, tubular lift-shaft and a sprawling staircase, the whole theatre drenched in a rich, chocolate brown. For the opening number, Judas Iscariot burst out of a huge dodecahedron, shadowed by two dancers echoing his every move. The production *rocked*: so much so that Tim Rice and Andrew Lloyd Webber, the lyricist and composer, invited Sharman and Thomson to direct and design the London season. In London, Thomson and Sharman collaborated with New Zealand ex-patriot Richard O'Brien to produce *The Rocky Horror Show* (1973), a satire of B-grade science fiction staged Upstairs at The Royal Court. From this production, of course, came the feature film *The Rocky Horror Picture Show* (1975), directed by Sharman. It is for this work that Sharman is most recognised internationally. Strangely enough, it was this man, the cool, in-touch 'idol of the young' who was to do justice to Patrick White's plays.

Returning to Australia, Sharman directed White's *The Season at Sarsaparilla* (1976) for the Old Tote, the state-subsidised theatre working in the Sydney Opera House. Its success prompted White to set to work on a new piece, *Big Toys*, directed by Sharman the following year with Thomson designing. The production 'bore resemblances to *The Rocky Horror Show* in the sophistication of its staging', wrote one commentator; 'White's late plays have increasingly become like high literary parallels to *The Rocky Horror Picture Show* ... [integrating] an element of high camp visual wit'.[11] Published editions of the text integrated Thomson and Sharman's design into the stage directions. A production of Strindberg's *Dreamplay* at NIDA (1977), for which Sharman had a mounded beach spilling off the stage into the audience, so affected White that he set about dedicating his late masterpiece, *The Twyborne Affair*, to Jim Sharman.

In these productions, Sharman was tapping into a vein of theatricality as far as possible removed from the 'rep company sets' and naturalism that was the Old Tote's house style. What Kruse read as a 'high camp visual wit', Sharman would understand as the essence of theatricality: that an audience sees before they listen. Sharman suggests that his achievement in working in the new genre of musical theatre in the early 1970s has to be understood in terms of a Brechtian, rather than Broadway musical tradition: Sharman's was a gestic theatre from the first, at least partly out of a regard for Brecht (and an expressionistic lineage from Shakespeare through Strindberg, Wedekind and **Reinhardt** to Brecht) but also from a number of other influences, among them his fascination with Asian theatre, developed during a study tour to Japan in the late 1960s. Sharman cites his own early experiences of musical theatre (he talks of being captivated as a teenager by a 1960s production of *Oliver!*), and, perhaps most significantly, of carnival and vaudeville. 'I grew up' Sharman has written,

> in a world of travelling sideshows, carnivals, circuses, boxing troupes, Chinese acrobats and tent-show vaudeville ... boxing matches fought in sawdust-strewn tents (an appropriate preparation for directing Strindberg!), Chinese acrobats in silk pyjamas spinning plates and then, barechested, leaping through hoops of fire. All this non-verbal theatre constituted a kind of dance, communicated without words, beyond words.[12]

This is a non-literary performance genealogy: Sharman recalls the Sorlie family's travelling tent shows, themselves a hold-over from the booming vaudeville circuits of the late nineteenth century.[13]

Between school terms, Sharman worked for his father, drumming up audiences for his father's boxing ring show. Little wonder that for his graduation project for NIDA, Sharman proposed a *Threepenny Opera* staged on a carousel revolve, seeing himself, one suspects, as the sideshow organ-grinder: Brecht's *Moritat* singer.[14]

When the Old Tote folded in 1978, Sharman and Rex **Cramphorn** brought together an ensemble of actors with a view to producing the Old Tote's planned season of new Australian plays. The new company was named for the marvellous art-deco cinema they rented in East Sydney: The Paris. In the spirit of optimism kindled by the project, Sharman spoke of his desire for 'a less naturalistic, or more poetic and more imaginative theatre',[15] something more than 'people in small rooms worrying about themselves'.[16] The first season was to include texts by Dorothy Hewitt, Louis Nowra (*Visions*) and Patrick White (*A Cheery Soul*). The season was a disaster: audiences stayed away in droves. The opening production was Hewitt's *Pandora's Cross* (1978), set in a constructivist ensemble of catwalks and elevator vertical spaces dominated by a Hollywood sign-esque letter 'P'.

The Paris company collapsed, but not before the idea of a permanent ensemble of actors *and* playwrights dedicated to developing a contemporary Australian sensibility had taken root. That idea was realised when, in 1982, Sharman was appointed Artistic Director of the State Theatre Company of South Australia, which he promptly renamed the Lighthouse Company. Working with a dozen actors, three playwrights (White, Nowra and Stephen Sewell) and (later) associate director Neil **Armfield**, The Lighthouse's first season was, in the words of one critic, 'not for the trivial-minded or the faint-hearted'.[17] Revealingly, Sharman refused to include popular favourite David Williamson's *The Perfectionist* at the Lighthouse in 1982, asserting that 'we are not looking for proven box-office smashes – we are looking to create our own' plays, pursuing 'an epic theatricality akin to that of Elizabethan theatre. Domestic comedy is not our forte' (Ackerholt 1995: 556). Instead, he premiered new work by White (*Netherwood*, 1983) and Nowra (*Royal Show*, 1982; *Sunrise*, 1983), European work such as Brecht's *Mother Courage* (1982) and Lorca's *Blood Wedding* (1983), and a Shakespeare (*A Midsummer Night's Dream*, 1982). For two seasons, indulged by the generous funding of the South Australian Ministry of the Arts, the ensemble was able to generate work 'of a scale, complexity and ambition seen neither before, nor since, on Australian stages'.[18]

Notes

1 Marr, D. (1991) *Patrick White: A Life*, Sydney: Random House: 588.
2 Ackerholt, M., personal correspondence.
3 Marr (1991: 570).
4 White, P. (1981) *Flaws in the Glass: A Self-portrait*, London: Jonathan Cape: 247.
5 Ibid.: 243.
6 Marr (1991: 559–560).
7 White (1981: 244).
8 Ibid.: 245.
9 Brisbane, K. (1985) 'Foreword' to *Patrick White: Collected Plays Volume 1*, Sydney: Currency Press: 7.
10 Thomas, M. (1989) 'Brian Thomson: Picturing the Stage(s)', *New Theatre: Australia* 12: 19–25.
11 Kruse, A. (1981) 'Patrick White's Later Plays' in Holloway, Peter (ed.) *Contemporary Australian Drama*, rev. edn, Sydney: Currency Press: 310.
12 Sharman, J. (1996) 'In the Realm of the Imagination: An Individual View of Theatre', *Australasian Drama Studies* 28: 22–23.
13 See Waterhouse, R. (1990) *From Minstrel Show to Vaudeville: The Australian Popular Stage 1788–1914*, Kensington, NSW: New South Wales University Press.
14 Sharman directed *Threepenny Opera* for the Old Tote Theatre Company in 1973 – the first use of the Drama Theatre at the Sydney Opera House.
15 Radic, L. (1991) *The State of Play: The Revolution in the Australian Theatre since the 1960s*, Ringwood, Vic.: Penguin Books: 147.
16 Otherwise unattributed quotes from Sharman are from personal conversations with the author.
17 Radic (1991: 184).
18 Ibid.: 191.

Further reading

Ackerholt, M. (1995) *The Currency Companion to Australian Theatre*, Sydney: Currency Press.

Carroll, D. (1995) *Australian Contemporary Drama*, Sydney: Currency Press.

IAN MAXWELL

ANNE BOGART (1951–)

In a career that spans more than thirty years and a hundred productions, Anne Bogart has distinguished herself both as an innovative director with eclectic interests and as a dedicated teacher who has changed the course of theatre training in the United States. She grew up as the daughter of a career naval officer, whose changing

commissions led to a peripatetic family life, including periods in
Rhode Island, California, Virginia and Japan. She received an MA in
directing from New York University in 1977 and, two years later,
began teaching and directing in NYU's newly formed Experimental
Theatre Wing. Her 1984 production there of Rodgers and
Hammerstein's *South Pacific*, which treated the musical as if it were
being performed by war veterans hospitalised for post-traumatic
stress syndrome, stirred controversy and won a Bessie Award. Her
1988 staging of excerpts from the theoretical writings of Bertolt
Brecht, titled *No Plays No Poetry But Philosophical Reflections Practical
Instructions Provocative Descriptions and Pointers From A Noted Critic
and Playwright*, won an Obie Award for Best Direction. She received
a second Obie four years later, when she directed the premiere of
Paula Vogel's *The Baltimore Waltz*, with Cherry Jones, at Circle
Repertory Company.

In 1989 Bogart replaced Adrian Hall as artistic director of Trinity
Repertory Company in Providence, Rhode Island, only to resign a
year later after a showdown with its board of directors. Then, in
1992, she joined with renowned Japanese director Tadashi **Suzuki**
to form the Saratoga International Theatre Institute (subsequently
known as the SITI Company) as an organisation dedicated to
training young theatre artists, creating new performance work, and
international collaboration. With the SITI Company, Bogart has
directed more than a dozen original creations, sometimes in
conjunction with a playwright or adaptor, as well as such standards
of the repertoire as *Hay Fever* (2002) and *A Midsummer Night's
Dream* (2004). In 1995 the Actors Theatre of Louisville celebrated
Bogart as a 'Modern Master' with a month-long festival of plays
directed by her, a weekend of lectures, workshops and panel discussions, and a book of essays about her work. Since 1994 she has
taught directing at Columbia University, and is the recipient of a
Guggenheim fellowship.

As one of six influential 'downtown directors' featured in a 2002
exhibition at the Exit Art Gallery in New York, Bogart divided her
body of work into six categories: Classic Explosions, mostly of
modernist masterworks and twentieth-century American favorites;
Site Specific, early experiments in borrowed spaces around New
York, including her own Brooklyn apartment; Dance/Theatre,
pieces driven more by movement than text, showing a curiosity
about the enigma of male/female relationships; Living Playwrights,
including collaborations with Mac Wellman, Eduardo Machado,
Charles Mee, Naomi Iizuka and Paula Vogel; Music Theatre, ranging

from Broadway musicals turned on their heads to Laurie Anderson's *Songs and Stories from Moby Dick* (1999) and to contemporary grand opera; and Devised Works, original collage pieces, woven out of texts from a single playwright or around a major cultural figure, mostly created with the members of the SITI Company. These groupings reflect the tremendous heterogeneity of Bogart's directing interests, which are united by an insatiable intellectual curiosity, a commitment to ensemble work and the sovereign actor, the pursuit of a permanent company to create new work, and a fascination with the nature of artistic creation and, especially, theatrical process. This has led to the creation of original pieces about important twentieth-century artists (Virginia Woolf, Orson Welles, Leonard Bernstein, Andy Warhol, Robert **Wilson**, among others) and to an ongoing enquiry into the aesthetic contract with the audience.

Bogart's concern with the audience is evident in her pioneering site-specific pieces of the late 1970s in which she would personally guide spectators to a variety of borrowed spaces, including an abandoned schoolhouse, a detective agency, a Romanian meeting hall and 'many other places ripe for invasion' (Bogart 2001: 11). In the late 1990s at the Actors Theatre of Louisville, she conducted an audience project in which she invited regular theatregoers to go behind the scenes and observe rehearsals of her *Private Lives* (1998); a year later she used interview material with these volunteers as partial text for a metatheatrical meditation titled *Cabin Pressure* (1999). Over the years her productions have often included one or more supernumeraries who function as on-stage spectators, drawing attention to the action as something to be watched, witnessed and scrutinised. This practice reflects Bogart's characterisation of herself as the first audience for a piece that is in the process of being created. Once the groundwork has been laid – a text selected or assembled, a cast chosen, a design and groundplan mapped out, and certain ground rules established – her rehearsal strategy is to sit back and watch what happens. She relies on her collaborators to make discoveries and generate possibilities. She looks and listens without particular expectation or a finished form in mind. As much as possible, she allows the shape of each production to reveal itself through the rehearsal process. She is patient and, when the time comes, decisive. Through her casual leadership and the rigorous quality of her attention, she creates a working space in which others can create, earning her a reputation as a nurturing, non-authoritarian director.

Bogart traces this approach to a job she had in the late 1970s leading an ongoing theatre workshop at a halfway house for schizophrenics. When attendance dropped, she acceded to the participants' wish to work on musical comedies and found that the group erupted with excitement and creativity. She provided enough structure to channel their energy back into the work, a practice she has maintained ever since. Bogart explains: 'That is how I learned that is what I do. I don't try to control things. I ride what is happening' (interview with the author, 21 April 2003, New York). In a professional setting, this strategy asks for actors who share a vocabulary and an aesthetic and who are well-trained, disciplined, inventive and prepared to take responsibility for their own performances. This is one reason why Bogart has always placed a premium on having a company, a difficult prospect in the United States. Since its establishment in 1992, the SITI Company has evolved into a creative collective that has enabled Bogart to pursue her vision of a theatre of enquiry, thanks in no small part to the commitment of her actors to the company ideal.

Most original SITI works are conceived by Bogart as a process of investigation built around three overlapping givens: a social or political question, often prompted by her own personal experience; an anchor, often an important artistic or cultural figure; and a structure, a device or conceit for shaping the performance, often borrowed from another work or form. For instance, the SITI Company's *Culture of Desire* (1997) used the figure of Andy Warhol as an anchor and aspects of Dante's *Inferno* as a structure to examine the question of what it means to be raised and educated in the United States as a consumer rather than a citizen. The performance that eventuated from this approach took a form that was musical, metaphorical and kaleidoscopic rather than rhetorical, narrative or psychological. The piece is composed of three interwoven semi-independent continuities or texts: a verbal text, often amounting to a collage of quotations collected during a preliminary research phase; a performance text, gestures, movements and actions worked out with choreographic exactitude by the actors in rehearsal; and a design text, including a simple, metaphoric set by Neil Patel, functional costumes by James Schuette, muscular lighting by Mimi Jordan Sherin, and an active, often insistent soundscape by Darron L. West. In her *mise-en-scène*, Bogart withholds some or all of the logic that has drawn these three texts together, thereby activating the audience's role as the final collaborator by giving them gaps to bridge (or not) with their own meanings, associations and responses. In this regard, her work can be seen as postmodern.

Around 1980, at New York University, Bogart met and worked with dancer Mary Overlie, who was developing a theory of choreography that she called the 'Six Viewpoints', after her idea of the six basic elements of a dance. In coming years, not without some controversy, Bogart adapted these ideas for theatre training and directing as the Viewpoints, changing some nomenclature and adding elements in the process. As a simple semiotics of movement in time and space, the Viewpoints – shape, spatial relationship, floor pattern, architecture, repetition, gesture, tempo, duration and kinesthetic response – form the basis for a series of physical improvisations that help actors to articulate their presence with clarity and precision, to establish a common vocabulary and create work quickly, and to find shape and vary the rhythms of performance. In Bogart's teaching and directing work, the Viewpoints feed into what she calls Composition, a method for creating short, quick, impulsive pieces as raw material that might become part of a larger piece under development. Both the Viewpoints and Composition advance Bogart's promotion of the actor as more a creative than an interpretive artist. As a co-ordinated system of training, the SITI Company has combined the Viewpoints and Composition with the rigorous exercises developed by Suzuki in the 1970s and 1980s. The Suzuki Method develops a performer's lower-body strength, concentration and vocal power through a series of precise physical forms or disciplines that are repeated with military precision. The synergy of the Viewpoints, Suzuki and Composition work has proved to be a fruitful platform for the SITI Company's original creations and a source of continuing inspiration for a younger generation of theatre artists.

As a senior at Bard College, when she could not decide which Ionesco play she wanted to direct, Bogart compiled her favorite bits and pieces into an Ionesco miscellany, which she staged. She has pursued much the same collage strategy ever since:

> I am a scavenger. I am not an original thinker and I am not a true creative artist. So the notion of scavenging appeals to me. That is what I do. Like a bird that goes and pulls different things and makes a nest. I think it is more a nesting impulse, of taking this and that and weaving it together to make some sort of marriage of ideas. I read a lot and I take little bits of what I read and I put them together into thoughts and ideas. I juxtapose ideas. I like the satisfaction of putting things together like that.
>
> (Interview with the author, 21 April 2003, New York)

Bogart's association of her 'scavenger mentality' with a nest-building impulse points to the heart of her work. She 'steals', as she calls it, from wide-ranging sources in order to create an environment or structure within which certain challenges and difficulties, including violence, stereotype, memory, embarrassment, eroticism and the terror of everyday life, can be confronted. Her abiding concern and major achievement is to engender in actors and audiences the capacity to pay attention without making it an act of will, to look, listen, feel and respond to what is already happening in the surrounding world. In this regard, Anne Bogart advocates and practices a theatre of consciousness.

Further reading

Bogart, Anne (2001) *A Director Prepares: Seven Essays on Art and Theatre*, London: Routledge.

Bogart, Anne and Landau, Tina (2004) *The Viewpoints Book: A Practical Guide to Viewpoints and Composition*, New York: Theatre Communications Group.

Cummings, Scott T. (2005) *Anne Bogart and Charles Mee: Remaking American Theater*, Cambridge: Cambridge University Press.

Dixon, Michael Bigelow and Smith, Joel A. (eds) (1995) *Anne Bogart: Viewpoints*, Lyme, NH: Smith & Kraus.

SCOTT T. CUMMINGS

LLUÍS PASQUAL (1951–)

After almost seven years in Paris, Lluís Pasqual returned to his native Catalonia in 1997 to assume co-ordination of the city's Ciutat del Teatre project. A year later he replaced actor/director Lluís Homar as co-artistic director of the Teatre Lliure, the theatre he had co-founded in 1976 with a group of collaborators including writer/dramaturg Guillem-Jordi Graells, director Pere Planella and designer Fabià Puigserver. These two events served to consolidate a commitment to re-establishing Pasqual as a permanent feature of the Catalan theatrical landscape, of which he had formed such a crucial component during the 1970s and early 1980s before assuming the artistic directorship of Madrid's Centro Dramático Nacional (1983–89) and Paris' Odéon-Théâtre de l'Europe, where he succeeded Giorgio **Strehler** in 1990.

Although perceived as a director who is most comfortable working within the classical repertory, Pasqual's career has been shaped by eclectic directorial choices. These include devised work (*La setmana tràgica*, 1975; *Camí de nit 1854*, 1977), contemporary writing (Genet's *El balcó*, 1980; Salvador Espriu's *Una altra Fedra, si us plau*, 1978) as well as revelatory readings of Spanish twentieth-century works that suffered neglect during the difficult years of the Franco regime (1939–75). A sixteen-year working relationship with the Polish-trained scenographer Fabià Puigserver generated twenty-three productions that, in their provocative re-imaginings of theatrical space, transcended the parameters of baroque design that had hitherto dominated the Spanish mainstream stage.

Pasqual and Puigserver first collaborated in 1975 on *La setmana tràgica*, a **Mnouchkine**-inspired production devised from improvisational work with students from the Escola de Teatre de l'Orfeo de Sants in Barcelona. It served to challenge customary actor–audience relationships through an orchestration of space whereby the actors encircled the audience, thereby subverting habitual framing boundaries. Their subsequent projects were notable both for stripping the stage of superficial decor and for the presence of visual analogies for the dramatic tensions in the text. At the Teatre Lliure, with its multipurpose auditorium, Pasqual and Puigserver worked with plays that veered away from the obvious, where the language was poetic and the emphasis was on showing rather than telling. The productions provided alternative spectator/performer configurations that disallowed complacent aestheticisation.

During the years following Pasqual's residencies at the National Theatre of Warsaw (where he assisted Adam Hanuszkiewicz on his 1976 production of Chekhov's *Platanov*) and Milan's Piccolo Teatro (1978) (where he worked as Strehler's assistant), his collaborations with Puigserver demonstrated a fascination with working in the round and an extraordinary capacity to conjure magical stage moments from elemental ingredients. He credits his time in Poland as crucial in shaping his capacity to 'watch and observe' performers, registering 'the communication between one actor and another; the triangle that develops between the actors and the audience'.[1] He cites both Strehler and **Brook** as key formative influences on his work, acknowledging that from the former he discovered 'the idea of the illusionist, the magician, of making what doesn't exist appear, done in a majestic, artistic way' and from the latter 'simplicity, authenticity, purity, where earth is earth and wood is wood'.[2]

A glance at the Lliure's programming between 1976 and 2001, or even Pasqual's choice of repertoire while artistic director of the Centro Dramático Nacional or the Odéon-Théâtre de l'Europe, indicates a marked attraction to works that defy linear logic and concern themselves with the relationship between differing registers of reality. Pasqual has been credited with bringing to the stage dramatic works that had previously been branded 'impossible' and lain dormant for decades. These include Ramón del Valle-Inclán's *Luces de bohemia* (1984), which Pasqual set on a brilliant mirrored floor, recognising the existence of conflicting articulations and dispensing with psychological identity as the sole pivot on which the interpretation of character turns. The premieres of Federico García Lorca's 'unknown' plays, *El público* (1986) and *Comedia sin título* (1989), reinvented both works as reflections on the function of theatre at a time of great social and cultural change in Spain. Questioning popular conceptions of García Lorca as a folkloric dramatist, the stagings, seen in Paris and Milan as well as Madrid's Centro Dramático Nacional, promoted Hispanic cultural heritage abroad without reducing it to a single hegemonic product.

With *El público*, Pasqual dispensed with a reverential reading that might have presented this excavated play-script to a curious audience with rigidly sacred precision. Instead, Pasqual chose a more playful approach that celebrated not only the complex interaction of differing linguistic and dramatic discourses in the play, but also the specific functions of the eccentric stage directions. Rather than simply seeing their task as extracting meaning from García Lorca's text, Pasqual and Puigserver recognised their own engagement in a creative dialogue with the play. Removing the stage and the orchestra stalls of the Teatro María Guerrero provided an expansive almost circular playing area of sparkling blue sand that simultaneously evoked a circus ring, a lunar landscape, a beach and a *corral*. Costumes alluded to the play's variant generic registers and were not located in any definable period or tradition.

With *Comedia sin título*, also, Pasqual's visual aesthetic revolved around the politics of visibility. Hinging on the slight plot of a revolution breaking out outside a theatre where rehearsals for *A Midsummer Night's Dream* are taking place, the play's narrative style, like that of *El público*, was oblique and fragmentary. In Puigserver's design, the ornate splendour of the Teatro María Guerrero was decisively placed on display, providing a frame for the rehearsals of Shakespeare's play that Pasqual included in his staging. Alternative theatrical configurations undermined the spectators' sense of themselves as a cohesive group. Actors were planted in the audience. 'Rehearsals' were disrupted by the tensions erupting around the stage. A rumbling noise on the street outside, symbolic of the 'other' feared by the audience, consistently threatened to invade their complacent and illusionist existence. Eventually, panic set in and the boundaries between the private space of the auditorium and the undefined public space of the world beyond collapsed. Disorder enveloped the auditorium as an explosion from outside ruptured a section of the stage. Spectators rushed out in haste, unaware that this was an illusion conjured by Pasqual and Puigserver. In terms of its provocative spirit and the manner in which it reframed Shakespeare's disembodied play, the production stood up against the boundaries of accepted taste, the 'cultura de plastico'[3] which Pasqual has repeatedly denounced for its corrupting and debilitating complacency.

It is significant that Pasqual chose *Comedia sin título* both to close his tenure at the Centro Dramático Nacional and as his inaugural production as artistic director of the Odéon-Théâtre de l'Europe in 1990. Staging *Comedia sin título* both in French as *Sans Titre* and in Castilian Spanish – and assuming the role of the Autor (Author) in the Spanish-language production – he sought to emphasise a cultural specificity that was enacted both through a focus on the problems inherent in translating García Lorca into French and through the different performance traditions of French and Spanish actors. Rather than erase difference in search of some naive concept of cultural globalisation, Pasqual sought to emphasise diversity and particularity. Referring to himself as more Spanish in Paris than he is in Spain, Pasqual strongly refuted the concept of international theatre, looking instead at the Odéon to create the possibility for a European theatre that goes beyond political institutions or bland standardisation. *Comedia sin título/Sans Titre* was about the inauguration of a theatrical strategy that could offer a means of interrogating what the oscillating discourses of a new Europe might be and how theatre might participate in the debates raging through the shifting boundaries of the continent.

The death of Puigserver in 1991 saw Pasqual negotiate new design partnerships. With Frederic Amat, Pasqual realised *Haciendo Lorca (Making Lorca)* in 1996. Originally conceived as a reworking of *Bodas de sangre (Blood Wedding)* for Nuria Espert and Alfredo Alcón, it mutated during rehearsal into a meditation on the play centring on the characters of Death and the Moon. Adapted, dismantled and reorganised, the piece emerged, like Peter Brook's performed essay on *Hamlet, Qui est là?*, as a process of weaving together research, reflections, selected sections of the play and fragments of other texts. The emphasis was on narrative discontinuity where bodies of inherited meaning come together to comment on the conflicts played out in the writings. The core design metaphor of the crane, provided by Amat and operated by a team of four technicians, alluded to Puigserver's canvas membrane for Víctor García's *Yerma* (1970), both in its concrete physicalisation of the dramatics of the piece and in its creation of a visual environment which emphatically rejected mimetic realism in its vertical organisation of space.

For *Tirano Banderas* (1992), a Spanish-language adaptation of Valle-Inclán's monumental novel on despotism in an unnamed Latin-American state, Amat created a dazzling visual correlation for the unstable political situation in a spinning merry-go-round set. For the controversial *Roberto Zucco*, produced first with the Lliure in 1993 and then with the Maly Drama Theatre of St Petersburg (directed by Lev **Dodin**) in 1994, he went on to craft a technological set of intrusive video monitors that exemplified a hostile visual world of uncompromising violence where surveillance is the order of the day. For *Waiting for Godot* (1999), Amat offered a horizontal set of cinematic dimensions. Against a white wall resembling a blank film screen, a solitary and twisted iron tree stood out from a set of abandoned chairs and other discarded detritus encrusted into a mound of rock. Thrown onto this rubbish tip of society, Anna Lizaran's animated Vladimir and Eduard Fernández's Estragon were mercilessly picked out by harsh spotlights, illuminated before an audience for whom they performed their vaudeville rituals of endless waiting. As with so much of Pasqual's stage work, performance and all its physical trappings served as the production's defining metaphor.

In the 1988 *Bengues* – the gypsy word for devils – a collaboration with Antonio Canales' dance company saw García Lorca's *La casa de Bernarda Alba* reinvented through the violent idiom of flamenco. Flamenco, which Pasqual had always consciously avoided, was here stripped of its showy folkloric adornments. The body functioned as the text on which the intersecting discourses of political and cultural history are written. Dismantling classical texts, as he had done with *La vida del Rey Eduardo II de Inglaterra*, *Bodas de sangre*, *Comedia sin título* and *La casa de Bernarda Alba*, Pasqual confronted his audiences with alternative ways of seeing. As with all his productions, the performance turned out to be a brilliant game of mirrors where reflections on truth and lies merged in a playful but often unsettling celebration of the subliminal artifice of the stage.

Notes

1 Pasqual quoted in Delgado, Maria M. (1998) 'Redefining Spanish Theatre: Lluís Pasqual on Directing, Fabiá Puigserver, and the Lliure', *Spanish Theatre 1920–1995: Strategies in Protest and Imagination (3)*, *Contemporary Theatre Review* 7 (4): 91–92.
2 Pasqual quoted in Delgado, Maria M. and Heritage, P. (eds) (1996) *In Contact with the Gods? Directors Talk Theatre*, Manchester and New York: Manchester University Press: 214.
3 Pasqual, Lluís and Muñoz, Diego (1995) 'No me encuentro bien bajo la cultura catalana que representa Jordi Pujol', *La Vanguardia*, 8 May: 39.

Further reading

Delgado, M.M. (2003) *'Other' Spanish Theatres: Erasure and Inscription on the Twentieth Century Spanish Stage*, Manchester: Manchester University Press.

Smith, P.J. (1998) *The Theatre of García Lorca: Text, Performance, Psychoanalysis*, Cambridge: Cambridge University Press.

MARIA M. DELGADO

EIMUNTAS NEKROSIUS (1952–)

Lithuanian-born Eimuntas Nekrosius trained under Andrey Goncharov at the State Institute for Theatre Arts in Moscow. Until the early 1990s he worked at the State Youth Theatre in Vilnius. His productions there include Eliseeva's *The Square* (1980), Korostylev's *Pirosmani, Pirosmani* (1981), *Love and Death in Verona* (1982, a rock opera based on *Romeo and Juliet*), Aitmatov's *A Day Longer than a Century* (1983), Chekhov's *Uncle Vanya* (1986) and Gogol's *The Nose* (1991). He subsequently worked for several years with the festival LIFE (Lithuanian International Theatre Festival), which produced three of his shows: Pushkin's *Mozart and Salieri* (1994), Chekhov's *Three Sisters* (1995) and Shakespeare's *Hamlet* (1997). From 1998 he headed his own theatre, MenoFortas, in Vilnius, where he directed *Macbeth* (1999) and *Othello* (2000).

Nekrosius' early productions at the Youth Theatre focused on characters who experience a last burst of energy before their imminent death. Some of these productions were structured as journeys into the past. *The Square* concerned a teacher who corresponded with a prisoner. She then visited him, they fell in love and she became pregnant. The teacher remembers on stage, the space of her memory visually cordoned off by a red ribbon, which was cut at the beginning to open up the space of the past. The latter space was then sealed off again at the end, when the narrative returned to the present. *Pirosmani, Pirosmani* also used the form of retrospection and focused on the last day in the life of the late nineteenth-century Georgian primitive painter. Pirosmani reflects about his life and engages in dialogue with the animated characters of his paintings. The painter cannot reconcile creativity with reality – a dilemma captured in a key image of the production when Pirosmani draws a figure on the frosted window and, from the other side, his muse Iya appears and wipes the window. She destroys the painting, but herself becomes the new object of the picture as she stands in the frame. In *The Nose*, his last production at the Youth Theatre, Nekrosius turned Major Kovalyov's nose into a penis, thus alluding to Gogol's alleged aversion towards the female sex. Instead of losing his nose, Kovalyov is castrated. Nekrosius had Gogol preside over the adventures of his characters, thus underlining the absurd games the writer plays with his characters. In these productions, Nekrosius placed little importance on the text: plays were often truncated, stories adapted, or the dialogue hastily written before the premiere (as was the case for *The Square*). His main concern was creating a series of images that tell the story.

In his two Chekhov productions, Nekrosius offered a fresh reading of the great Russian playwright, whose plays have often been crippled by the constraints of the Moscow Art Theatre's psychological realism and often turned into melodramas. In *Uncle Vanya*, he parodied the pseudo-progressive doctor who shows Russia's forests on a map the size of a stamp, which he picks up with tweezers and inspects under a huge looking glass the shape and size of a television screen. A similarly parodic view appears when the doctor, allegedly enlightened by modern medicine, applies the house remedy of 'cupping' (placing suction jars to draw the heat from a fevered patient) to treat Vanya's temperature. The stylish life of the landowners of the *fin de siècle* is shown to be essentially inactive and decadent. Elena Sergeyevna is sexually attractive to all the men. The servants continually flit across the stage with felt-padded shoes to polish the floors, while failing to respond to the requests of their masters. The time for change, for the masters to be replaced by the servants, has come. Before this happens, however, they all pose together for a final photograph, recording their image for posterity to the accompaniment of Verdi's 'Choir of the Prisoners' ('*Va pensiero*') from *Nabucco*.

Three Sisters also undermines the traditional perception of Chekhov in its portrayal of the Prozorov sisters as lacking in manners. They smoke like men, wipe their noses on the table-cloth, carry birch logs and jump on to vaulting-horses. They do not belong to the educated class, but are daughters of military men who, physically strong, ape the behaviour of their late father and his military colleagues. *Three Sisters* contains, above all, an element that anticipates a central theme of *Hamlet*: that of playing games. Both the military and the Prozorov family are almost constantly engaged in fitness exercises, turning the props on the stage into objects for this use. Physical exercises and games serve to cover the absurdity of their existence. The sisters are aware of the ordinary nature of their lives, but pretend to be extraordinary as they play games to create the illusion that their lives are active and meaningful. Nekrosius chose to set the play in a living room dominated by a tower of birch logs which can be dismantled and reassembled to form the walls. The logs, chopped from the trees of the Prozorovs' estate, suggest that the estate is doomed. For Nekrosius, Chekhov's dramas are comedies in that the characters are aware of their destiny and witness the end of their era, but engage in a series of games between the crucial events (in Chekhov, always off-stage) which constitute their lives.

After adapting *Romeo and Juliet* to the rock opera *Love and Death in Verona* and an aborted *King Lear* in the early 1990s, Nekrosius turned to *Hamlet*, *Macbeth* and *Othello*, reducing their texts to concentrate on the central and universal themes of life and death. The crucial theme in *Hamlet* and *Macbeth* was the continuity of time, captured in the design of *Hamlet* by the eroding drizzle falling onto a rusty saw suspended over the stage centre and, in *Macbeth*, by a swaying wooden bar. This was contrasted with the transience of human lives and how they are disrupted through the task of revenge (the father challenging the son to exert a God-like function), or through fate and circumstance (the witches' manipulation of Macbeth). In *Othello*, time is static: it is measurable like the water level on a bar placed at the centre of the stage.

In *Hamlet*, Nekrosius is interested in the theme of taking life. Hamlet's father reaches the sad realisation that he gave the wrong role to his son by demanding he take revenge. In *Macbeth* the witches play with Macbeth's life, until it is too late. Both productions end with unwanted, yet predictable, deaths. People inflict destruction on the lives of the protagonists while demanding justice (Hamlet's father) or attention in a game with love and power (the witches). Othello, however, takes Desdemona's life as well as his own. He knows from the outset that his love for Desdemona has no chance because of its intensity. He is enamoured with the girl he once knew, and when Desdemona takes the future of their love into her own hands by eloping with him, the floodgates of betrayal, suspicion and denunciation are flung wide open. In the first two productions the forces that wreaked havoc were not ordinary human beings, but, in *Othello*, ordinary human beings cause the tragedy.

With *Othello* Nekrosius turns from the historical and universal perspectives explored in *Hamlet* and *Macbeth* to the individual, since the play is about a personal tragedy. Othello kills Desdemona and commits suicide when he realises that he has wrongly suspected her of adultery. Nekrosius explores, in his Shakespearean tragedies, the relationships between characters in terms of the games they play with each other while they are fully aware of what is in store for them at the end of the game. Gradually, as the game becomes more and more difficult to play, the tragic tone slows down the pace of the production, ultimately leaving the key players immobile.

Nekrosius' productions impress by their powerful images and by the clarity with which he conveys his interpretation through theatrical devices. His is a highly visual theatre. He explains the motivations of a character's action through gestures and the ritual of everyday life. He presents the author's *Weltanschauung*, as evident in the text, with great clarity. There may be recurring images in Nekrosius' productions, but each one of them operates within a closed system of images and gestures. There is nothing superfluous on stage in that the text and its meaning are stripped to the bone.

Nekrosius works within his own closed world of references. We may recognise his images, devices or moves in the work of other directors, but more important is the point that he creates a closed system of images. It is not the single, independent image that matters, but the narrative created through a series of images and their variations. His productions are visually highly complex, yet Nekrosius' reading of each text is amazingly clear, precise and extremely sharp once the spectator has deciphered the visual imagery.

For Nekrosius, images, not words, tell the story. Images do not serve the purpose of illustration, but offer a parallel narrative to the verbal score. He therefore often fragments the text to break up its linearity, cuts scenes or reorganises them in a different sequence. His theatre is almost cinematic in its use of poetic images, its close-ups and zooms on characters, and its montage of the text.

His images rely on the spectators' ability to read them imaginatively, but are never prescriptive and unequivocal. For example, fire can destroy or illuminate; water can be life-giving and refreshing, or erosive; metal can represent stability, but can also corrode; and wood may be supple or hard.

Nekrosius does not require a psychological reading from actors, but an externalised vision of the situation, expressed in movement and gesture. Since movement supersedes the word, the actors need to be agile and versatile as they develop their roles in rehearsal together with the director. They invent their own visual interpretation and their own inter-media. He tends to work with the same group of actors, often drawing on non-professionals. Hamlet was played by the rock star Andrius Mamontovas; and Nekrosius invited the ballerina Egle Spokaite to play the part of Desdemona. His choice underscores Desdemona's ability to engage in expressive and playful movements and to perform the 'dance' of death with Othello. Similarly, her agility can be contrasted with Othello's wooden and weighty movements.

Under Nekrosius the set design develops during rehearsal to allow for the stage props to be encompassed in the core scenic image, which is static, since none of the productions has a set change. This set creates the conditions for the actors' play. Nekrosius has worked with an almost unchanged team of collaborators: the set designers, Adomas Jacovskis and Nadezhda Gultiayeva, and the composer, Faustas Latenas. The close collaboration with actors, musicians and designers reflects well that the central image is not dictated by the director but is developed collectively.

Further reading

Beumers, Birgit (1999) 'Erosion through Time: the Rest is not Silence', *Theatre Forum* 14: 68–74.

Popenhagen, Ludvika (1999) *Nekrosius and Lithuanian Theatre*, New York: Peter Lang.

BIRGIT BEUMERS

DECLAN DONNELLAN (1953–)

Donnellan, together with his designer and partner Nick Ormerod, both graduates in law of Cambridge University, founded Cheek by Jowl in 1981 as a national and international touring company. Its commitment to an ensemble ethos was a tall order in a society imbued with the individualistic and competitive values of Margaret Thatcher's government, whose destruction of the public sector and cuts to arts subsidies weakened the institutional status of theatre makers and the quality of their work. Donnellan and Ormerod's iconoclastic attitude towards the prevailing dogmas injected new life and excitement into the British theatre of the 1980s.

Cheek by Jowl's remit to re-invigorate the classics and make them vital to a wide public involved demystifying the canon, not least Shakespeare, that most canonical of English dramatists. The company's critique of a certain kind of establishment 'Englishness' was also evident in its casting of local black actors in major roles; similarly, in its promotion of foreign classics, many of them never having been performed in the country before. Donnellan's productions of Racine's *Andromaque* (1984), Corneille's *Le Cid* (1986) and Ostrovsky's *A Family Affair* (1988) were British premieres. They also demonstrated, by stripping away national stereotypes – Corneille's 'French' rhetoric and flourish, for instance – Donnellan's fearless approach to the very idea of a canon as such.

Donnellan is neither militant nor didactic; at the time of his *Measure for Measure* (1994), an exposé of the cant of state authority and corruption in government whose topical interest was evident – given current scandals involving politicians – he is quoted as saying that 'theatre doesn't answer political questions, though it asks them' (*Guardian*, 14 June 1994). Asking pertinent questions, always in relation to actuality, is central to his focus on texts as repositories of thought not taken for granted as being there, immanent in the words on the page but discovered and ascribed by actors as they probe the possibilities of play. The actor, for Donnellan, is neither an interpreter of pre-existing meaning nor a creator by sheer dint of inventive or 'creative' power. He/she is an 'intrepid explorer' and 'finds rather than creates and controls' (Donnellan 2002: 133).

In this can be detected Donnellan's implicit critique of **Stanislavsky**'s notion of the actor-creator, which reappears in his emphasis on how the actor discovers a universe from without rather than from within his/her self. What is found, contra Stanislavsky, is not a storehouse of conscious as well as unconscious experiences and memories 'inside' the actor waiting to be drawn out, but a whole host of pragmatically ascertainable options 'outside' in the ambient world. Each one of these is a 'target', as Donnellan calls it: something concrete to guide the actor's actions – a question to be raised, a decision to be made, an object to be perceived. The actor is confronted by shifting targets, since they move at every given moment of play. Nothing is fixed, and the director's task is not to map, but to enable this journey through constantly changing goals.

Donnellan's outside-oriented approach to direction aims for transparency. Its assumptions appear to underlie three abiding principles of his work: care for the text as a discrete verbal composition requiring pristine exposition, enunciation and diction, which facilitate the actor's discovery of targets; uncluttered space in which the dialogue uttered can maintain its integrity, this condition being met by Ormerod's minimalist design; and concentration on the actor through whom are crystallised the contradictory motives, emotions and actions of characters, contradiction and irresolution being part of the flux of the evolving text for performance. Donnellan's concern with the conflicting tensions that activate each moment indicates why a shifting target is always accessible, this being part of the transparency of the *mise-en-scène*.

Transparency, however, is not a matter of monological presentation. As Donnellan puts it, what is at stake for the actor is not a 'paralysing "one" ' issue to be played, but a 'dynamic "two" ' (ibid.: 53). In the case of Juliet, for example:

What is at stake is not:
   'that Juliet will run away with Romeo.'

What is at stake is:
   'that Juliet will run away with Romeo' and
   'that Juliet will not run away with Romeo'.

Both the positive and the negative are present at the same time, both the hope and the fear, both the plus and the minus.

(Ibid.: 51)

One pole alone – positive *or* negative – is 'paralysing' because, obsessive, it demands a categorical and thus unattainable answer.

The early Shakespeare productions, notably *Midsummer Night's Dream* (1985) and *Romeo and Juliet* (1986), probe this idea of the 'dynamic "two" ', leading to its joyful exploration of doubling in *As You Like It* (1991), which toured the world, and then again in 1994. The production's all-male cast is neither used as a 'Shakespearean' convention nor as gay pride, but as a celebration of sex and gender ambiguities and of love, regardless of sexual inclination; it shows how everybody does and does not run away with their love because emotion and reason and abandon and constraint operate in each impulse. A black Rosalind (Adrian Lester) makes a point not so much about racial and ethnic mixing as about the tricks of perception which filter through highly subtle and funny performances from all as they toss off verbal and gestural jokes (a flick of a wrist, a twitch of an eye), make quick, often unexpected entrances and exits, and weave a network of sensual character relationships.

In all his Shakespeare productions, Donnellan scrupulously follows the rhythms of Shakespeare's blank verse, but has it spoken in conversational tones. He found this natural quality in the Russian translation he chose of *The Winter's Tale*, directed with the Maly Drama Theatre of St Petersburg (1997) and which toured Britain in 1998. An extraordinarily powerful study of political and domestic oppression (Leontes' condemnation of Hermione is a show-trial scene recalling Stalin's purges of the 1930s), its resolution shows the power of love, reconciliation and forgiveness.

These are themes to which Donnellan returns, not least in his 1998 *Le Cid* in French for the Avignon Festival and which was performed in London with English surtitles in 1999. Here, too, Donnellan respects the textual language – in this case, Corneille's alexandrines – but has it spoken without the sonorous monotony to which these twelve-metre rhyming couplets so easily lend themselves. Corneille's heroics, in which paternal tyranny, honour, duty and revenge impede love, are cut down to size through such devices as the ghost figure (not in Corneille) of Chimène's father, whom Rodrigue, the protagonist and Chimène's lover, kills to avenge the death of his own father. This 'ghost' stalks the lovers more like a voyeur than a disapproving father fixated on the rules of duty. (Chimène is meant to avenge her father by renouncing Rodrigue). His gaze is upon Chimène, which illustrates Donnellan's notion of 'target' – *she* is the actor's target rather than his character's internal feelings. Similarly, it draws attention to her tormented state of mind, objectifying her passion rather than focusing on how it surges from within, or letting it dominate the stage.

Donnellan's style is deliberate. Groupings are formal, even self-consciously placed, especially in his openings. Scenes overlap, as happens when Rodrigue's father slaps Chimène's father while a guitar concert ends to applause at Court. Actors freeze while others complete scenes or introduce new ones. Or else they freeze to contain emotions, as occurs at the end of *The Winter's Tale* when emotion is so intense that movement would have broken its grip. The past collapses into the present. Time is suspended, or its passage is emblematically configured – in *The Winter's Tale* by an old woman sweeping the floor who, when time facilitates healing, is transformed into a radiant young woman. Different locations appear simultaneously. Violence is stylised, as in *Le Cid*, when a mimed duel casts huge shadows on the back wall. The acting is incisive, precise and devoid of sentimentality. Movements and gestures are simple and frequently geometrically assigned.

Ormerod's design is sparse. Green banners drop from the flies in *As You Like It* to indicate the forest of Arden. A desk, a chair and a working light are the setting for *Measure for Measure*. Similar items reappear in *Homebody/Kabul* (2002), where carpets are pulled back to reveal boards suggesting a parched Kabul. Chairs delineate space in *Much Ado About Nothing* (1998). A billowing sheet of grey silk, light and thunder claps represent the heath in *King Lear* (2002). Costumes are austere. The classics are dressed in militaristic-style, slightly decorated suits, grey business suits, casual chic and evening wear – black, for instance, for the sisters in *King Lear*. And while modern dress, especially for Shakespeare, has become a cliché of contemporary British theatre, Ormerod and Donnellan consistently integrate it into the central ideas of each production.

Contemporary drama, when staged, is almost exclusively by Tony Kushner. Donnellan directed the two-part British premiere of *Angels in America* during his tenure as associate director of the National Theatre in London (1989–97). *Millennium Approaches* (1992) is a fast, fluent production whose corrosive jokes and brutal emotions show Donnellan at his toughest. He accentuates Kushner's argument that the 1980s Aids epidemic was exploited to witch-hunt homosexuals; and stresses Kushner's metaphor of Aids for the intolerance, greed and corruption of the Reagan period, linking this to Thatcher's Britain. In *Perestroika* (1993), he disciplines the play's 'sprawling episodes' to 'stylistic unity' with an 'armour-plated' production (Irving Wardle, *Independent on Sunday*, 21 November 1993). He puts his finger on the pulse of his time again with *Homebody/Kabul*, which refers to the political and religious struggles of Afghanistan and which he staged in New York, despite protests against Kushner's fortuitous lines on the Taliban coming to New York, written before 9/11.

Homebody/Kabul was the first Cheek by Jowl production after Donnellan and Ormerod had disbanded the company in 1998 in order to deepen their engagement with the theatre in Europe. It was Russian theatre that had the greatest impact on Donnellan's direction, starting with the Maly's phenomenal ensemble playing and Lev **Dodin**'s approach to actor training. Donnellan had discovered them when staging *Macbeth* with the National Theatre of Finland in 1986.

He and Ormerod came to know the Maly actors so well that they were able to cast *The Winter's Tale* in one morning (unpublished interview with author, London, 30 December 1998). In addition, Donnellan observes: 'I'm more interested in training the actor than in imposing specific interpretations on a play – something else I have in common with the Russians' (*Daily Telegraph*, 4 May 1999). Not since **Craig**'s *Hamlet* at the Moscow Art Theatre has a British director-designer (a couple, here, rather than one person) staged Shakespeare in Russia. In 1999, *The Winter's Tale* received the Golden Mask in Moscow, Russia's equivalent of the Olivier award. Donnellan was also nominated for best director, a distinction never before conferred upon a foreigner.

No British director, past or present, has had such an intense relationship with the Russian theatre. Donnellan's *Boris Godunov* (2001), with Russian actors from various theatres in Moscow, combines breathtaking ensemble performance, sharp anachronisms (Godunov dressed like President Putin juxtaposed against archaic monks) and an equally pointed connection between the political–ethical dilemmas addressed by Pushkin and those confronting post-communist Russia. The production toured Europe, including Paris and London, to fulsome acclaim. Donnellan's work with his Russian team continued with *Twelfth Night* at the 2003 Chekhov Festival in Moscow. His summer school for English actors, the Royal Shakespeare Academy Company, which performed *King Lear*, was also inspired by Russian principles of actor training.

Further reading

Donnellan, Declan (2002) *The Actor and the Target*, London: Nick Hern Books.

Reade, Simon (1991) *Cheek by Jowl: Ten Years of Celebration*, London: Absolute Classics.

MARIA SHEVTSOVA

NEIL ARMFIELD (1955–)

In January 1998, Company B Belvoir, Sydney, and the Perth-based Black Swan Theatre Company premiered Neil Armfield's production *Cloudstreet* for the Festival of Sydney. In *Cloudstreet* it was possible to discern, if not the high-water mark of Armfield's career, then at the very least the consummate collocation of a number of themes, threads, craft and passion characterising that career. In *Cloudstreet*, we see at once: Armfield's absolute regard for, and privileging of, the actor; his commitment to developing new writing through ensemble work conducted in collaboration with playwrights; his visual and spatial flair; his concern with the development of an expressive, poetic Australian stage language; a desire to people the Australian stage with indigenous actors and characters; his passion for a good story, well told; and a recurring thematic concern with familial belonging. As Armfield himself pointed out, 'the thing I am drawn to is the moment of passing from isolation to community, and when I think of the images of my work that I remember and treasure most, that is the drama that is being enacted, the story that is being told'.[1]

A sprawling, five-hour adaptation of Tim Winton's novel, *Cloudstreet* is the story of two down-on-their-luck families, the Lambs and the Quicks, sharing a house in Perth in the years following the Second World War. Armfield's production was staged in an empty shipping warehouse on the quayside of Sydney's Walsh Bay. Scenic elements were piled against dun-coloured calico sheets, draped down the side and upstage walls, surrounding a vast, empty, blond-wood and sand stage. A vomitory entrance bisected raked bleachers, seating 600. Audience and performers shared the same cavernous space: there was no proscenium, curtain, tabs or masks. Props – a bathtub, furniture, netting, a boat – were rolled or carried out into the playing space by the actors. The effect was not so much explicitly Brechtian, as a recreation, in this vast, hollowed-out industrial space, of the intimacy, openness and lack of artifice that had, for over a decade, become the house style of Company B under Armfield's artistic directorship in the Upstairs Theatre at Belvoir Street – itself located in a converted industrial building. Similarly, Enright and Monjo's adaptation adopted a *pre*sentational voice (an early stage direction reads 'QUICK speaks directly to the audience, as he and other characters will do from time to time throughout the play'),[2] less out of an intellectual regard for breaking the illusion of verisimilitude, but precisely because, in Armfield's theatre, this moment of contact between the fantastical world of the narrative and the world of the audience is where theatre takes place.

Two moments in *Cloudstreet* illustrate Armfield's capacity to create, in this space shared between audience and performers, work that is distinctly *theatrical*. When the brothers Fish and Quick go night-fishing, Armfield directed two of his cast to wheel a rowing boat into the arena from beneath the audience. Fish and Quick clambered in as two other actors placed basins of water on the stage on either side. As the scene started, a cluster of naked light-bulbs, visible throughout the performance but now slowly lowered into the centre of the space, became an incandescent firefly-halo around the boys' heads. The boat was gently rotated on its trolley while other cast members gently lapped at the water in the basins. Daniel Wyllie, playing Fish, leant over the bow, gazing into the suddenly evoked night depths of the Swan River – and, in an instant, the audience was transported: we were there, too. It was a moment of transcendent theatricality, with no attempt to create a convincing illusion. Instead, the conjurer had carefully allowed us to see the workings of the trick as it was performed. The elements constituting the scene were assembled, piece by piece, there, in front of the audience, creating a magical transformation, a whole considerably more than the sum of its parts.

In the play's final moments, the cast assembled downstage, facing their audience. Wyllie/Fish stepped forward, speaking as narrator, offering the final speech, his longest of the play:

FISH: I know my story for just long enough to see how we've come, how we've all battled in the same corridor that time makes for us, and I'm Fish Lamb for those seconds it takes to die, as long as it takes to drink the river, as long as it took to tell you all this, and then my walls are tipping and I burst into the moon, sun and stars of who I truly am. Being Fish Lamb. Perfectly. Always. Everyplace. Me.[3]

The actor turned upstage and started to run, hard, towards the back wall of the building, where the dun curtains parted, a slender slit through which the audience could see the dark harbour night outside, the cityscape of casino and restaurants twinkling in the mid-distance. And the actor kept running, running through the labial folds of the curtain, into the dark and leapt, caught momentarily in a spotlight, plunging into the unseen water below. As a piece of theatre, it was, simply, stunning; a breathtaking *coup de théâtre* celebrated minutes later as the dripping Wyllie returned to take his bows.

Armfield's first professional engagement came when his productions for the Sydney University Dramatic Society caught the eye of John Bell and Ken Horler at the Nimrod Theatre Company, at that time the 'alternative' to the mainstream, Sydney Opera House-based Old Tote Theatre Company (and its successor from 1979, the

Sydney Theatre Company). From 1979 until 1981 Armfield was Co-Artistic Director at the Nimrod, and directed a characteristic (of the Nimrod) mix of new Australian work, notably by Stephen Sewell and Louis Nowra, reworked classics (Jonson's *Volpone*) and contemporary English plays (Frayn, Hare). The Nimrod's theatre was a converted salt factory building on Belvoir Street, in inner Sydney's Surry Hills, a working-class suburb of warehouses and public housing. The main auditorium, now known simply as The Upstairs Theatre, consists of a broad, open, idiosyncratic, kite-shaped stage, built into the corner of the building and thrusting to a blunt apex between three converging seating banks: an intimate arena space seating 320 spectators.

Through the ensuing twenty years, the bulk of Armfield's directorial work has been seen on this stage. It was to this stage that he returned in the late 1980s, and it is here that he has worked in his capacity, since 1994, as the Artistic Director of the resident company, Company B. The space has been formative of Armfield's theatrical aesthetic in two important, related respects. The first is the absolute centrality of the actor to Armfield's theatre. The second is a design sensibility in which scenic elements are subordinated to the preeminence of the actor in space. Armfield's designers tend to furnish him with elegant, minimalist settings, treating the walls and the surface of the stage, and leaving to the actor the run of the space. The idiosyncrasies of the space itself, bearing the traces of its industrial history (exposed structural joists, concrete and brick walls, a rolling loading-dock door upstage), and the awkwardness of access to the stage (the only entrances to a hidden off-stage are on the prompt side, or through a central vomitory) have, in Armfield's hands, lent themselves to a 'presentational' style not dependent upon naturalistic illusion, but exploitative of the transformational power of theatre.

Subsequently, as a guest director at the Lighthouse Company, Armfield was able to work on a large, purpose-built proscenium stage for the first time, directing the premiere of Patrick White's *Signal Driver* for the 1982 Adelaide Festival. The production was 'remarkable for its visual and design effects, including an electrified overhead wire and the symbolic mushroom cloud which swelled up at the end, enveloping the Playhouse audience'.[4] The following year, after the Australia Council funded a study tour to Europe, Armfield was appointed as Associate Director at the Lighthouse, under the mentorship of Jim **Sharman**. During the Lighthouse years Armfield was supported by generous state subsidies and was therefore able to work with a consistent ensemble of actors, one of the only occasions in recent Australian theatre when such an ensemble has been possible. It was during this period that he developed his relationship with the three resident playwrights Nowra, Sewell and White. Their cross-pollinating experiments with dramatic form ranged from the epic/didactic (Sewell) and the surreal/expressionist (White) to the lyrical/'emblematic' (Nowra). The three writers shared a concern with the development of a theatrical voice that pushed beyond the clipped, sardonic, masculine working-class vernacular that had dominated the attempts of nationalist playwrights of the 1960s to establish a distinctly Australian stage voice. In its place, all three sought – and found – a poetic idiom through which complex emotional and political material could be expressed on Australian stages. In the hothouse environment of the ensemble, Armfield both contributed his own sense of the possibility of such a language, and developed his own confidence in an indigenisation of European theatre texts. Armfield's comfortableness with an identifiably Australian vocality has carried into his subsequent work on classic texts, from Shakespeare to Chekhov, Gogol and Ibsen.

In 1988 Nowra wrote of a 'sense of family [being] a feature of Armfield's working'.[5] With Company B, Armfield has championed the ideal of the ensemble, even as funding dries up and the ideal becomes even more impossible to attain. Armfield has responded by gathering around him a 'family' of co-workers – actors, writers, designers, composers – all of whom are comfortable with his rehearsal habits and with whom he is able to create the 'domestic' space within which he can work. This discourse of 'family' is extended throughout the company's marketing: subscribers are invited to be part of the Belvoir Company, and favourite actors are referred to as 'our Cate [Blanchett]' or 'our Geoffrey [Rush]'. For Armfield, 'a production can only be truly great if it is an expression of all of its participants, if it is owned by its performers'.[6] Indeed, Armfield has a reputation for leaving 'rehearsals so open-ended that chaos still prevails just days before opening':[7]

> Some actors working for the first time with Neil are invariably confused. I have heard actors complaining or wondering plaintively, especially in the early days of rehearsal, if he actually knows what he's doing. He's not dominating, doesn't thrust interpretations down the throats of his cast and has a tendency to watch, absorb and contemplate without giving many hints as to what he's after.[8]

Armfield's work is in fact meticulously planned. An account of Armfield's 1995 rehearsal of Stephen Sewell's *The Blind Giant is Dancing* draws attention to his 'extremely precise instructions', and observes that '(w)hile creating the effect of an unhurried, democratic atmosphere', Armfield's blocking of the actors was 'often prescriptive and auteur-like'.[9]

In the late 1990s, Armfield's work appeared to be pushing in two directions. On the one hand, Company B ran on a shoestring budget and evolved a 'poor theatre' aesthetic out of economic necessity. *The Seagull* was staged in a rehearsal room in which the designers had reproduced the church hall in which the production had been worked up, furnishing the set with bits and pieces from local second-hand shops. Beatrix Christian's *The Governor's Family*, set in colonial Sydney, was staged on the blackened, burnt-out set from *The Seagull*, its floor removed and replaced by a square of earth. On the other hand, in a rehearsal room barely 100 metres from Belvoir Street, Armfield worked just as comfortably within the high-budget, tightly scheduled world of Opera Australia. Here he brought the freshness and vigour engendered in his theatre practice to productions of Janacek's *Cunning Little Vixen* (1997) and *Jenufa* (1998). For the opera, Armfield's focus was tight and his staging thoroughly theatrical. Performances were carefully crafted, and plot treated with absolute clarity. The visual sense nurtured Upstairs at Belvoir Street was given full flower in a series of magical revolves and elegant mechanical transformations. For example, *Billy Budd* (1998/99) was staged on a simple constructivist platform, mounted on a revolve and pitching on hydraulic rams.

In *Cloudstreet*, the scale and complexity of an operatic staging and the informality and intimacy of The Upstairs Theatre came together to produce an intimate epic. The production established Armfield as the pre-eminent Australian stage director of his generation.

Notes

1 Armfield, N. (1998) 'Australian Culture: Creating It and Losing It: The Fourth Philip Parsons Memorial Lecture', Belvoir Street Theatre, Sydney, 9 November, printed in edited form as 'Dare to Touch the Divine, Mr Prime Minister', *Sydney Morning Herald*, 11 November: 15.

2 Winton, Tim, Enright, Nick and Monjo, Justin (1999) *Cloudstreet: Play*, Redfern, NSW: Currency Press: 3.

3 Ibid.: 122.

4 Radic, L. (1991) *The State of Play: The Revolution in the Australian Theatre since the 1960s*, Ringwood, Vic.: Penguin Books: 186.

5 Nowra, L. (1988) 'Neil Armfield – Radical Classicist', *New Theatre: Australia* 3: 7

6   Armfield (1998).
7   Cosic, Miriam (1999) 'Boy From Company B' in *The Australian Magazine*, 20–21 February: 16.
8   Nowra (1988): 7.
9   Fewster, R. (2002) 'A Director in Rehearsal: Neil Armfield and the Company B Production of *The Blind Giant is Dancing* by Stephen Sewell', *Australasian Drama Studies* 40: 106–118.

Further reading

Golder, J. and Madelaine, R. (1998) 'Elsinore at Belvoir St: Neil Armfield talks about *Hamlet*', *Australasian Drama Studies* 26 (April): 55–80.
Ridgman, J. (1983) 'Interview: Louis Nowra, Stephen Sewell and Neil Armfield', *Australian Drama Studies* 1 (April): 105–123.

IAN MAXWELL

ROBERT LEPAGE (1957–)

In 1985 Robert Lepage's *The Dragon's Trilogy* was about an hour long. By 1987 it was more than six hours long. In two years it had gained five hours, a monstrous snowball of a performance that had grown and changed with a vitality that has become a hallmark of Lepage's productions. In 1994 *The Seven Streams of the River Ota* ran to about three hours. By 1996 it was seven hours long, having ravenously devoured all the influences of its playing conditions – the countries the company visited, the translations they required, the local actors they used. 'What we're doing is more or less a public rehearsal',[1] said Lepage ingenuously, seemingly unaware that he had done more to redefine the term 'work in progress' than any living director.

For Lepage, an opening night is just another moment in the evolution of a production that reaches its final form only when the company ceases to perform it. For Lepage theatre is most vibrantly itself when it resists solidifying into a fixed structure, when plays develop a life of their own and discover themselves through the course of a run of performances. Under Lepage's direction, performing becomes an adventure, an exploration of uncharted terrain, and the pleasure it yields is directly related to the risk that such an approach implies. Lepage makes the comparison with the enjoyment of sport where players' skills are tested in an uncertain forum, where there are no guarantees and where even the spectators feel that, by cheering themselves hoarse, they are contributing to the result that is finally obtained.

A performance that is forever evolving is by definition a performance that is created collectively by a company. As there is no set script, the evolution of a performance becomes a communal endeavour, the result of improvisations in which action rather than text becomes the principal medium in which theatre is conceived. In Lepage's work, performance is no different to rehearsals, which, too, begin not with a text but with an idea. Work on *Seven Streams of the River Ota* (1994), for instance, began with nothing more concrete than a desire to do something about Hiroshima. Similarly, *Tectonic Plates* (1988) began with 'just an intuition. Then everyone in the company gives their impression':[2]

> Our creative work begins with a huge brain-storming and a collective drawing session where ideas are grouped together. Then, we discuss ideas that have been singled out, which leads us to improvisation. Then there's the phase of structuring the improvisations, which we rehearse, and eventually perform publicly. These performances, rather than being the culmination of the process, are really further rehearsals for us, since the show is not written down or fixed.
>
> (Lepage 1995: 177)

There is no reason why a company in rehearsal should not stumble upon a form that everyone finds satisfactory. In performance, however, there is the constant spur of changing playing conditions and audiences, which Lepage relies upon to shape the work and add to it the tension that comes from uncertainty. Like a team coach who discusses strategy with the players but does not know how precisely things will go in the course of a match, so also the actors prepare their scenarios but are uncertain as to whether they will be successful. Not that the fear of failure deters Lepage: for him, consternation is a tonic, the goad that keeps a performance from atrophying.

A striking by-product of Lepage's preoccupation with involving the actors in the process of developing performances is the proliferation of the most exquisite stage images in his dramas. Whether it is the manner in which a parking attendant's booth becomes a staircase leading down into a basement in *The Dragon's Trilogy* or a huge syringe injecting narcotics into a gigantic silhouetted arm in *Needles and Opium* (1991), Lepage's productions speak with a vibrant visual eloquence. As Lepage's actors work with movement as well as language, they retain the possibility of allowing action to influence speech rather than having gestures follow forever on the heels of words penned in the absence of theatrical imperatives. His stage images are the result of this inversion, a demonstration of the ability of action to imitate – and even surpass – the capacity of language to communicate in metaphors. The transformation of Stella in *The Dragon's Trilogy* is a good example of the irony by which a prosaic concern with theatrical practicalities generates a moment of rare poetry on stage:

> In *The Dragon's Trilogy*, Lorraine Cote played both a nun and Stella…. There wasn't enough time for Lorraine to change costumes so I told her to wear Stella's costume under her nun's tunic and when she ran backstage she would only have to take off one set of clothing. But this still didn't work. So we had to have her take her tunic off in front of the whole audience … so that Lorraine was gradu- ally transformed into Stella…. We invented a whole ritual to give the transformation meaning and it became one of the most beautiful moments of the entire six hours of *Trilogy*. All because one actor didn't have the time to change costumes.
>
> (Ibid.: 31)

Lepage speculates that some of Shakespeare's best monologues were written to hold the attention of the audience during elaborate scene changes. In both cases the mundane business of staging gener- ates an inadvertent lyricism whose appeal is far in excess of anything one might expect, given the sense of compromise and contrivance that marks their invention.

As actors use the concrete co-ordinates of space rather than the abstract vehicle of language as the medium in which their perfor- mances are constructed, they stumble not only upon mesmerising individual images but also on ways of narrating stories that are radi- cally different from anything writers are able to produce when they work at desks rather than in theatres. In *The Dragon's Trilogy*, for example, the story of Crawford's life, from youth to old age, is compressed into a few seconds as his coat is worn in turn by the three actors who play him at different ages through the course of the drama. In the same performance, shoes are used to depict the most affecting events with a force that is proportional to their simplicity:

In *The Dragon's Trilogy*, shoes were a powerful resource for story-telling. A pair was taken out of a suitcase to show a child's first steps, and then bigger and bigger shoes showed the child's growth. Another pair was put into a suitcase to signify a mother's death. Shoes were also carefully lined up all along the set by another character, only to be trampled by soldiers walking on ice skates – an unusual but most powerful evocation of the Second World War's destruction. Thus, the most modest of stage props, the most common objects of daily life were used to show birth, life and death, the love of a father and mother and the hideous devastation of war.

(Ibid.: 8–89)

This is Lepage at his best – and his most typical. To critics schooled in the virtues of good dramatic language, this is sleight of hand. To those who are able to appreciate the potential for semiotic elegance within non-linguistic structures, this is the work of a magician.

Part of the appeal of this essentially visual rather than aural mode of communication is that it requires the implicit co-operation of the audience. Lepage has long argued that today's audiences have so much exposure to cinema and television that they bring to the theatre techniques of decoding action that the theatre does not sufficiently utilise:

We tend to do theatre in a manner where we're using an old way of telling stories because we think people are obtuse, and that they only have this old fashioned way of understanding a story. In fact people are extremely modern … they watch TV, they know what a flash-back is, they understand the codes of a flash forward, they know what a jump cut is. They know all these things that we didn't know when we started to go and see theatre. And if you don't use that, you don't trigger that, of course they're bored.[3]

Ironically the poetry that attaches to the use of cinematic tech-niques in the theatre is far greater than that which accrues to a film that uses the same methods. Cinema is far too literal a medium to be able to use theatricality without seeming needlessly obtuse and extravagant. It is because theatre is so limited by comparison that its potential for the use of the imagination is so great.

245

Lepage's facility with the use of cinematic techniques derives from the fact that he works in both fields – and often on the same material. This has made possible a degree of cross-fertilisation that has produced a plethora of interesting effects. In *Circulations* (1984), for instance,

> there's a scene in which two guys and a girl are smoking a joint in a motel, quietly talking in the moonlight that's streaming in through a skylight above them. Then the stage goes to black and when the lights come up we see the same scene but through the skylight, in other words, from the point of view of the moon. It was the first time we used an inverted perspective in our work. The actors were stretched out horizontally, giving the audience the impression they were watching the characters from the sky, from above. And it was the use of drugs that made this kind of poetic transposition possible.
>
> (Ibid.: 75)

The important thing here is not so much the use of the inverted perspective but the fact that this relates directly to the subject matter of the drama. Lepage is not gratuitously indulging his flair for multiple media: he is stretching the resources of his medium so as to make it better able to reflect, in external terms, the interior narrative of his characters. It is this ability to coax his resources to *enact* rather than merely *narrate* their content that makes Lepage's drama so poetic.

In Lepage's drama, the ability of form to echo content is not merely poetic but symptomatic of his preoccupation with connectedness generally. Almost all Lepage's plays make connections between intuitively dissimilar things. *Seven Streams of the River Ota* deals both with French Canadian independence and the Japanese phoenix rising out of the ashes of Hiroshima. The more recent *Geometry of Miracles* (1999) puts the esoteric philosophy of Gurdjieff together with the architecture of Frank Lloyd Wright. 'I think that things are connected deeply and as an author or director, you have to know how to be a bit of an anthropologist or archaeologist',[4] says Lepage. This sense of almost mystical oneness underlying the fractured surface of our perception of the world gives Lepage's plays an anchor. While Lepage's theatre can sometimes be multifaceted to the point of being chaotic, his almost sacred sense of the importance of coincidence keeps his theatre firmly rooted in a safety net of serendipitous affinities. For Lepage, a coincidence is a revelation of the concealed synchronicity of life, a harbinger of 'a sense of spiritu-ality'[5] that the theatre alone can discover. What Wright's architecture has in common with Gurdjieff's dance sequences is that they are both attempts to distil, within the confines of a physical form, a metaphysical perception that defies corporeal assimilation. For Lepage, theatre is itself a similar enterprise, an attempt to find, in the critical moment of performance, a trace of the harmony that is obscured by the abundance and diversity of material existence.

Notes

1 Delgado, Maria M. and Heritage, P. (eds) (1996) *In Contact With the Gods? Directors Talk Theatre*, Manchester and New York: Manchester University Press: 141.
2 National Theatre, *Platform Papers* 3: 29.
3 Delgado and Heritage (1996: 148).
4 National Theatre: 38.
5 Delgado and Heritage (1996: 144).

Further reading

Lepage, R. (1995) *Connecting Flights*, trans. Wanda Romer Taylor, London: Methuen.

SHOMIT MITTER

SIMON McBURNEY (1957–)

In the late 1970s, Simon McBurney studied English at Cambridge University, where he was a performer and writer in the Cambridge Footlights alongside Emma Thompson, Hugh Laurie and Annabel Arden. After graduating, he trained at the Jacques Lecoq school in Paris before returning to London in 1983 to co-found Theatre de Complicite with Annabel Arden, Marcello Magni and Fiona Gordon. Having created almost thirty productions in the past twenty years, many of which have toured extensively, Complicite has established itself as one of Europe's most popular, critically lauded and influential theatre companies. Successfully navigating the apparent divide between avant-garde experiment and a popular mainstream, Complicite has become known internationally for the physical dexterity and darkly comic inventiveness of its collabora-tively devised work,[1] and the fluid dramaturgies of its productions of classic texts[2] and adaptations of contemporary fiction.[3] As artistic director of Complicite, McBurney has directed almost all of the company's shows in the past ten years to produce a body of work of remarkable focus, energy and diversity. At the same time, he has continued to work internationally as a freelance theatre director and an actor in both film and television.[4]

Having trained as a performer with Lecoq, McBurney brings an embodied understanding of the predicament of performers to his work as a director, and in particular to the necessity for collaborators to generate a common language. At the outset of any devising process – all of McBurney's work should be viewed through the lens of devising, including work on existing texts[5] – his primary concern is to try to invent the conditions for invention through the preparation of bodies, voices and imaginations: 'I prepare them so that they are ready: ready to change, ready to be surprised, ready to seize any opportunity that comes their way' (McBurney 1999: 71). A number of McBurney's long-term collaborators also trained with Lecoq, and they share a certain short-hand in terms of exercises, discourses and dispositions towards the making of performance. Over the years, however, Complicite has become an increasingly loose alliance of collaborators rather than a permanent company, with new members joining those with some greater continuity for particular projects. In addition, McBurney's free-lance work brings him into contact with actors largely unfamiliar with the unpredictable and difficult joys of devising, the occasional terrors of setting off into the unknown and getting very lost. In recent years, for example, he has directed productions for the National Actors' Theatre in New York (**Brecht**'s *The Resistible Rise of Arturo Ui* in 2002, with Al Pacino, John Goodman and Steve Buscemi), and with members of Tokyo's Setagaya Public Theatre (*The Elephant Vanishes* in 2003).

McBurney happily admits to the legacies of Lecoq in his work: the centrality of the ensemble as a kind of multi-headed storyteller, swarming as one multiple organism, 'like a flock of starlings' (ibid.: 74); the ideals of embodied lightness and *disponibilité* as prerequisites for the emergence of forms and images in complicitous play, of emotion from motion, of laughter that is both celebratory and critically corrosive; the creation of suggestive, incomplete forms that invite imaginative complicity from spectators, activating their creative agency. Above all, he holds to an amplified quality of atten-tive listening to and engagement with rhythm, tempo, musicality and the dynamics of space as core components in elaborating and evaluating live theatre:

> an analysis through the use of movement of how a piece of
> theatre works: how it actually functions in terms of space, in

terms of rhythm, almost like music in terms of counter-point, harmony: image and action, movement and stillness, words and silence.

(McBurney 1994: 18)

At the outset of a rehearsal process, particular emphasis is placed on the establishment of a play space, with all sorts of objects, materials, research documentation, games and other rule or event-based practices available for individual and collective exploration. McBurney has used the word 'playground', and often re-iterates a connection with team sports. The precise nature and use of texts, music, objects and other scenographic materials within a production, as well as the detailed texture of its compositional weave, are all determined over time in the studio according to a pragmatics of what seems to support and feed the emergence of a shared, deep-breathing 'world'. In broad terms, the devising model stems from Lecoq's *autocours*, a heuristic pedagogy of the imagination in contexts where collaborative work takes place, a flexing and toning of the 'muscle of the imagination' in search of a 'moment of collective imagining' (McBurney 1999: 71). On another level, it relates to the informed sink-or-swim predicament of street theatre and stand-up, or the patient immersive hothouse of certain choreographic or physical theatre practices that endeavour to spatialise the topographies of internal journeys. On yet another level, perhaps less visible but materially constitutive, McBurney's *modus operandi* is informed by the psycho-physical attunements, layerings and expressive unfoldings afforded by a close study of Feldenkrais technique with the remarkable teacher Monika Pagneux.

Aesthetically and dramaturgically, McBurney is no less catholic in his sources for stimulus, drawing on aspects of **Brook**, **Meyerhold**, Brecht and **Kantor**, as well as the neo-expressionist dance-theatre of Pina **Bausch** and Josef Nadj, the transformative manipulations of object-theatre and puppetry, the spatio-temporal polyrhythms and mobilities of film languages, and the critical intelligence of John Berger's fiction, to create something unique in contemporary popular theatre. McBurney's work since the early 1990s proposes a distinctly European, multilingual, poetic integrating image, narrative and a choreography of bodies, objects and space to produce a contemporary *Gesamtkunstwerk*. Within this symphonic form, the creative agency of performers and their bodies comprises the very foundation for a compassionate celebration of the extraordinary in the everyday and the marginalised, and an articulate humanist enquiry into a 'politics of the imagination' (McBurney 1994: 22).

One of McBurney's most remarkable attributes is his facility for creating images that defamiliarise and redirect the geometry of conventional, received attention to reality, and etch themselves into our imaginations. Here 'image' is not simply pictorial representation or *coup de théâtre*, but rather a complex, dynamic syntax allying and layering movement, rhythm, text, music and object, engendered by the poetic logic of the forms and narratives at play within a production: image as the fusion of form and content in an embodied if fleeting 'world'. *Mnemonic* (1999), for example, is haunted by the ambiguities of new technologies of communication (the mobile phone) and recording (video). The phone line breaks up at moments of intense 'proximity', painfully re-instating distance and absence, and memory is replayed and fast-forwarded repeatedly, as if it were a VCR, in an obsessive search for the 'real' and for 'origins'. At times the discontinuous rhythm of the remote control or the edit suite consciously determines the staging itself: live sequences are 'rewound' at vertiginous speed and replayed again and again in a cycle of repetitions with difference.

McBurney's dramaturgies of emergence and dissolution allow highly focused 'image-worlds' to appear from the deployments, interactions and transpositions of bodies and objects, and to crystallise into ephemeral sharp-edged form before their constituent elements are dispersed and returned to a state of energised potentiality. In *The Three Lives of Lucie Cabrol* (1994), for example, an explosive manipulation of wooden planks is used to represent the dynamics of desire and the precarious uncertainty of refuge as Jean and Lucie make love in a 'barn'. In *Mnemonic*, a broken wooden chair (already a mnemonic-by-association for the main character, Virgil's father, and his absent lover) is puppeted then laid out to represent the leathery remains of a 5000–year-old Neothilic 'iceman' recently discovered in the Tyrolean Alps. With the economy of a haiku, a white cloth is thrown over it, and the chair becomes a glacier. As the father says in *The Street of Crocodiles* (1992): 'The migration of forms is the essence of life'. Since the elastic temporalities and magical metamorphoses of this astonishing production, within which the laws of Newtonian physics seemed to be momentarily suspended as books flapped and flew like birds, and a spectral figure strolled vertically down the back wall and into the space, displacement, connectivity and the fluidity of memory and identity have become recurrent themes in McBurney's work.

Accordingly, in all of his productions the material components of scenography are encouraged to mutate and recompose, to displace, transform and reinvent themselves temporarily, adopting ephemeral configurations and identities within a theatre language that itself is always migrating, transforming, always on the move. The only constant is change, the protean 'play' of people and things in their becomings: *tout bouge.*[6]

From his early days in knockabout clown-inflected work to more recent investigations of alienated, sped-up hyper-modernity using sophisticated video mediation in live performance (*Mnemonic, The Elephant Vanishes*), McBurney has returned consistently to material of substantial existential gravity, political resonance or ethical complexity. There is anxiety about mortality, for example, in the painfully funny *A Minute Too Late* (1984), in part a response to the recent death of his father; the fragility of imaginative life under repressive regimes in *The Street of Crocodiles*, which directly referenced the murder of the Polish writer Bruno Schulz by the Nazis, and in *The Noise of Time* (2000), in which Shostakovich's String Quartet no. 15 in E Minor was re-membered in the context of Soviet history and the composer's troubled life under Stalinism; exile, desire, loss and the slipperiness of relations between history, archaeology and memory in *Mnemonic*; the tyrannies of extremism and xenophobic fear in *The Resistible Rise of Arturo Ui*, McBurney's New York production offering an explicit critical engagement with the ideologies of a hawkish and morally bankrupt US administration.

McBurney seeks to contest and affirm – often at the same moment – and his work might be characterised paradoxically in terms of both its philosophical seriousness and its consistent light-ness of touch. Within these tragic farces, celebration co-exists with desolation, reparation with separation, reverie with nightmare, grace with gravity. In McBurney's best work, the social and aesthetic act of collaboration itself eloquently affirms the vibrant creative potential of encounter, attention, imagination and connective energy, while the transience of the theatre event and of the forms that are its building blocks asks us to engage with the precariousness and trans-formative potentialities of our own lives as social and creative beings. 'We have to invent our own circumstances, as we have now to reinvent our theatre' (McBurney 1999: 77).

Notes

1　These include *Put it on your Head* (1983), *A Minute Too Late* (1984), *More Bigger Snacks Now* (1985), *Anything for a Quiet Life* (1987), *Burning*

Ambition for BBC2 (1988), *Mnemonic* for both theatre (1999) and radio (2000) and *The Noise of Time* (2000) with the Emerson String Quartet.

2   Dürenmatt's *The Visit* (1989), Shakespeare's *The Winter's Tale* (1992), Brecht's *The Caucasian Chalk Circle* (1997), Ionesco's *The Chairs* (1997).

3   *The Street of Crocodiles* (1992), adapted from texts by Bruno Schulz; *Out of a House Walked a Man* (1994), from Daniil Kharms; *The Three Lives of Lucie Cabrol* (1994), from John Berger's *Pig Earth*; *Foe* (1996), from J.M. Coetzee; *To the Wedding* (1997), from John Berger, for BBC Radio 3; *Light* (2000), from Torgny Lindgren; *The Elephant Vanishes* (2003), from Haruki Murakami.

4   As an actor, McBurney's film credits include *Sleepy Hollow*, *Kafka*, *Tom and Viv*, *Mesmer*, *Cousin Bette*, *Onegin* and the title role in *Eisenstein*.

5   'There is a curious and very different sensation when you apparently have something in your hands – a play – and when you have nothing but fragments, scraps and imaginings when you are devising; yet strangely I feel I start from the same place: until I start to feel and experience something, there is nothing' (McBurney 1999: 67).

6   *Tout bouge* ('Everything moves') was the title of the lecture-demonstration Jacques Lecoq performed internationally to great acclaim from the late 1960s onwards. As McBurney points out in his foreword to Lecoq's *The Moving Body*, it was also 'a central tenet of his teaching' (Lecoq 2000: x).

Further reading

Lecoq, Jacques (2000) *The Moving Body: Teaching Creative Theatre*, trans. David Bradby, London: Methuen. Foreword by Simon McBurney.

McBurney, Simon (1994) 'The Celebration of Lying', interview in Tushingham, David (ed.) *Live 1: Food for the Soul*, London: Methuen: 13–24.

—— (1999) Interview, in Giannachi, Gabriella and Luckhurst, Mary (eds) *On Directing: Interviews with Directors*, London: Faber & Faber: 67–77.

Theatre de Complicite (2003) *Complicite Plays 1 (The Street of Crocodiles, The Three Lives of Lucie Cabrol, Mnemonic)*, London: Methuen.

Theatre de Complicite website: http://www.complicite.org

DAVID WILLIAMS

PETER SELLARS (1958–)

A graduate of Harvard University, where he staged numerous allegedly outrageous productions, Sellars is a polymath who directs theatre, opera, television film, feature film and rock video. He has appeared in Bill Moyers' *Miami Vice* and *The Equalizer* as well as in Jean-Luc Godard's film of *King Lear* (1987). Sellars had performed in his own undergraduate *Lear* in 1980, when an on-stage Lincoln

Continental, purportedly the symbol of Lear's power, was ostentatiously stripped down to its chassis every night.

Precocity and zeal combined when he served as the artistic director of the Boston Shakespeare Company (1983–84) and the American National Theater (ANT) at the Kennedy Center in Washington (1984–86). Sellars relinquished the latter after leading it into controversy over his spectacular profligacy, incandescent inventiveness (technological experiments, use of visible stage machinery, heightened movement, clowning) and highly critical productions of contemporary America. Thus he typically set his anti-Vietnam War *Ajax* (1986) in the Pentagon, its text by Sophocles adapted by his dramaturg Robert Auletta to his political stance, not least of which was his policy of interracial casting. Its performance needs – Sellars' is primarily an aesthetics of gesture – were largely provided for by the sign language of the deaf-mute actor Howie Segal in the title role. Washington was not the place for his reformist mission as regards the state of the nation, and the ANT closed down, while Sellars moved on. The creative abandon of this period was to be symptomatic of the rest of his career, which, on so many points of theatrical style and political motivation, recalls **Meyerhold**, who had been his inspiration during his student days.

Sellars was the artistic director of the 1990 and 1993 Los Angeles Festivals, expanding the Festival's remit to incorporate various minority communities in its proceedings and events. This included designating performance venues in black neighbourhoods, among them those of the 1992 Los Angeles race riots. Crossing social borders, prejudices, phobias and taboos was to remain a permanent feature of Sellars' work, entailing, as well, his engagement with community performance, where he mixes professional and non-professional actors. In recent years, this type of activity has notably involved his direction of Genet's *Les Paravents* as *Los Biombos/The Screens* (1998) with the hispanic community of Boyle Heights in East Los Angeles, the Cornerstone Theatre Company and the Los Angeles Poverty Department (whose acronym is a satirical take on the Los Angeles Police Department). The production transposed the oppressive relationship displayed by Genet between coloniser and colonised in Algeria to what might be termed the internal colonisation of Mexican language and culture within the United States through its hegemonic power.

A similarly community-oriented approach guided Sellars when he was appointed director of the 2002 Adelaide Festival. However, his absences from planning, discussion and decision making, coupled with 'monumental costs' and 'idealistic folly' (*The Advertiser*, 13 November 2001), ended in a debacle; 'idealistic folly' essentially referred to his activist community-arts attitude, especially as regards the integration and reconciliation issues concerning the Aboriginal peoples of Australia, which were, and continue to be, of monumental importance to the country. Sellars holds a teaching position as Professor of World Arts and Cultures at the University of California Los Angeles.

The dissolution of hierarchies, by which distinctions between 'high' and 'low' and 'classical' and 'popular' culture are no longer operative is as central to Sellars' concerns as his interest in multimedia for the theatre. Television monitors, computers, screened images, movie clips, amplified sound, microphones and other equipment layer his productions in order to embed the working modern world within them. Their purpose is also to remind audiences of the negative impact of the media on their lives, and to urge them to seek alternative, more truthful systems of information such as the theatre itself. The theatre, for Sellars, can only be *of* the present and committed wholly to it: 'Our task as artists is to respond, to make a record of what's going on and to put something on stage that actually reflects society' (Sellars 1997: 205). Furthermore, 'when we talk about making theatre, we're really talking about making a society' (ibid.: 193), so much so that 'a production has to be – like a government – a discussion among equals; and there has to be a kind of energy that comes from a democratically charged environment' (ibid.: 194).

The theatre as forum for open discussion and debate defines, according to Sellars, its fundamental democratic role. His major productions after *Ajax* adopt strategies not only for a 'discussion among equals', but for the development of people's sense of their civic responsibilities. *The Persians* (1993), once again in collaboration with Auletta and Segal, denounces America's role in the Gulf War. By transposing Aeschylus' tragedy into a contemporary context (facilitated by Auletta's adaptation) and by speaking from the standpoint of the 'alien' defeated, as Aeschylus had done, Sellars was able to use an austere space, sharp light, and physical and vocal rhetoric, much of it dehumanised by technological gadgetry, to draw attention to the effects on perception of war propaganda. He staged **Artaud**'s (in)famous radio diatribe, *For an End to the Judgement of God*, as the ravings of an American General spin-doctoring the cause of war on Iraq (2003); and nothing could have been more topical at the time. An American flag, podium, microphone and non-stop movie of atrocities set the scene for a virtuoso monologue of violence presented as a Pentagon press conference. It was coupled with Afro-American poet, June Jordan's *Kissing God Goodbye*, whose vision of a better humanity was presented via reflections upon the violence of the anti-abortion campaigns in the United States 'in the name of God'.

Sellars used a comparable method of rewriting established texts while retaining their essential meaning when he directed *The Children of Herakles* (2002) by Euripides. Once again, a Greek play provided him with a model since, after September 11, 'there's been a tangible chill on free speech in America. The limit of what can be discussed on the op-ed page of the *New York Times* is appalling' (Sellars 2002: 3). The theatre, he argues, 'provides some of the last public spaces left in this country' and its 'civil discourse ... makes democracy possible because it provides a place where you don't have to be polite, where the gloves are taken off, but where nobody is actually taking the blows' (ibid.). The production co-ordinated Euripides' tale of orphaned children seeking asylum in Athens with the international refugee crisis. It was a three-part event comprising a panel discussion on US immigration policy, the performance, and after-performance films on the terror-ridden places of the globe that that have generated its asylum-seekers. The production represented some of the children of Herakles with real-life refugee and immigrant youth in non-speaking parts (from the Boston area, when performed there, and from Kurdish groups, for example, when performed in Germany).

The community dimension of *Herakles* was doubled by a multicultural one. The latter had distinguished *The Merchant of Venice* (1994) with a black Shylock and a Chinese-American Portia in an acerbic study of capitalism. Perhaps nowhere is Sellars' commitment to multiculturalism more explicitly articulated than in *Peony Pavilion* (1998) by Tang Xianzu, the most celebrated epic of Chinese Kun opera. The work was written about the time of *Romeo and Juliet* and also dealt with the subject of absolute love, a fact exploited by Sellars in how he organises his material around the idea of cultural interchange. With crossover Chinese-Western music by Tan Dun, the production doubles physically restrained Kun performers, notably the celebrated Hua Wenyi, with Chinese-American actors performing in a graphic modern style. Perspex installations and mirror images, including miniatures screened on hand-held video cameras, accentuate the criss-cross between tradition and modernity of the whole. *Peony Pavilion* toured Europe, as have most of Sellars' theatre productions after the early 1990s, re-confirming his reputation abroad.

With more than 100 productions to his name, Sellars is probably at his best as a director of opera, whose civic function he also stresses. His three Mozart operas in several similar versions, *Così fan tutte* (1986, 1987, 1989) *Don Giovanni* (1987, 1989) and *The Marriage of Figaro* (1988), are landmarks for their radical recasting: Sellars does not update operas, but reshapes their thematics while retaining their musical structures. *Così* is set in a Californian diner full of visibly American trappings, including plastic ketchup containers. Dorabella and Fiodiligi admire photographs of handsome men in fashion magazines, and, in flowered pants, bright shirts, dangling plastic earings and sunglasses are like suburban mums on holiday. The men who test their love are dressed in a similar fashion, and, beer cans in hand, sing a 'little toast to the God of Love', Mozart's beautiful trio, as if it were an advertisement on television. Despina mops the floor in short skirts, stiletto heels and fishnet tights, while Don Alfonso epitomises an abusive has-been who continues to taunt her. Full of gestures familiar from hosted television shows and soap operas, this *Così* places Mozart's subject matter at the heart of everyday, explicitly sexual, relationships which pay tribute to the less obvious, pervasively underlying sexual passions explored with such humanity by Mozart.

Don Giovanni is set in a seedy New York neighbourhood, while its titular hero is a brutal drug addict cum rapist who is accompanied by Leperello, his greedy sidekick. The characters wear blue jeans and are black. Donna Anna, whom Don Giovanni attempts to rape, is white, and shoots up heroin on the stage. Donna Elvira is a tart, and so on, in a production that demystifies seducers as it homes in on a dangerous street culture. *The Marriage of Figaro* takes place in the Trump Tower in New York. Mozart's Count is replaced by a local multimillionaire who uses and abuses his valet Figaro and his maid Susanna. Apart from allusions to the city's skyscrapers, the design features Susanna's cramped quarters which display a washing machine, washing powder, an iron and ironing board and the rest of the paraphernalia that distinguishes her working day from the lifestyle of her employers.

Making Mozart about Americans – this principle extends to all of Sellars' classical opera stagings, most consistently to Handel's oratorio *Theodora* (1996), whose pagan ruler evokes a power-hungry President bent on subjecting dissenters to his authority. The latter are early Christians in Handel and Quakers and Shakers in Sellars, judging by their gestures, movements and dress (once again Sellars relies on his team, costume and stage designers, Dunya Ramicova and George Tsypin and lighting designer James Ingalls). *Theodora*, much like *Giulio Cesare* by Handel (1985, 1987 and 1990, invited to Paris by **Chéreau**) and especially his Mozart works, is highly choreographed, all movement being deliberate without exploiting 'popular' mannerisms (vaudeville, chorus-line, musical theatre), as occurs most notably in *Così*. His production of *The Rake's Progress* by Stravinsky (1998) at the Netherlands Opera is set in a Californian jail and is a masterpiece of choreographic and musical form and civic concern, music providing Sellars, here and elsewhere, with a controlling structure for his free imagination.

Despite controversy over his recast opera, Sellars is a favourite at Glyndebourne, where his most recent production was Mozart's *Idomeneo* with references to Iraq (2003). Yet he is a bold advocate of contemporary opera, where he is able to focus on America-in-the-world in an American idiom. His collaboration with John Adams has given *Nixon in China* (1987) in modern suits and *The Death of Klinghoffer* (1991), intended to provoke thought on the Arab–Israeli conflict, not least through the tragic scapegoating of the American Klinghoffer. Sellars' telefilm of this opera (2002) has a lighter counterpart in his last work with Adams to date, the oratorio-film-dance *El Niño*, premiered in Paris in 2002.

Further reading

Delgado, Maria M. (1999) ' "Making Theatre, Making a Society": an Introduction to the Work of Peter Sellars', *New Theatre Quarterly* 15 (3): 204–217.

Littlejohn, David (1990) 'Reflections on Peter Sellars' Mozart', *Opera Quarterly* 7: 2, 6–36.

Maurin, Frédéric (ed.) (2003) *Peter Sellars*, Paris: CNRS Editions.

Sellars, Peter (1997) 'Theatre, Opera, Society: the Director's Perspective', *Grand Street 61*, 16 (1): 192–207.

—— (2002) 'The Balm of Ancient Words', *American Repertory Theatre: Articles Online*, http://www.amrep.org 1 (2): 1–4.

MARIA SHEVTSOVA

DEBORAH WARNER (1959–)

In 1988 Deborah Warner directed Fiona Shaw in a landmark production of Sophocles' *Electra* for the Royal Shakespeare Company. Previously known for her starkly uncompromising productions of canonical texts with her company Kick, Warner's production of *Electra* began a collaborative relationship with Shaw which has been central to their status as major figures in the contemporary British theatre scene, and their work has played an important role in theatre practice since the 1980s. Warner has also developed work separately in opera, notably with *Turn of The Screw* (1997) and *Fidelio* (2001); in site-specific performance such as the *St Pancras Project* (1995) and *The Tower Project* (1998); and in feature film with *The Last September* (1999).

Warner's productions are caught within three competing modes of theatrical representation. There is Warner's loyalty to the text: she sees herself as working in the service of the universal human truths of canonical play-texts and situates herself within the traditions of 'classical' British theatre. Warner emphasises the need for 'transparent' theatre productions which remove ideological and historical filters from the audience's experience of these plays, and this transparency often translates into a heightened form of naturalism in her work. Then there is Warner and Shaw's emphasis on experimentation and risk in performance, garnered from their interest in the European modernist avant-garde. Warner has been particularly influenced by the work of Peter **Brook**, which shows in her search for truth in performance and in her minimal use of set, props and costumes. Finally, there is the central role Shaw's virtuosity plays in Warner's productions, which supports and, simultaneously, disrupts the authority of the play-text. Shaw's position as a 'great' classical actress affirms the hierarchy of canonical texts, but her star status also interrupts this hierarchy by drawing attention to her own work as an actor. While an interest in text, acting and experimentation are not necessarily contradictory, Shaw's virtuoso experimentalism is frequently at odds with the transparency required by text-centred performance in Britain. The tension between these elements has resulted in her developing some of the most interesting performances of femininity in contemporary British theatre.

Warner's approach to gender in performance places a particular strain on the convergence of tradition and experiment in her work. Warner and Shaw have publicly disavowed the importance of gender to Warner's work, arguing that they prefer to concentrate on the universal human experience. Ironically, Warner's focus on the 'universal' has produced some of the most important renditions of femininity on the British classical stage in recent years, particularly in her *Electra*, *Good Person of Sichuan* (1989), *Hedda Gabler* (1990), *Footfalls* (1994), *The Wasteland* (1995) and *Medea* (2000). The tension between Warner's focus and her inadvertent exploration of gender politics shows how Shaw's performances have produced complex and theatrical portraits of femininity which also tend to oppose confining stage images of masculinity, femininity and Irishness. In *Electra*, Shaw's androgynous characterisation in the lead role contrasted with the stereotyped portraits of femininity that are Clytaemnestra and Chrysothemis. In *The Good Person of Sichuan*, her complex and intelligent representation of femininity in the character of Shen Teh countered her one-dimensional portrait of masculinity as Shui Ta. In *Hedda Gabler* and *Medea*, Shaw's rebellious female characters were placed in opposition to a repressive and homogenous Irish masculinity. The Irish context of *Hedda Gabler* was referenced by the 'big house' and the parochialism of small-town Ireland in which this masculinity held sway. Warner's tendency to oppose complex feminine identity with a stereotyped masculine or national identity often places a sympathetic heroine in conflict with the repressive forces of a homogenous and repressive patriarchal nationalism. While Shaw has always played these heroines with intelligence, constructing a subversive vision of feminine identity by default, the focus of these productions has been on an exploration of universal, rather than gendered, identity.

The universal is often conflated with the individual in Warner's work in that she focuses on figures who somehow transcend their gender and nationality in their search for greater 'human' truths. Yet her concept of the universal as operating 'outside' cultural or gendered boundaries creates contradictions in her approach to representations of gender and nationality in her productions. This showed, in particular, in her *Richard II* (1995) at the National Theatre in London, Shaw playing the title role. Warner's lack of interest in the politics of gender resulted in a cross-dressed experiment with an unidentified aesthetic or political aim, which was evident in Shaw's claim: 'I'm not interested in cross-gender plays, I'm interested in experiment'.[1] The production was mainly disliked by those critics who objected to the ways in which masculinity and monarchy were disrupted and disturbed by a cross-dressed woman in the lead role. However, although gender was troubled by monarchy, gender also troubled monarchy by subverting the normally masculine reading of history in contemporary productions of Shakespeare's history plays. Shaw's cross-dressed performance paradoxically re-affirmed stereotypes of feminine identity even as it re-gendered history; and there was a split between the masculine and realist medieval world of Bolingbroke and the feminine and theatrical world of Richard.

The production was set in a corridor-like space lit by candles, with the audience sitting on either side of the long narrow playing area, as if in the Houses of Parliament or at a jousting match. Shaw was in a different theatrical register to the other actors through the stylisation of her costume, her excessive movement and the display of her body, which feminised her portrait of the king. From her shoulders to her ankles, she was wrapped in bandages that were fully visible beneath her medieval-style costume, disrupting the realist field of the performance. Shaw's performance was visceral, hyperactive and non-naturalistic, and her body was abstracted and stylised in comparison to the naturalist play of the other actors. This distinction relied, in part, on the difference between the 'star' player and the rest of the cast, but it also had an effect on how Shaw's king was positioned and gendered. Shaw's performance created the sense that Richard's identity was fluid and continually being materialised through performance and display, while the other performances produced a more static and stable conception of characterisation and psychology. Moreover, the contrasts between Shaw and the other actors were exacerbated by the fact that Shaw was the only cross-dressed figure. Her Richard unsettled the consistency of Warner's psychological and faithful approach to the text.

The tensions in Warner's work between naturalism and experimentation and the authority of the text and that of the actor could be found in the complex response demanded by Shaw's performance. Shaw claimed that she could access universal human truths in *Richard II* in a way not possible in her previous, female roles. However, while Shaw played Richard with ambiguity and intelligence, the fact that she played a male role traditionally represented as feminine and effeminate problematised her usual critical engagement with gender. As Irving Wardle pointed out: 'much of her performance conforms to the womanish stereotype: irrationally obstinate, unable to make up her mind, forever retreating from public issues into personal relationships' (*Independent on Sunday*, 11 June 1995). Shaw's usually critical portraits of feminine *women* now contrasted with her much more conventional portrait of femininity when playing a *man*. Warner's defence of her casting choice – arguing that Richard was a feminine character and that Shaw's femaleness should be ignored in favour of a focus on the universal truths of the role – had the knock-on effect of defining femininity by the qualities which Richard embodies: ineffectualness, indecision and irrationality. Casting Shaw as Richard both essentialised Richard's qualities as feminine and Shaw as female, and endorsed rather than critiqued the stereotypes associated with women. While Shaw claimed that playing a man gave her access to universal human truths, she performed, in fact, the most stereotypically feminine role of her career.

Warner's production asked the audience to identify with this feminine king rather than with the masculine realism of Bolingbroke's world. Although Shaw's cross-dressed performance constructed restricted images of femininity, the longing the production expressed for Richard's moment was deeply subversive of the commonplace construction of history as masculine. Warner displayed 'an unexpected nostalgia for a different lost way',[2] and this nostalgia was the most radical component of her production. Warner's reverence for the past was shown through the celebratory use of ritual – the choral laments sung by female singers and the evident loss felt, even by Bolingbroke, at the destruction of Richard's world. She constructed a medieval past which was ruled by a figure who combined masculine, feminine and childlike traits. Warner made the more modern world of Bolingbroke more familiar but, at the same time, placed the star actor, Shaw, in opposition to this world, and demanded sympathy for Richard's world and Richard's downfall.

In doing so, Warner challenged an English sense of history and monarchy, evoking a feminised, ambiguous past as ideal over the masculine and powerful world of Bolingbroke more typical of the representations of English history on the stage (and in films such as *Henry V* by Laurence Olivier or Kenneth Branagh). By placing the 'inappropriate' body of Shaw in the role of a king, Warner challenged the intertwined relationship of Englishness, history and masculinity, offering a different sense of historical possibility in its place. The feminine king became a cultural ideal for the present. As Susan Bennett argues, 'often what is perceived as "lost" is reasserted by its cultural representation'.[3] By expressing nostalgia for Richard's historical moment, Warner asked spectators to share in a longing for an English *present* which was ambiguous, feminine and theatrical. The critical resistance to Warner's production can be seen as a resistance to this vision of Englishness and history, and Shaw's cross-dressing was seen by critics as a threat to the 'reality' of monarchy, and to Shakespeare himself. The English cultural investment in history plays was highlighted by Warner's production and her use of cross-dressing revealed how the representation of monarchy and history is a volatile and political affair. Warner and Shaw demonstrated that the individual, and the universal, can also be *female* in performance.

Notes

1 Armistead, Claire (1995) 'Kingdom under Siege', *Guardian*, 31 May: 10–11.
2 Holland, Peter (1997) *English Shakespeares: Shakespeare on the English Stage in the 1990's*, Cambridge, New York and Melbourne: Cambridge University Press: 247.
3 (1996) *Performing Nostalgia: Shifting Shakespeare and the Contemporary Past*, London and New York: Routledge: 3.

Further reading

Chillington, Rutter Carol (1997) 'Fiona Shaw's Richard II: The Girl As Player-King As Comic', *Shakespeare Quarterly* 48 (3): 314–324.
Howard, Jean E, and Rackin, Phyllis (1997) *Engendering A Nation: A Feminist Account Of Shakespeare's English Histories*, London and New York: Routledge.
Shank, Theodore (1996) 'The Multiplicity Of British Theatre', in Shank (ed.) *Contemporary British Theatre*, London: Macmillan: 3–19.
Worthen, W.B. (2000) 'The Rhetoric Of Performance Criticism', in Shaughnessy, Robert (ed.) *Shakespeare In Performance*, London: Macmillan: 95–151.

AOIFE MONKS

CALIXTO BIEITO (1963–)

When Calixto Bieito made his Edinburgh Festival debut in 1997 with a staging of *La verbena de la paloma* (*The Festival of the Dove*), an 1894 *zarzuela* (or popular operetta) by Tomás Breton, few had heard of this young Catalan director. He had, however, already made a name for himself in Barcelona as an innovative and versatile director, equally at home working within musical theatre (Sondheim, Barbieri, Schönberg), with more contemporary writers (Shaw, Plath, Lorca, Bernhard) and in the handling of classical texts (Shakespeare, Molière). Bieito chose to set *La verbena de la paloma* in an urban wasteland outside a tram shed, thereby undermining the celebratory tone in which the piece is habitually read and locating the drama within the prism of an overt social criticism of bourgeois complacency and corruption. The production served to announce the dominant facets of Bieito's directorial aesthetic: economical stagecraft; close attention to character construction within a spirited performance style which juggles high theatricality with a commitment to realistic detail; and a bare stage where décor is reduced to its essentials, allowing the construction of a multi-dimensional world where the real and the poetic can exist cheek by jowl.

These elements were clearly in evidence in Bieito's 1998 English-language production of Pedro Calderón de la Barca's *Life is a Dream* for The Royal Lyceum Company. Widely praised for its wry humour, dynamic urgency and delicate interrogation of the ever-shifting relationship between illusion and reality, Bieito's staging evolved on a grey, sandy set dominated by a gigantic, suspended mirror. The mirror functioned as a metaphorical tool, providing both a dazzling image of an elusive world that can never be entirely controlled and a commentary on a play that continuously questions what we mean by 'reality' and 'fiction'. The furious pace of this pared-down version of Calderón's metaphysical reflection on the illusory nature of human existence, presented in Castilian in 2000 as part of the 400th anniversary celebrations of Calderón de la Barca's birth, may have succeeded in generating positive critical responses, but purist audiences in Spain responded with shock to Bieito's pacy staging.

Bieito's eclectic body of work has never been tame. His productions are often marked by a sexual charge that has not found favour with conservative audiences. He has boldly re-envisaged canonical Spanish texts for the stage – as with his rough, aggressive Edinburgh Festival production of Valle-Inclán's *Barbaric Comedies* (2000) and his abrasive reading of *La casa de Bernarda Alba* (*The House of Bernarda Alba*, 1998). It is perhaps in opera that Bieito's revisionist approach has been most contested. Here his questioning of the assumptions that have built up around the language of opera has resulted in a series of stagings that have generated frenzied indignation from critics who have judged his productions to be abusive, vulgar and tasteless misreadings of works that defy such radical treatment. In many ways such responses recall those engendered by another *enfant terrible* of the opera world, Peter **Sellars**. And indeed, there are solid points of contact between the two directors: both highlight rather than erase the contentious elements of the works they stage; both push their performers against a reliance on easy acting vocabularies and towards a physical choreography which comments on musical patterns; and both are reliant on cultural juxtapositions which recast their work through a complex contemporary reference system. Indeed, Bieito's work shares profound parallels with that of a number of other radical directors, such as Planchon and **Chéreau**, who have re-viewed some of the seminal works of the Western canon through the prism of a decaying society where moral indignation is tempered by a spirit of disquieting enquiry.

As artistic director of Barcelona's Romea theatre (alongside the Principal and the Liceu, part of a triptych of theatres which marks out the city's theatrical heritage over the twentieth century), Bieito has worked to re-establish a purpose for the theatre – the traditional home of Catalan theatre – in a city that now boasts a Catalan National Theatre which has partly usurped the Romea's mandate. Here he has invited innovative young companies such as Kràmpack, who have secured a young audience for the venue, and built up a company who have juggled both Catalan and Castilian-language productions (as in Bieito's 2002 stagings of *Macbeth* and *The Threepenny Opera*), offering bilingual theatre in a city where theatre is often polarised around the Catalan/Castilian axis. His own Galician roots, his upbringing in Castile, his relocation to Catalonia at the age of fifteen, his bilingualism (in Castilian-Spanish and Catalan), his fluency in English, French and Italian have ensured that in a European climate of collapsing borders he remains a powerful symbol of a multilingual Spain of co-existing identities.

Bieito's productions consistently ask radical questions about *how* and *what* texts mean to different generations. With the classics especially, he has demonstrated the ability to re-invent texts, stripping them of the legacy of past productions and re-imagining them for contemporary audiences. For the Grec, Barcelona's summer theatre festival, he provided pared-down re-readings of *Two Gentlemen of Verona* (1989), *A Midsummer Night's Dream* (1991), *King John* (1995) and *The Tempest* (1997); for the Teatre Nacional de Catalunya a disquieting *Measure for Measure* (1999). His attraction is often to the Bard's marginalised, more awkward works. As with Sellars, his approach has never been one of ignoring that which is not easily understood, but rather of foregrounding gaps in the writing and of recognising the layers of interpretation present when any cultural artefact from an earlier era is restaged in contemporary times.

More recently he has provided German, Catalan and Castilian-language stagings of *Macbeth* (2001–03), thus further exploring the subtleties and complexities of working across different languages, with plays repositioned within alternative linguistic, cultural and social contexts. In 2002–03 *Macbeth* was performed by the Romea company in both Castilian and Catalan, each language making different demands on the performers. This process has involved a progressively more active collaboration with living translators (Miquel Desclot, Josep Galindo) who have worked with Bieito on the translations of *The Tempest* and *Macbeth*. Increasingly this process of reworking has involved bold dramaturgical reshaping: in *Macbeth*

Bieito shifted the order of certain scenes and reconfigured characters. Certain roles were condensed and others enhanced. There was no porter, no witches, no Siward, no messengers or murderers: their lines were redistributed, with Lenox taking the porter's lines and becoming a wry, detached observer on the action. Ross took over the role of the murderers in Act 3 and the messenger and murderers in Act 4, thus becoming Macbeth's mafioso henchman. Seyton took over the lines of the witches and became a cackling seer at the heart of the family, seeking to usurp Lady Macbeth's role.

While Bieito's reading may have been regarded as sacrilegious by some critics, it developed conceptual links between the social structures of the play and the reference points of contemporary audiences. Set in a family unit (and what more brilliant metaphor for the divisive loyalties of the domestic world than the mafia, which Bieito uses to provide the initial landscape for his staging), this is a community increasingly at war, espousing loyalty and honour but brutally chasing the seductive allure of the material. And it was in a garish, tawdry world of disposable consumables that Bieito and designer Alfons Flores chose to set the action. Macbeth, Lady Macbeth and Duncan were conceived as the monarchs of the contemporary era, an era defined by the director as 'a hedonistic, drug and drink-fuelled culture with no bounds'[1] where each protagonist prowls, bounces and charges across the stage in the ruthless pursuit of power and the prestige that such power brings.

While this was a world of modern gangsters and molls envisaged through the violent and threatening prism of popular TV iconography, it was also the story of a couple scarred by childlessness. Bieito's reading conspicuously gravitated around domestic politics: it was through the iconography of the toys and the paddling pool of the Macduff children that Bieito located the destructive anguish that fuelled the Macbeths' avarice. The domestic iconography was also used to orchestrate some of the production's most exquisitely choreographed sequences – including the silent murder of Lady Macduff and her children with a jug of hot coffee, an iron flex and a coke bottle. This was no idealised world where children are protected. Bieito's staging constructed a hierarchical edifice where Fleance was the victim of his father Banquo's pent-up aggression. Indoctrination into the absolute and inflexible codes of masculinity, to which Duncan, Macbeth and their 'troops' adhere, was shown to begin in childhood when the boys are given clear guidelines on how to behave so as to secure their position within a pecking order.

It is this profound engagement with the conditions of our existence that makes Bieito, in the words of Michael Billington, 'not some brutal sensationalist dancing on the corpses of old masterpieces'[2] but rather a profoundly moral artist engaging with the key issues and debates of our amoral age.

Notes

1   Bieito, quoted in Delgado, Maria M. (2003) 'Calixto Bieito: Reimagining the Text for the Age in which it is being Staged', *Contemporary Theatre Review* 13 (3): 62.
2   Billington, M. (2002) 'Blood and Guts', *Guardian (Saturday Review)*, 30 March: 4.

Further reading

Billington, Michael (2001) 'Sex, Booze, Drugs and Mozart', *Guardian*, 30 May: 14–15.

Delgado, Maria M. (2000) 'A Contentious Production of Ramón del Valle-Inclán's *Barbaric Comedies*', *Western European Stages* 12 (3): 61–70.

—— (2001) 'Calixto Bieito's *Don Giovanni* outrages the British Critics', *Western European Stages* 13 (3): 53–58.

—— (2003) '*A Masked Ball, Die Fledermaus, Threepenny Opera*: Calixto Bieito's 2002', *Western European Stages* 15 (1): 91–100.

MARIA M. DELGADO

INDEX